ILLUSTRATED COURSE GUIDES

Microsoft® Access® 2010

Basic

Lisa Friedrichsen

COURSE TECHNOLOGY
CENGAGE Learning™

Australia • Brazil • Japan • Korea • Mexico • Singapore • Spain • United Kingdom • United States

COURSE TECHNOLOGY
CENGAGE Learning

Illustrated Course Guide: Microsoft® Access® 2010 Basic

Lisa Friedrichsen

Vice President, Publisher: Nicole Jones Pinard

Executive Editor: Marjorie Hunt

Associate Acquisitions Editor: Brandi Shailer

Senior Product Manager: Christina Kling Garrett

Associate Product Manager: Michelle Camisa

Editorial Assistant: Kim Klasner

Director of Marketing: Cheryl Costantini

Senior Marketing Manager: Ryan DeGrote

Marketing Coordinator: Kristen Panciocco

Contributing Authors: Carol Cram, Elizabeth Eisner Reding

Developmental Editors: Lisa Ruffolo, Pamela Conrad, Jeanne Herring

Content Project Manager: Melissa Panagos

Copy Editor: Mark Goodin

Proofreader: Harold Johnson

Indexer: BIM Indexing and Proofreading Services

QA Manuscript Reviewers: John Frietas, Serge Palladino, Susan Pedicini, Jeff Schwartz, Danielle Shaw, Marianne Snow

Print Buyer: Fola Orekoya

Cover Designer: GEX Publishing Services

Cover Artist: Mark Hunt

Composition: GEX Publishing Services

Trademarks:

Some of the product names and company names used in this book have been used for identification purposes only and may be trademarks or registered trademarks of their respective manufacturers and sellers.

Microsoft and the Office logo are either registered trademarks or trademarks of Microsoft Corporation in the United States and/or other countries. Course Technology, Cengage Learning is an independent entity from Microsoft Corporation, and not affiliated with Microsoft in any manner.

Library of Congress Control Number: 2010936044

ISBN-13: 978-0-538-74839-1
ISBN-10: 0-538-74839-7

Course Technology
20 Channel Center Street
Boston, MA 02210
USA

Cengage Learning is a leading provider of customized learning solutions with office locations around the globe, including Singapore, the United Kingdom, Australia, Mexico, Brazil, and Japan. Locate your local office at:
international.cengage.com/region

Cengage Learning products are represented in Canada by Nelson Education, Ltd.

To learn more about Course Technology, visit **www.cengage.com/coursetechnology**

To learn more about Cengage Learning, visit **www.cengage.com**

Purchase any of our products at your local college store or at our preferred online store
www.cengagebrain.com

Printed in the United States of America
2 3 4 5 6 7 8 9 18 17 16 15 14 13 12 11

Brief Contents

Contents

Office 2010

Access 2010

Web Apps

Preface

Welcome to *Illustrated Course Guide: Microsoft®
Access® 2010 Basic.* If this is your first experience with the Illustrated Course Guides, you'll
see that this book has a unique design: each
skill is presented on two facing pages, with
steps on the left and screens on the right. The
layout makes it easy to learn a skill without
having to read a lot of text and flip pages to
see an illustration.

This book is an ideal learning tool for a wide
range of learners—the "rookies" will find the
clean design easy to follow and focused with
only essential information presented, and the
"hotshots" will appreciate being able to move
quickly through the lessons to find the information they need without reading a lot of text.
The design also makes this a great reference
after the course is over! See the illustration on
the right to learn more about the pedagogical
and design elements of a typical lesson.

What's New In This Edition

- **Fully Updated.** Highlights the new
  features of Microsoft Access 2010
  including the new Backstage view, new
  database templates, and enhanced
  datasheet formatting tools. A new
  appendix covers cloud computing
  concepts and using Microsoft Office Web
  Apps. Examples and exercises are
  updated throughout.

- **Maps to SAM 2010.** This book is
  designed to work with SAM (Skills
  Assessment Manager) 2010. **SAM
  Assessment** contains performance-based,
  hands-on SAM exams for each unit of
  this book, and **SAM Training** provides
  hands-on training for skills covered in
  the book. Some exercises are available in
  SAM Projects, which is auto-grading
  software that provides both learners and
  instructors with immediate, detailed
  feedback (SAM sold separately.) See
  page xii for more information on SAM.

Each two-page spread focuses on a single skill.

Introduction briefly explains why the lesson skill is important.

A case scenario moti-vates the the steps and puts learning in context.

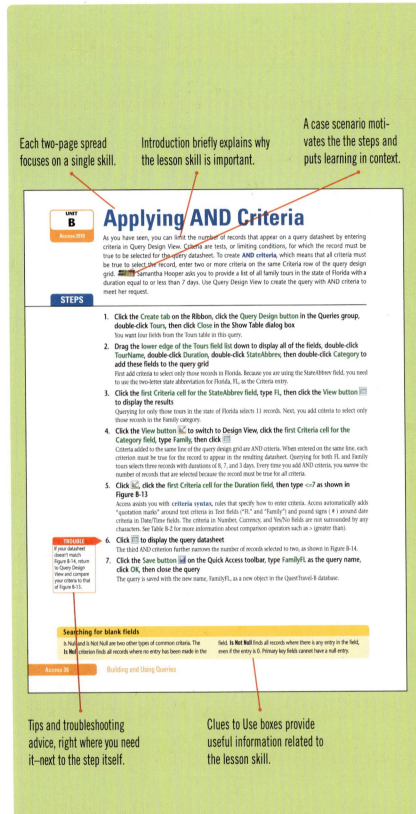

Tips and troubleshooting advice, right where you need it—next to the step itself.

Clues to Use boxes provide useful information related to the lesson skill.

Assignments

The lessons use Quest Specialty Travel, a fictional adventure travel company, as the case study. The assignments on the light yellow pages at the end of each unit increase in difficulty. Assignments include:

- **Concepts Review** consist of multiple choice, matching, and screen identification questions.

- **Skills Reviews** are hands-on, step-by-step exercises that review the skills covered in each lesson in the unit.

- **Independent Challenges** are case projects requiring critical thinking and application of the unit skills. The Independent Challenges increase in difficulty, with the first one in each unit being the easiest. Independent Challenges 2 and 3 become increasingly open-ended, requiring more independent problem solving.

- **SAM Projects** is live-in-the-application autograding software that provides immediate and detailed feedback reports to learners and instructors. Some exercises in this book are available in SAM Projects. (Purchase of a SAM Projects pincode is required.)

- **Real Life Independent Challenges** are practical exercises in which learners create documents to help them with their every day lives.

- **Advanced Challenge Exercises** set within the Independent Challenges provide optional steps for more advanced learners.

- **Visual Workshops** are practical, self-graded capstone projects that require independent problem solving.

Large screen shots keep learners on track as they complete steps

Brightly colored tabs indicate which section of the book you are in.

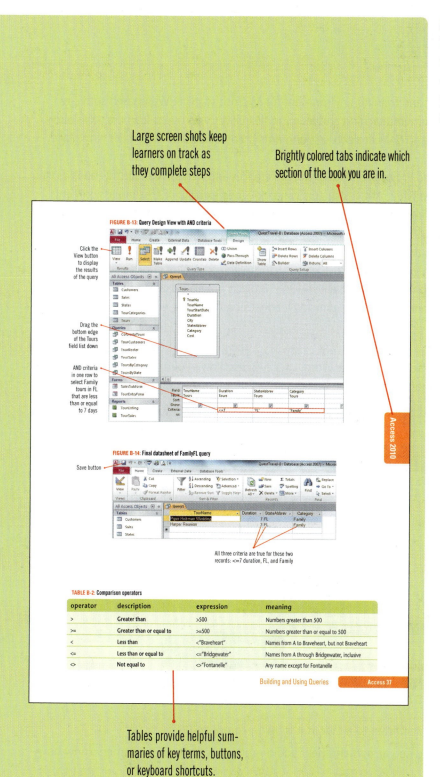

Click the View button to display the results of the query

Drag the bottom edge of the Tours field list down

AND criteria in one row to select Family tours in FL that are less than or equal to 7 days

Save button

All three criteria are true for these two records: <=7 duration, FL, and Family

Access 2010

FIGURE B-13: Query Design View with AND criteria

FIGURE B-14: Final datasheet of FamilyFL query

Building and Using Queries   Access 37

TABLE B-2: Comparison operators

operator	description	expression	meaning
>	Greater than	>500	Numbers greater than 500
>=	Greater than or equal to	>=500	Numbers greater than or equal to 500
<	Less than	<"Braveheart"	Names from A to Braveheart, but not Braveheart
<=	Less than or equal to	<="Bridgewater"	Names from A through Bridgewater, inclusive
<>	Not equal to	<>"Fontanelle"	Any name except for Fontanelle

Tables provide helpful summaries of key terms, buttons, or keyboard shortcuts.

About SAM

SAM is the premier proficiency-based assessment and training environment for Microsoft Office. Web-based software along with an inviting user interface provide maximum teaching and learning flexibility. SAM builds learners' skills and confidence with a variety of real-life simulations, and SAM Projects' assignments prepare learners for today's workplace.

The SAM system includes Assessment, Training, and Projects, featuring page references and remediation for this book as well as Course Technology's Microsoft Office textbooks. With SAM, instructors can enjoy the flexibility of creating assignments based on content from their favorite Microsoft Office books or based on specific course objectives. Instructors appreciate the scheduling and reporting options that have made SAM the market-leading online testing and training software for over a decade. Over 2,000 performance-based questions and matching Training simulations, as well as tens of thousands of objective-based questions from many Course Technology texts, provide instructors with a variety of choices across multiple applications from the introductory level through the comprehensive level. SAM Projects is auto-grading software that lets learners complete projects using Microsoft Office and then receive detailed feedback on their finished projects.

SAM Assessment

- Content for these hands-on, performance-based tasks includes Word, Excel, Access, PowerPoint, Internet Explorer, Outlook, and Windows. Includes tens of thousands of objective-based questions from many Course Technology texts.

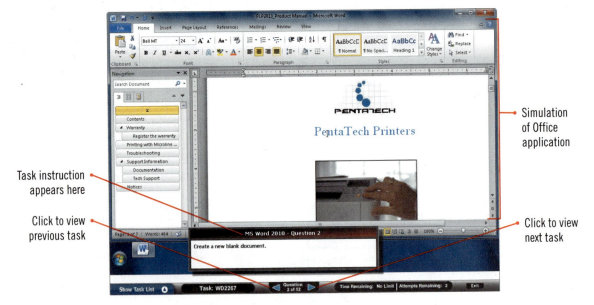

Simulation of Office application

Task instruction appears here

Click to view previous task

Click to view next task

SAM Training

- Observe mode allows the learners to watch and listen to a task as it is being completed.
- Practice mode allows the learner to follow guided arrows and hear audio prompts to help visual learners know how to complete a task.
- Apply mode allows the learner to prove what they've learned by completing a project using on-screen instructions.

SAM Projects

- Live-in-the-application assignments in Word, Excel, Access and PowerPoint allow learners to create a project using the Microsoft Office software and then receive immediate, detailed feedback on their completed project.
- Learners receive detailed feedback on their project within minutes.
- Unique anti-cheating detection feature is encrypted into the data files to ensure learners complete their own assignments.

Instructor Resources

The Instructor Resources CD is Course Technology's way of putting the resources and information needed to teach and learn effectively into your hands. With an integrated array of teaching and learning tools that offer learners a broad range of technology-based instructional options, we believe this CD represents the highest quality and most cutting edge resources available to instructors today. The resources available with this book are:

- **Instructor's Manual**—Available as an electronic file, the Instructor's Manual includes detailed lecture topics with teaching tips for each unit.

- **Sample Syllabus**—Prepare and customize your course easily using this sample course outline.

- **PowerPoint Presentations**—Each unit has a corresponding PowerPoint presentation that you can use in lecture, distribute to learners, or customize to suit your course.

- **Figure Files**—The figures in the text are provided on the Instructor Resources CD to help you illustrate key topics or concepts. You can create traditional overhead transparencies by printing the figure files. Or you can create electronic slide shows by using the figures in a presentation program such as PowerPoint.

- **Solutions to Exercises**—Solutions to Exercises contains every file learners are asked to create or modify in the lessons and end-of-unit material. Also provided in this section, there is a document outlining the solutions for the end-of-unit Concepts Review, Skills Review, and Independent Challenges. An Annotated Solution File and Grading Rubric accompany each file and can be used together for quick and easy grading.

- **Data Files for Learners**—To complete most of the units in this book, learners will need Data Files. You can post the Data Files on a file server for learners to copy. The Data Files are available on the Instructor Resources CD-ROM, the Review Pack, and can also be downloaded from cengagebrain.com. For more information on how to download the Data Files, see the inside back cover.

Instruct learners to use the Data Files List included on the Review Pack and the Instructor Resources CD. This list gives instructions on copying and organizing files.

- **ExamView**—ExamView is a powerful testing software package that allows you to create and administer printed, computer (LAN-based), and Internet exams. ExamView includes hundreds of questions that correspond to the topics covered in this text, enabling learners to generate detailed study guides that include page references for further review. The computer-based and Internet testing components allow learners to take exams at their computers, and also saves you time by grading each exam automatically.

Content for Online Learning.

Course Technology has partnered with the leading distance learning solution providers and class-management platforms today. To access this material, visit www.cengage.com/webtutor and search for your title. Instructor resources include the following: additional case projects, sample syllabi, PowerPoint presentations, and more. For additional information, please contact your sales representative. For learners to access this material, they must have purchased a WebTutor PIN-code specific to this title and your campus platform. The resources for learners might include (based on instructor preferences): topic reviews, review questions, practice tests, and more.

Acknowledgements

Instructor Advisory Board

We thank our Instructor Advisory Board who gave us their opinions and guided our decisions as we updated our texts for Microsoft Office 2010. They are as follows:

Terri Helfand, Chaffey Community College

Barbara Comfort, J. Sargeant Reynolds Community College

Brenda Nielsen, Mesa Community College

Sharon Cotman, Thomas Nelson Community College

Marian Meyer, Central New Mexico Community College

Audrey Styer, Morton College

Richard Alexander, Heald College

Xiaodong Qiao, Heald College

Student Advisory Board

We also thank our Student Advisory Board members, who shared their experiences using the book and offered suggestions to make it better: **Latasha Jefferson**, Thomas Nelson Community College, **Gary Williams**, Thomas Nelson Community College, **Stephanie Miller**, J. Sargeant Reynolds Community College, **Sarah Styer**, Morton Community College, **Missy Marino**, Chaffey College

Author Acknowledgements

Lisa Friedrichsen This book is dedicated to my students, and all who are using this book to teach and learn Access. Thank you. Also, thank you to all of the professionals who helped me create this book.

Read This Before You Begin

What are Data Files?

A Data File is a partially completed Access database or another type of file that you use to complete the steps in the units and exercises to create the final document that you submit to your instructor. Each unit opener page lists the Data Files that you need for that unit.

Where are the Data Files?

Your instructor will provide the Data Files to you or direct you to a location on a network drive from which you can download them. For information on how to download the Data Files from cengagebrain.com, see the inside back cover. **Note**: These Access data files are set to automatically compact when they are closed. This requires extra free space on the drive that stores your databases. We recommend that your storage device (flash drive, memory stick, hard drive) always have at least 30 MB of free space to handle these processes.

What software was used to write and test this book?

This book was written and tested using a typical installation of Microsoft Office 2010 Professional Plus on a computer with a typical installation of Microsoft Windows 7 Ultimate.

The browser used for any Web-dependent steps is Internet Explorer 8.

Do I need to be connected to the Internet to complete the steps and exercises in this book?

Some of the exercises in this book require that your computer be connected to the Internet. If you are not connected to the Internet, see your instructor for information on how to complete the exercises.

What do I do if my screen is different from the figures shown in this book?

This book was written and tested on computers with monitors set at a resolution of 1024 × 768. If your screen shows more or less information than the figures in the book, your monitor is probably set at a higher or lower resolution. If you don't see something on your screen, you might have to scroll down or up to see the object identified in the figures.

The Ribbon—the blue area at the top of the screen—in Microsoft Office 2010 adapts to different resolutions. If your monitor is set at a lower resolution than 1024 × 768, you might not see all of the buttons shown in the figures. The groups of buttons will always appear, but the entire group might be condensed into a single button that you need to click to access the buttons described in the instructions.

COURSECASTS Learning on the Go. Always Available...Always Relevant.

Our fast-paced world is driven by technology. You know because you are an active participant—always on the go, always keeping up with technological trends, and always learning new ways to embrace technology to power your life. Let CourseCasts, hosted by Ken Baldauf of Florida State University, be your guide into weekly updates in this ever-changing space. These timely, relevant podcasts are produced weekly and are available for download at http://coursecasts.course.com or directly from iTunes (search by CourseCasts). CourseCasts are a perfect solution to getting learners (and even instructors) to learn on the go!

Getting Started with Microsoft Office 2010

Files You Will Need:

OFFICE A-1.xlsx

Microsoft Office 2010 is a group of software programs designed to help you create documents, collaborate with coworkers, and track and analyze information. Each program is designed so you can work quickly and efficiently to create professional-looking results. You use different Office programs to accomplish specific tasks, such as writing a letter or producing a sales presentation, yet all the programs have a similar look and feel. Once you become familiar with one program, you'll find it easy to transfer your knowledge to the others. 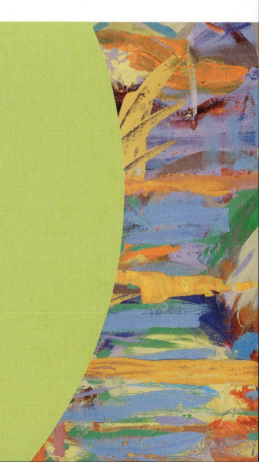 This unit introduces you to the most frequently used programs in Office, as well as common features they all share.

OBJECTIVES

Understand the Office 2010 suite

Start and exit an Office program

View the Office 2010 user interface

Create and save a file

Open a file and save it with a new name

View and print your work

Get Help and close a file

Understanding the Office 2010 Suite

Microsoft Office 2010 features an intuitive, context-sensitive user interface, so you can get up to speed faster and use advanced features with greater ease. The programs in Office are bundled together in a group called a **suite** (although you can also purchase them separately). The Office suite is available in several configurations, but all include Word, Excel, and PowerPoint. Other configurations include Access, Outlook, Publisher, and other programs. Each program in Office is best suited for completing specific types of tasks, though there is some overlap in capabilities.

DETAILS

The Office programs covered in this book include:

- **Microsoft Word 2010**

  When you need to create any kind of text-based document, such as a memo, newsletter, or multipage report, Word is the program to use. You can easily make your documents look great by inserting eye-catching graphics and using formatting tools such as themes, which are available in most Office programs. **Themes** are predesigned combinations of color and formatting attributes you can apply to a document. The Word document shown in Figure A-1 was formatted with the Solstice theme.

- **Microsoft Excel 2010**

  Excel is the perfect solution when you need to work with numeric values and make calculations. It puts the power of formulas, functions, charts, and other analytical tools into the hands of every user, so you can analyze sales projections, calculate loan payments, and present your findings in style. The Excel worksheet shown in Figure A-1 tracks personal expenses. Because Excel automatically recalculates results whenever a value changes, the information is always up to date. A chart illustrates how the monthly expenses are broken down.

- **Microsoft PowerPoint 2010**

  Using PowerPoint, it's easy to create powerful presentations complete with graphics, transitions, and even a soundtrack. Using professionally designed themes and clip art, you can quickly and easily create dynamic slide shows such as the one shown in Figure A-1.

- **Microsoft Access 2010**

  Access helps you keep track of large amounts of quantitative data, such as product inventories or employee records. The form shown in Figure A-1 was created for a grocery store inventory database. Employees use the form to enter data about each item. Using Access enables employees to quickly find specific information such as price and quantity without hunting through store shelves and stockrooms.

Microsoft Office has benefits beyond the power of each program, including:

- **Common user interface: Improving business processes**

  Because the Office suite programs have a similar **interface**, or look and feel, your experience using one program's tools makes it easy to learn those in the other programs. In addition, Office documents are **compatible** with one another, meaning that you can easily incorporate, or **integrate**, an Excel chart into a PowerPoint slide, or an Access table into a Word document.

- **Collaboration: Simplifying how people work together**

  Office recognizes the way people do business today, and supports the emphasis on communication and knowledge sharing within companies and across the globe. All Office programs include the capability to incorporate feedback—called **online collaboration**—across the Internet or a company network.

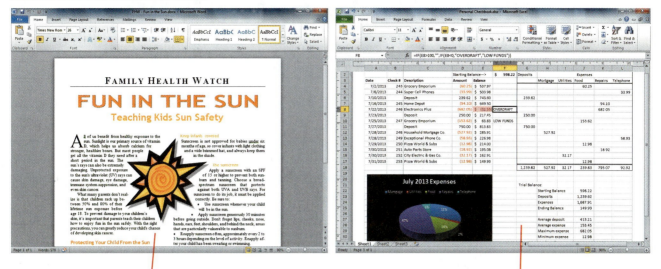

Newsletter created in Word

Checkbook register created in Excel

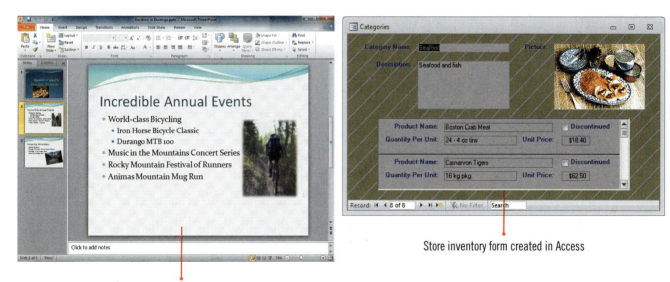

Tourism presentation created in PowerPoint

Store inventory form created in Access

Deciding which program to use

Every Office program includes tools that go far beyond what you might expect. For example, although Excel is primarily designed for making calculations, you can use it to create a database. So when you're planning a project, how do you decide which Office program to use? The general rule of thumb is to use the program best suited for your intended task, and make use of supporting tools in the program if you need them. Word is best for creating text-based documents, Excel is best for making mathematical calculations, PowerPoint is best for preparing presentations, and Access is best for managing quantitative data. Although the capabilities of Office are so vast that you *could* create an inventory in Excel or a budget in Word, you'll find greater flexibility and efficiency by using the program designed for the task. And remember, you can always create a file in one program, and then insert it in a document in another program when you need to, such as including sales projections (Excel) in a memo (Word).

UNIT A
Office 2010

Starting and Exiting an Office Program

The first step in using an Office program is to open, or **launch**, it on your computer. The easiest ways to launch a program are to click the Start button on the Windows taskbar or to double-click an icon on your desktop. You can have multiple programs open on your computer simultaneously, and you can move between open programs by clicking the desired program or document button on the taskbar or by using the [Alt][Tab] keyboard shortcut combination. When working, you'll often want to open multiple programs in Office and switch among them as you work. Begin by launching a few Office programs now.

STEPS

QUICK TIP

You can also launch a program by double-clicking a desktop icon or clicking the program name on the Start menu.

1. **Click the Start button 🔵 on the taskbar**

   The Start menu opens. If the taskbar is hidden, you can display it by pointing to the bottom of the screen. Depending on your taskbar property settings, the taskbar may be displayed at all times, or only when you point to that area of the screen. For more information, or to change your taskbar properties, consult your instructor or technical support person.

2. **Click All Programs, scroll down if necessary in the All Programs menu, click Microsoft Office as shown in Figure A-2, then click Microsoft Word 2010**

   Word 2010 starts, and the program window opens on your screen.

QUICK TIP

It is not necessary to close one program before opening another.

3. **Click 🔵 on the taskbar, click All Programs, click Microsoft Office, then click Microsoft Excel 2010**

   Excel 2010 starts, and the program window opens, as shown in Figure A-3. Word is no longer visible, but it remains open. The taskbar displays a button for each open program and document. Because this Excel document is **active**, or in front and available, the Excel button on the taskbar appears slightly lighter.

QUICK TIP

As you work in Windows, your computer adapts to your activities. You may notice that after clicking the Start button, the name of the program you want to open appears in the Start menu above All Programs; if so, you can click it to start the program.

4. **Point to the Word program button 🔲 on the taskbar, then click 🔲**

   The Word program window is now in front. When the Aero feature is turned on in Windows 7, pointing to a program button on the taskbar displays a thumbnail version of each open window in that program above the program button. Clicking a program button on the taskbar activates that program and the most recently active document. Clicking a thumbnail of a document activates that document.

5. **Click 🔵 on the taskbar, click All Programs, click Microsoft Office, then click Microsoft PowerPoint 2010**

   PowerPoint 2010 starts and becomes the active program.

6. **Click the Excel program button 🔲 on the taskbar**

   Excel is now the active program.

TROUBLE

If you don't have Access installed on your computer, proceed to the next lesson.

7. **Click 🔵 on the taskbar, click All Programs, click Microsoft Office, then click Microsoft Access 2010**

   Access 2010 starts and becomes the active program. Now all four Office programs are open at the same time.

8. **Click Exit on the navigation bar in the Access program window, as shown in Figure A-4**

   Access closes, leaving Excel active and Word and PowerPoint open.

Using shortcut keys to move between Office programs

As an alternative to the Windows taskbar, you can use a keyboard shortcut to move among open Office programs. The [Alt][Tab] keyboard combination lets you either switch quickly to the next open program or file or choose one from a gallery. To switch immediately to the next open program or file, press [Alt][Tab]. To choose from all open programs and files, press and hold [Alt], then press and release [Tab] without releasing [Alt]. A gallery opens on screen, displaying the filename and a thumbnail image of each open program and file, as well as of the desktop. Each time you press [Tab] while holding [Alt], the selection cycles to the next open file or location. Release [Alt] when the program, file, or location you want to activate is selected.

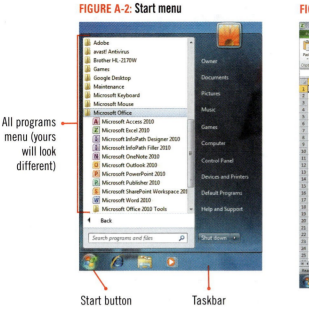

All programs
menu (yours
will look
different)

Start button   Taskbar

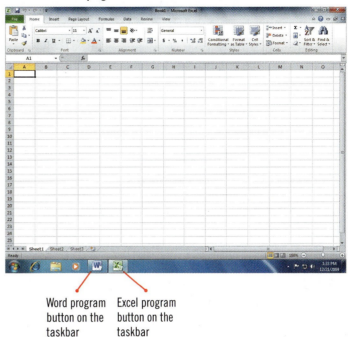

Word program
button on the
taskbar

Excel program
button on the
taskbar

FIGURE A-4: Access program window

File tab

Navigation bar

Exit command

Windows Live and Microsoft Office Web Apps

All Office programs include the capability to incorporate feedback—called online collaboration—across the Internet or a company network. Using **cloud computing** (work done in a virtual environment), you can take advantage of Web programs called Microsoft Office Web Apps, which are simplified versions of the programs found in the Microsoft Office 2010 suite. Because these programs are online, they take up no computer disk space and are accessed using

Windows Live SkyDrive, a free service from Microsoft. Using Windows Live SkyDrive, you and your colleagues can create and store documents in a "cloud" and make the documents available to whomever you grant access. To use Windows Live SkyDrive, you need a free Windows Live ID, which you obtain at the Windows Live Web site. You can find more information in the "Working with Windows Live and Office Web Apps" appendix.

Viewing the Office 2010 User Interface

One of the benefits of using Office is that the programs have much in common, making them easy to learn and making it simple to move from one to another. Individual Office programs have always shared many features, but the innovations in the Office 2010 user interface mean even greater similarity among them all. That means you can also use your knowledge of one program to get up to speed in another. A **user interface** is a collective term for all the ways you interact with a software program. The user interface in Office 2010 provides intuitive ways to choose commands, work with files, and navigate in the program window. Familiarize yourself with some of the common interface elements in Office by examining the PowerPoint program window.

STEPS

QUICK TIP

In addition to the standard tabs on the Ribbon, **contextual tabs** open when needed to complete a specific task; they appear in an accent color and close when no longer needed. To minimize the display of the buttons and commands on tabs, click the Minimize the Ribbon button ⌃ on the right end of the Ribbon.

1. **Click the PowerPoint program button 🅿 on the taskbar**

   PowerPoint becomes the active program. Refer to Figure A-5 to identify common elements of the Office user interface. The **document window** occupies most of the screen. In PowerPoint, a blank slide appears in the document window, so you can build your slide show. At the top of every Office program window is a **title bar** that displays the document name and program name. Below the title bar is the **Ribbon**, which displays commands you're likely to need for the current task. Commands are organized onto **tabs**. The tab names appear at the top of the Ribbon, and the active tab appears in front. The Ribbon in every Office program includes tabs specific to the program, but all Office programs include a File tab and Home tab on the left end of the Ribbon.

2. **Click the File tab**

   The File tab opens, displaying **Backstage view**. The navigation bar on the left side of Backstage view contains commands to perform actions common to most Office programs, such as opening a file, saving a file, and closing the current program. Just above the File tab is the **Quick Access toolbar**, which also includes buttons for common Office commands.

3. **Click the File tab again to close Backstage view and return to the document window, then click the Design tab on the Ribbon**

   To display a different tab, you click the tab on the Ribbon. Each tab contains related commands arranged into **groups** to make features easy to find. On the Design tab, the Themes group displays available design themes in a **gallery**, or visual collection of choices you can browse. Many groups contain a **dialog box launcher**, an icon you can click to open a dialog box or task pane from which to choose related commands.

QUICK TIP

Live Preview is available in many galleries and menus throughout Office.

4. **Move the mouse pointer ☿ over the Angles theme in the Themes group as shown in Figure A-6, but do not click the mouse button**

   The Angles theme is temporarily applied to the slide in the document window. However, because you did not click the theme, you did not permanently change the slide. With the **Live Preview** feature, you can point to a choice, see the results right in the document, and then decide if you want to make the change.

QUICK TIP

If you accidentally click a theme, click the Undo button ↺ on the Quick Access toolbar.

5. **Move ☿ away from the Ribbon and towards the slide**

   If you had clicked the Angles theme, it would be applied to this slide. Instead, the slide remains unchanged.

QUICK TIP

You can also use the Zoom button in the Zoom group on the View tab to enlarge or reduce a document's appearance.

6. **Point to the Zoom slider ▽ on the status bar, then drag ▽ to the right until the Zoom level reads 166%**

   The slide display is enlarged. Zoom tools are located on the status bar. You can drag the slider or click the Zoom In or Zoom Out buttons to zoom in or out on an area of interest. **Zooming in**, or choosing a higher percentage, makes a document appear bigger on screen, but less of it fits on the screen at once; **zooming out**, or choosing a lower percentage, lets you see more of the document but at a reduced size.

7. **Drag ▽ on the status bar to the left until the Zoom level reads 73%**

FIGURE A-5: PowerPoint program window

Quick Access toolbar

Ribbon

Clipboard dialog box launcher

Title bar

Tabs

Document window

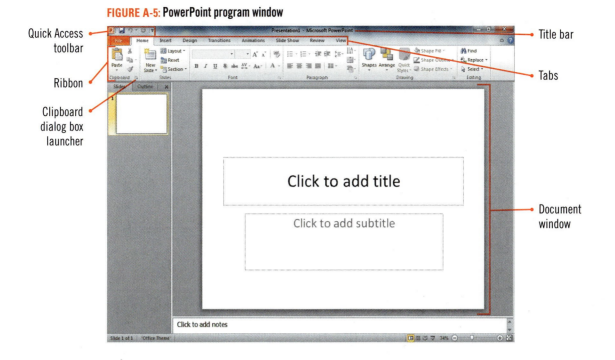

FIGURE A-6: Viewing a theme with Live Preview

Angles theme

Mouse pointer

Live Preview of Angles theme applied to document

Zoom slider

Zoom In button

Zoom level

Zoom Out button

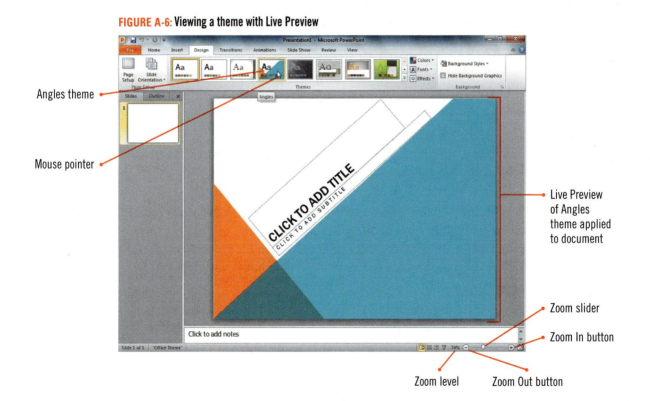

Using Backstage view

Backstage view in each Microsoft Office program offers "one stop shopping" for many commonly performed tasks, such as opening and saving a file, printing and previewing a document, defining document properties, sharing information, and exiting a program.

Backstage view opens when you click the File tab in any Office program, and while features such as the Ribbon, Mini toolbar, and Live Preview all help you work *in* your documents, the File tab and Backstage view help you work *with* your documents.

Creating and Saving a File

When working in a program, one of the first things you need to do is to create and save a file. A **file** is a stored collection of data. Saving a file enables you to work on a project now, then put it away and work on it again later. In some Office programs, including Word, Excel, and PowerPoint, a new file is automatically created when you start the program, so all you have to do is enter some data and save it. In Access, you must expressly create a file before you enter any data. You should give your files meaningful names and save them in an appropriate location so that they're easy to find. Use Word to familiarize yourself with the process of creating and saving a document. First you'll type some notes about a possible location for a corporate meeting, then you'll save the information for later use.

STEPS

1. **Click the Word program button 🖳 on the taskbar**

2. **Type Locations for Corporate Meeting, then press [Enter] twice**
   The text appears in the document window, and the **insertion point** blinks on a new blank line. The insertion point indicates where the next typed text will appear.

3. **Type Las Vegas, NV, press [Enter], type Orlando, FL, press [Enter], type Boston, MA, press [Enter] twice, then type your name**
   Compare your document to Figure A-7.

QUICK TIP

A filename can be up to 255 characters, including a file extension, and can include upper- or lowercase characters and spaces, but not ?, ", /, \, <, >, *, |, or :.

4. **Click the Save button 🖳 on the Quick Access toolbar**
   Because this is the first time you are saving this document, the Save As dialog box opens, as shown in Figure A-8. The Save As dialog box includes options for assigning a filename and storage location. Once you save a file for the first time, clicking 🖳 saves any changes to the file *without* opening the Save As dialog box, because no additional information is needed. The Address bar in the Save As dialog box displays the default location for saving the file, but you can change it to any location. The File name field contains a suggested name for the document based on text in the file, but you can enter a different name.

5. **Type OF A-Potential Corporate Meeting Locations**
   The text you type replaces the highlighted text. (The "OF A-" in the filename indicates that the file is created in Office Unit A. You will see similar designations throughout this book when files are named. For example, a file named in Excel Unit B would begin with "EX B-".)

QUICK TIP

Saving a file to the Desktop creates a desktop icon that you can double-click to both launch a program and open a document.

6. **In the Save As dialog box, use the Address bar or Navigation Pane to navigate to the drive and folder where you store your Data Files**
   Many students store files on a flash drive, but you can also store files on your computer, a network drive, or any storage device indicated by your instructor or technical support person.

7. **Click Save**
   The Save As dialog box closes, the new file is saved to the location you specified, then the name of the document appears in the title bar, as shown in Figure A-9. (You may or may not see the file extension ".docx" after the filename.) See Table A-1 for a description of the different types of files you create in Office, and the file extensions associated with each.

QUICK TIP

To create a new blank file when a file is open, click the File tab, click New on the navigation bar, then click Create near the bottom of the document preview pane.

TABLE A-1: Common filenames and default file extensions

file created in	is called a	and has the default extension
Word	document	.docx
Excel	workbook	.xlsx
PowerPoint	presentation	.pptx
Access	database	.accdb

FIGURE A-7: Document created in Word

Save button

Your name should appear here

Insertion point

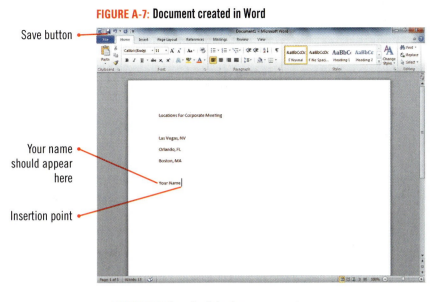

FIGURE A-8: Save As dialog box

Address bar

Navigation Pane; your links and folders may differ

File name field; your computer may not display file extensions

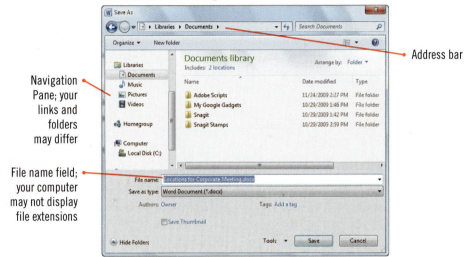

FIGURE A-9: Saved and named Word document

Filename appears in title bar

Using the Office Clipboard

You can use the Office Clipboard to cut and copy items from one Office program and paste them into others. The Office Clipboard can store a maximum of 24 items. To access it, open the Office Clipboard task pane by clicking the dialog box launcher in the Clipboard group on the Home tab. Each time you copy a selection, it is saved in the Office Clipboard. Each entry in the Office Clipboard includes an icon that tells you the program it was created in. To paste an entry, click in the document where you want it to appear, then click the item in the Office Clipboard. To delete an item from the Office Clipboard, right-click the item, then click Delete.

Opening a File and Saving It with a New Name

In many cases as you work in Office, you start with a blank document, but often you need to use an existing file. It might be a file you or a coworker created earlier as a work in progress, or it could be a complete document that you want to use as the basis for another. For example, you might want to create a budget for this year using the budget you created last year; you could type in all the categories and information from scratch, or you could open last year's budget, save it with a new name, and just make changes to update it for the current year. By opening the existing file and saving it with the Save As command, you create a duplicate that you can modify to your heart's content, while the original file remains intact. Use Excel to open an existing workbook file, and save it with a new name so the original remains unchanged.

STEPS

QUICK TIP
Click Recent on the navigation bar to display a list of recent workbooks; click a file in the list to open it.

1. **Click the Excel program button 🗷 on the taskbar, click the File tab, then click Open on the navigation bar**

   The Open dialog box opens, where you can navigate to any drive or folder accessible to your computer to locate a file.

2. **In the Open dialog box, navigate to the drive and folder where you store your Data Files**

   The files available in the current folder are listed, as shown in Figure A-10. This folder contains one file.

TROUBLE
Click Enable Editing on the Protected View bar near the top of your document window if prompted.

3. **Click OFFICE A-1.xlsx, then click Open**

   The dialog box closes, and the file opens in Excel. An Excel file is an electronic spreadsheet, so it looks different from a Word document or a PowerPoint slide.

4. **Click the File tab, then click Save As on the navigation bar**

   The Save As dialog box opens, and the current filename is highlighted in the File name text box. Using the Save As command enables you to create a copy of the current, existing file with a new name. This action preserves the original file and creates a new file that you can modify.

QUICK TIP
The Save As command works identically in all Office programs, except Access; in Access, this command lets you save a copy of the current database object, such as a table or form, with a new name, but not a copy of the entire database.

5. **Navigate to the drive and folder where you store your Data Files if necessary, type OF A-Budget for Corporate Meeting in the File name text box, as shown in Figure A-11, then click Save**

   A copy of the existing workbook is created with the new name. The original file, Office A-1.xlsx, closes automatically.

6. **Click cell A19, type your name, then press [Enter], as shown in Figure A-12**

   In Excel, you enter data in cells, which are formed by the intersection of a row and a column. Cell A19 is at the intersection of column A and row 19. When you press [Enter], the cell pointer moves to cell A20.

7. **Click the Save button 🖫 on the Quick Access toolbar**

   Your name appears in the workbook, and your changes to the file are saved.

Working in Compatibility Mode

Not everyone upgrades to the newest version of Office. As a general rule, new software versions are **backward compatible**, meaning that documents saved by an older version can be read by newer software. To open documents created in older Office versions, Office 2010 includes a feature called Compatibility Mode. When you use Office 2010 to open a file created in an earlier version of Office, "Compatibility Mode" appears in the title bar, letting you know the file was created in an earlier but usable version of the program. If you are working with someone who may not be using the newest version of the software, you can avoid possible incompatibility problems by saving your file in another, earlier format. To do this in an Office program, click the File tab, click Save As on the navigation bar, click the Save as type list arrow in the Save As dialog box, then click an option on the list. For example, if you're working in Excel, click Excel 97-2003 Workbook format in the Save as type list to save an Excel file so that it can be opened in Excel 97 or Excel 2003.

FIGURE A-10: Open dialog box

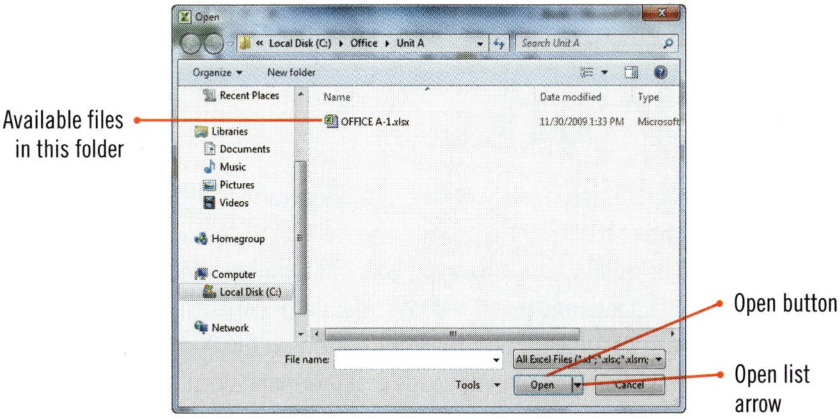

Available files in this folder → OFFICE A-1.xlsx

Open button
Open list arrow

FIGURE A-11: Save As dialog box

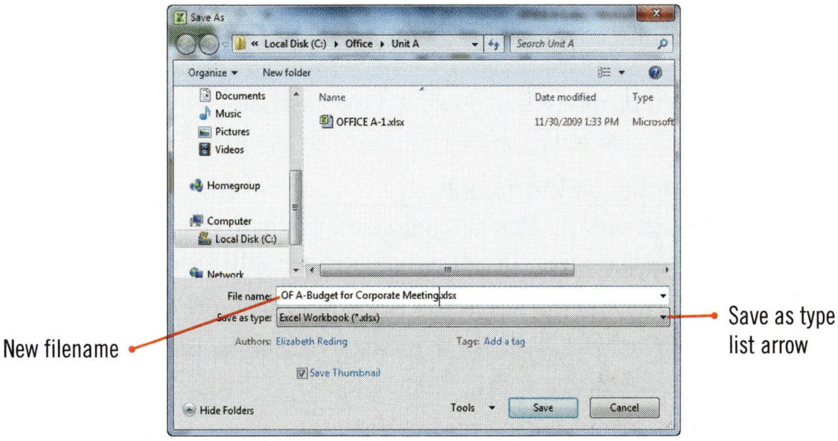

New filename → OF A-Budget for Corporate Meeting.xlsx

Save as type list arrow

FIGURE A-12: Your name added to the workbook

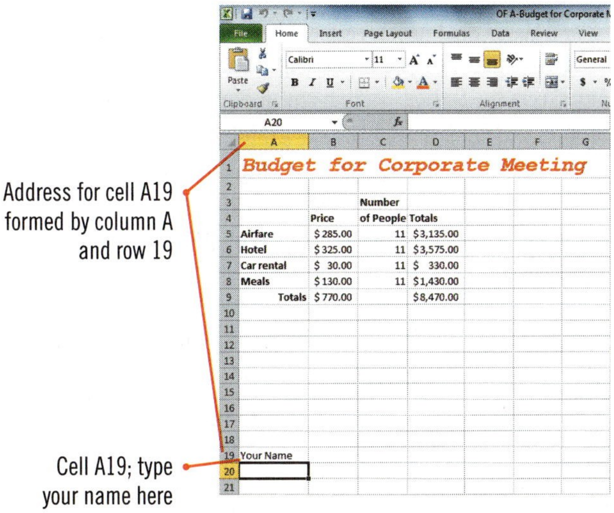

Address for cell A19 formed by column A and row 19

Cell A19; type your name here

	Price	Number of People	Totals
Airfare	$ 285.00	11	$3,135.00
Hotel	$ 325.00	11	$3,575.00
Car rental	$ 30.00	11	$ 330.00
Meals	$ 130.00	11	$1,430.00
Totals	$ 770.00		$8,470.00

Exploring File Open options

You might have noticed that the Open button on the Open dialog box includes an arrow. In a dialog box, if a button includes an arrow you can click the button to invoke the command, or you can click the arrow to choose from a list of related commands. The Open list arrow includes several related commands, including Open Read-Only and Open as Copy. Clicking Open Read-Only opens a file that you can only save with a new name; you cannot save changes to the original file. Clicking Open as Copy creates a copy of the file already saved and named with the word "Copy" in the title. Like the Save As command, these commands provide additional ways to use copies of existing files while ensuring that original files do not get changed by mistake.

Viewing and Printing Your Work

Each Microsoft Office program lets you switch among various **views** of the document window to show more or fewer details or a different combination of elements that make it easier to complete certain tasks, such as formatting or reading text. Changing your view of a document does not affect the file in any way, it affects only the way it looks on screen. If your computer is connected to a printer or a print server, you can easily print any Office document using the Print button on the Print tab in Backstage view. Printing can be as simple as **previewing** the document to see exactly what a document will look like when it is printed and then clicking the Print button. Or, you can customize the print job by printing only selected pages or making other choices. Experiment with changing your view of a Word document, and then preview and print your work.

STEPS

1. **Click the Word program button 🔳 on the taskbar**
   Word becomes the active program, and the document fills the screen.

2. **Click the View tab on the Ribbon**
   In most Office programs, the View tab on the Ribbon includes groups and commands for changing your view of the current document. You can also change views using the View buttons on the status bar.

3. **Click the Web Layout button in the Document Views group on the View tab**
   The view changes to Web Layout view, as shown in Figure A-13. This view shows how the document will look if you save it as a Web page.

4. **Click the Print Layout button on the View tab**
   You return to Print Layout view, the default view in Word.

5. **Click the File tab, then click Print on the navigation bar**
   The Print tab opens in Backstage view. The preview pane on the right side of the window automatically displays a preview of how your document will look when printed, showing the entire page on screen at once. Compare your screen to Figure A-14. Options in the Settings section enable you to change settings such as margins, orientation, and paper size before printing. To change a setting, click it, and then click the new setting you want. For instance, to change from Letter paper size to Legal, click Letter in the Settings section, then click Legal on the menu that opens. The document preview is updated as you change the settings. You also can use the Settings section to change which pages to print and even the number of pages you print on each sheet of printed paper. If you have multiple printers from which to choose, you can change from one installed printer to another by clicking the current printer in the Printer section, then clicking the name of the installed printer you want to use. The Print section contains the Print button and also enables you to select the number of copies of the document to print.

6. **Click the Print button in the Print section**
   A copy of the document prints, and Backstage view closes.

QUICK TIP
You can add the Quick Print button 🖨 to the Quick Access toolbar by clicking the Customize Quick Access Toolbar button, then clicking Quick Print. The Quick Print button prints one copy of your document using the default settings.

Customizing the Quick Access toolbar

You can customize the Quick Access toolbar to display your favorite commands. To do so, click the Customize Quick Access Toolbar button ⮟ in the title bar, then click the command you want to add. If you don't see the command in the list, click More Commands to open the Quick Access Toolbar tab of the current program's Options dialog box. In the Options dialog box, use the Choose commands from list to choose a category, click the desired command in the list on the left, click Add to add it to the Quick Access toolbar, then click OK. To remove a button from the toolbar, click the name in the list on the right in the Options dialog box, then click Remove. To add a command to the Quick Access toolbar on the fly, simply right-click the button on the Ribbon, then click Add to Quick Access Toolbar on the shortcut menu. To move the Quick Access toolbar below the Ribbon, click the Customize Quick Access Toolbar button, and then click Show Below the Ribbon.

FIGURE A-13: Web Layout view

Web Layout button →

View buttons on status bar →

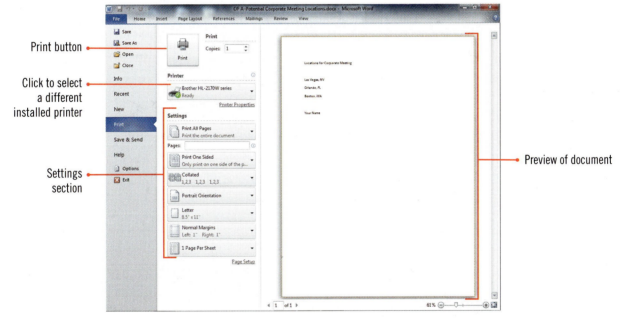

FIGURE A-14: Print tab in Backstage view

Print button →

Click to select a different installed printer →

Settings section →

→ Preview of document

Creating a screen capture

A **screen capture** is a digital image of your screen, as if you took a picture of it with a camera. For instance, you might want to take a screen capture if an error message occurs and you want Technical Support to see exactly what's on the screen. You can create a screen capture using features found in Windows 7 or Office 2010. Windows 7 comes with the Snipping Tool, a separate program designed to capture whole screens or portions of screens. To open the Snipping Tool, click it on the Start menu or click All Programs, click Accessories, then click Snipping Tool. After opening the Snipping Tool, drag the pointer on the screen to select the area of the screen you want to capture. When you release the mouse button, the screen capture opens in the Snipping Tool window, and

you can save, copy, or send it in an e-mail. In Word, Excel, and PowerPoint 2010, you can capture screens or portions of screens and insert them in the current document using the Screenshot button on the Insert tab. And finally, you can create a screen capture by pressing [PrtScn]. (Keyboards differ, but you may find the [PrtScn] button in or near your keyboard's function keys.) Pressing this key places a digital image of your screen in the Windows temporary storage area known as the **Clipboard**. Open the document where you want the screen capture to appear, click the Home tab on the Ribbon (if necessary), then click the Paste button on the Home tab. The screen capture is pasted into the document.

Getting Help and Closing a File

You can get comprehensive help at any time by pressing [F1] in an Office program. You can also get help in the form of a ScreenTip by pointing to almost any icon in the program window. When you're finished working in an Office document, you have a few choices regarding ending your work session. You can close a file or exit a program by using the File tab or by clicking a button on the title bar. Closing a file leaves a program running, while exiting a program closes all the open files in that program as well as the program itself. In all cases, Office reminds you if you try to close a file or exit a program and your document contains unsaved changes. Explore the Help system in Microsoft Office, and then close your documents and exit any open programs.

STEPS

TROUBLE

If the Table of Contents pane doesn't appear on the left in the Help window, click the Show Table of Contents button 📄 on the Help toolbar to show it.

1. **Point to the Zoom button on the View tab of the Ribbon**
   A ScreenTip appears that describes how the Zoom button works and explains where to find other zoom controls.

2. **Press [F1]**
   The Word Help window opens, as shown in Figure A-15, displaying the home page for help in Word on the right and the Table of Contents pane on the left. In both panes of the Help window, each entry is a hyperlink you can click to open a list of related topics. The Help window also includes a toolbar of useful Help commands and a Search field. The connection status at the bottom of the Help window indicates that the connection to Office.com is active. Office.com supplements the help content available on your computer with a wide variety of up-to-date topics, templates, and training. If you are not connected to the Internet, the Help window displays only the help content available on your computer.

QUICK TIP

You can also open the Help window by clicking the Microsoft Office Word Help button 📘 to the right of the tabs on the Ribbon.

3. **Click the Creating documents link in the Table of Contents pane**
   The icon next to Creating documents changes, and a list of subtopics expands beneath the topic.

4. **Click the Create a document link in the subtopics list in the Table of Contents pane**
   The topic opens in the right pane of the Help window, as shown in Figure A-16.

5. **Click Delete a document under "What do you want to do?" in the right pane**
   The link leads to information about deleting a document.

QUICK TIP

You can print the entire current topic by clicking the Print button 🖨 on the Help toolbar, then clicking Print in the Print dialog box.

6. **Click the Accessibility link in the Table of Contents pane, click the Accessibility features in Word link, read the information in the right pane, then click the Help window Close button ⬛**

7. **Click the File tab, then click Close on the navigation bar; if a dialog box opens asking whether you want to save your changes, click Save**
   The Potential Corporate Meeting Locations document closes, leaving the Word program open.

8. **Click the File tab, then click Exit on the navigation bar**
   Word closes, and the Excel program window is active.

9. **Click the File tab, click Exit on the navigation bar to exit Excel, click the PowerPoint program button 📙 on the taskbar if necessary, click the File tab, then click Exit on the navigation bar to exit PowerPoint**
   Excel and PowerPoint both close.

FIGURE A-15: Word Help window

Help toolbar

Search field

The colors of your links may differ if the links have been visited previously

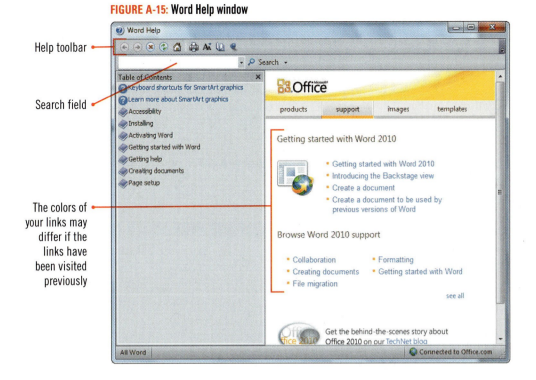

FIGURE A-16: Create a document Help topic

Print button

Icon indicates expanded topic

Create a document link

Create a document topic

Click to read how to perform the action described

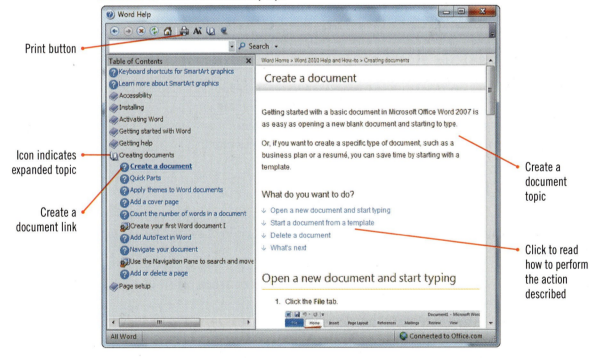

Recovering a document

Each Office program has a built-in recovery feature that allows you to open and save files that were open at the time of an interruption such as a power failure. When you restart the program(s) after an interruption, the Document Recovery task pane opens on the left side of your screen displaying both original and recovered versions of the files that were open. If you're not sure which file to open (original or recovered), it's usually better to open the recovered file because it will contain the latest information. You can, however, open and review all versions of the file that were recovered and save the best one. Each file listed in the Document Recovery task pane displays a list arrow with options that allow you to open the file, save it as is, delete it, or show repairs made to it during recovery.

Practice

For current SAM information, including versions and content details, visit SAM Central (http://www.cengage.com/samcentral). If you have a SAM user profile, you may have access to hands-on instruction, practice, and assessment of the skills covered in this unit. Since various versions of SAM are supported throughout the life of this text, check with your instructor for the correct instructions and URL/Web site for accessing assignments.

Concepts Review

Label the elements of the program window shown in Figure A-17.

FIGURE A-17

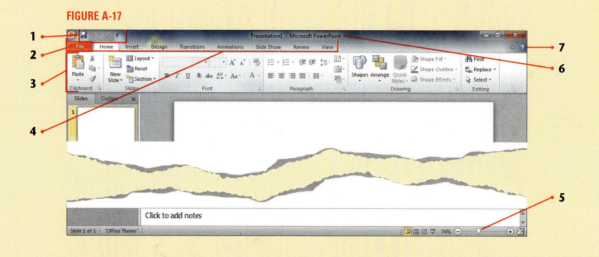

Match each project with the program for which it is best suited.

8. Microsoft Access   a. Corporate convention budget with expense projections

9. Microsoft Excel   b. Business cover letter for a job application

10. Microsoft Word   c. Department store inventory

11. Microsoft PowerPoint   d. Presentation for city council meeting

Independent Challenge 1

You just accepted an administrative position with a local independently owned produce vendor that has recently invested in computers and is now considering purchasing Microsoft Office for the company. You are asked to propose ways Office might help the business. You produce your document in Word.

a. Start Word, then save the document as **OF A-Microsoft Office Document** in the drive and folder where you store your Data Files.

b. Type **Microsoft Word**, press [Enter] twice, type **Microsoft Excel**, press [Enter] twice, type **Microsoft PowerPoint**, press [Enter] twice, type **Microsoft Access**, press [Enter] twice, then type your name.

c. Click the line beneath each program name, type at least two tasks suited to that program (each separated by a comma), then press [Enter].

Advanced Challenge Exercise

- Press the [PrtScn] button to create a screen capture.
- Click after your name, press [Enter] to move to a blank line below your name, then click the Paste button in the Clipboard group on the Home tab.

d. Save the document, then submit your work to your instructor as directed.

e. Exit Word.

Getting Started with Access 2010

In this unit, you will learn the purpose, advantages, and terminology of Microsoft Access 2010, the relational database program in the Microsoft Office 2010 suite of software. You will create and relate tables, the basic building blocks of an Access relational database. You'll also navigate, enter, update, preview, and print data. Samantha Hooper is the tour developer for United States group travel at Quest Specialty Travel (QST), a tour company that specializes in customized group travel packages. Samantha uses Access to store, maintain, and analyze customer and tour information.

OBJECTIVES

Understand relational databases

Explore a database

Create a database

Create a table

Create primary keys

Relate two tables

Enter data

Edit data

Understanding Relational Databases

Microsoft Access 2010 is relational database software that runs on the Windows operating system. You use **relational database software** to manage data that is organized into lists, such as information about customers, products, vendors, employees, projects, or sales. Many small companies track customer, inventory, and sales information in a spreadsheet program such as Microsoft Excel. Although Excel offers some list management features, Access provides many more tools and advantages for managing data. The advantages are mainly due to the "relational" nature of the lists that Access manages. Table A-1 compares the two programs. You and Samantha Hooper review the advantages of database software over spreadsheets for managing lists of information.

DETAILS

The advantages of using Access for database management include:

- **Duplicate data is minimized**
  Figures A-1 and A-2 compare how you might store sales data in a single Excel spreadsheet list versus three related Access tables. With Access, you do not have to reenter information such as a customer's name and address or tour name every time a sale is made, because lists can be linked, or "related," in relational database software.

- **Information is more accurate, reliable, and consistent because duplicate data is minimized**
  The relational nature of data stored in an Access database allows you to minimize duplicate data entry, which creates more accurate, reliable, and consistent information. For example, customer data in a Customers table is entered only once, not every time a customer makes a purchase.

- **Data entry is faster and easier using Access forms**
  Data entry forms (screen layouts) make data entry faster, easier, and more accurate than entering data in a spreadsheet.

- **Information can be viewed and sorted in many ways using Access queries, forms, and reports**
  In Access, you can save queries (questions about the data), data entry forms, and reports, allowing you to use them over and over without performing extra work to recreate a particular view of the data.

- **Information is more secure using Access passwords and security features**
  Access databases can be encrypted and password protected.

- **Several users can share and edit information at the same time**
  Unlike spreadsheets or word-processing documents, more than one person can enter, update, and analyze data in an Access database at the same time.

FIGURE A-1: Using a spreadsheet to organize sales data

	A	B	C	D	E	F	G	H	I
1	CustNo	FName	LName	SalesNo	SaleDate	TourName	TourStartDate	City	Cost
2	1	Gracita	Mayberry	13	11-Jul-12	Red Reef Scuba	07/24/2012	Islamadora	$1,500.00
3	2	Jacob	Alman	14	11-Jul-12	Red Reef Scuba	07/24/2012	Islamadora	$1,500.00
4	3	Julia	Bouchart	15	11-Jul-12	Red Reef Scuba	07/24/2012	Islamadora	$1,500.00
5	3	Julia	Bouchart	81	11-Jun-12	Piper-Heitman Wedding	06/17/2012	Captiva	$825.00
6	4	Kayla	Browning	5	01-Jun-12	American Heritage Tour	09/11/2012	Philadelphia	$1,200.00
7	4	Kayla	Browning	82	11-May-12	Red Reef Scuba	07/24/2012	Islamadora	$1,500.00
8	5	Samantha	Braven	16	11-Jul-12	Bright Lights Expo	12/19/2012	Branson	$200.00
9	5	Samantha	Braven	83	11-Jul-12	Red Reef Scuba	07/24/2012	Islamadora	$1,500.00
10	6	Kristen	Collins	1	30-Apr-12	Ames Ski Club	01/20/2013	Breckenridge	$850.00
11	6	Kristen	Collins	4	01-Jun-12	Yosemite National Park Great Cleanup	08/07/2012	Sacramento	$1,100.00
12	6	Kristen	Collins	8	07-Jul-12	Bright Lights Expo	12/19/2012	Branson	$200.00
13	6	Kristen	Collins	84	01-Jun-12	American Heritage Tour	09/11/2012	Philadelphia	$1,200.00

Customer information is duplicated each time that customer makes a purchase

Tour information is duplicated each time that tour is purchased

FIGURE A-2: Using a relational database to organize sales data

Customers table

Cust No	First	Last	Street	City	State	Zip	Phone
1	Gracita	Mayberry	222 Elm	Topeka	KS	66111	913-555-0000
2	Jacob	Alman	400 Oak	Lenexa	MO	60023	816-555-8877
3	Julia	Bouchart	111 Ash	Ames	IA	50010	515-555-3333

Sales table

Cust No	TourNo	Date	SalesNo
1	2	5/1/12	101
2	2	5/2/12	102
3	2	5/3/12	103

Tours table

TourNo	TourName	TourStartDate	City	Cost
1	Ames Ski Club	1/20/13	Breckenridge	$850
2	Red Reef Scuba	7/24/12	Islamadora	$1,500
3	American Heritage Tour	9/11/12	Philadelphia	$1,200

TABLE A-1: Comparing Excel to Access

feature	Excel	Access
Layout	Provides a natural tabular layout for easy data entry	Provides a natural tabular layout as well as the ability to create customized data entry screens called forms
Storage	Restricted to a file's limitations	Virtually unlimited when coupled with the ability to use Microsoft SQL Server to store data
Linked tables	Manages single lists of information—no relational database capabilities	Relates lists of information to reduce data redundancy and create a relational database
Reporting	Limited	Provides the ability to create an unlimited number of reports
Security	Limited to file security options such as marking the file "read-only" or protecting a range of cells	When used with SQL Server, provides extensive security down to the user and data level
Multiuser capabilities	Not allowed	Allows multiple users to simultaneously enter and update data
Data entry	Provides limited data entry screens	Provides the ability to create an unlimited number of data entry forms

Exploring a Database

You can start Access from the Start menu, from an Access shortcut icon, from a pinned program on the taskbar, or by double-clicking an Access database file on your computer. When you start the Access program from the Start menu, Access displays a window that allows you to open an existing database or create a new one from a template or as a blank database. Samantha Hooper has developed a database called QuestTravel-A, which contains tour information. She asks you to start Access and review this database.

1. **Start Access from the Start menu**

   Access starts, as shown in Figure A-3. This window helps you open an existing database, create a new database from a template, or create a new blank database. At this point, if you click the Home, Create, External Data, or Database Tools tabs, no options would be available because Access is running, but no database is open.

   > **TROUBLE**
   > If a yellow Security Warning bar appears below the Ribbon, click Enable Content.

2. **Click the Open button, navigate to the drive and folder where you store your Data Files, click the QuestTravel-A.accdb database file, click Open, then click the Maximize button** 🔲 **if the Access window is not already maximized**

   The QuestTravel-A.accdb database contains five tables of data named Customers, Sales, States, TourCategories, and Tours. It also contains four queries, two forms, and two reports. Each of these items (table, query, form, and report) is a different type of **object** in an Access database and is displayed in the **Navigation Pane**. The purpose of each object is defined in Table A-2. To learn about an Access database, you explore its objects.

   > **TROUBLE**
   > If the Navigation Pane is not open, click the Shutter Bar Open/Close button ≪ to open it and view the database objects.

3. **In the Navigation Pane, double-click the Tours table to open it, then double-click the Customers table to open it**

   The Tours and Customers tables open to display the data they store. A **table** is the fundamental building block of a relational database because it stores all of the data.

4. **In the Navigation Pane, double-click the TourSales query to open it, double-click any occurrence of Heritage (as in American Heritage Tour), type Legacy, then click any other row**

   A **query** selects a subset of data from one or more tables. In this case, the TourSales query selects data from the Tours, Sales, and Customers tables. Editing data in one object changes it in every other object of the database, which demonstrates the power and productivity of a relational database.

5. **Double-click the TourEntryForm to open it, double-click Tour in "American Legacy Tour", type Rally, then click any name in the middle part of the window**

   An Access **form** is a data entry screen. Users prefer forms for data entry rather than tables and queries because the information can be presented in an easy-to-use layout.

6. **Double-click the TourSales report to open it**

   An Access **report** is a professional printout. A report is for printing purposes only, not data entry. As shown in Figure A-4, the edits made to the American Legacy Rally tour name have carried through to the report.

7. **Click the File tab, then click Exit**

   Exiting Access closes the database on which you are working. If you made any changes to the database that should be saved, Access would remind you to do so before closing. Changes to data, such as the edits you made to the American Legacy Rally tour, are automatically saved as you work.

FIGURE A-3: Opening Microsoft Access 2010 window

File tab

Open an existing database

Recently used databases

Exit Access

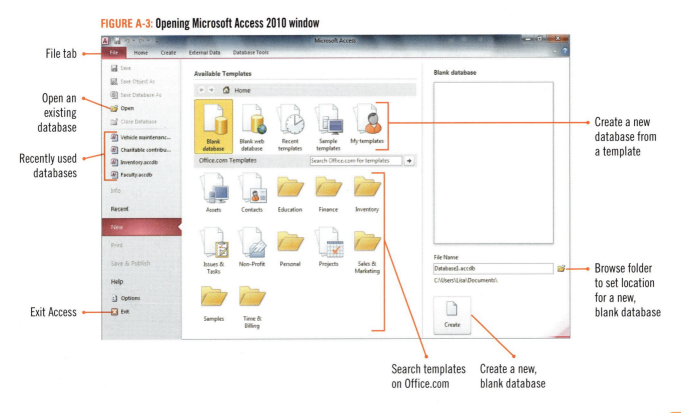

Create a new database from a template

Browse folder to set location for a new, blank database

Search templates on Office.com   Create a new, blank database

FIGURE A-4: Objects in the QuestTravel-A database

Customers table

Tours table

Shutter Bar Open/ Close button

Navigation Pane shows all objects; yours might display them in a different view

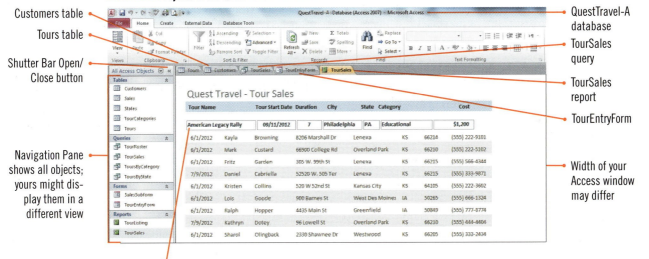

QuestTravel-A database

TourSales query

TourSales report

TourEntryForm

Width of your Access window may differ

American Legacy Rally tour name is updated in the TourSales report

TABLE A-2: Access objects and their purpose

object	Navigation Pane icon	purpose
Table		Contains all of the raw data within the database in a spreadsheet-like view; tables are linked with a common field to create a relational database, which minimizes redundant data
Query		Allows you to select a subset of fields or records from one or more tables; queries are created when you have a question about the data
Form		Provides an easy-to-use data entry screen
Report		Provides a professional printout of data that can contain enhancements such as headers, footers, graphics, and calculations on groups of records

Creating a Database

You can create a database using an Access **template**, a sample database provided within the Microsoft Access program, or you can start with a blank database to create a database from scratch. Your decision depends on whether Access has a template that closely resembles the type of data you plan to manage. If it does, building your own database from a template might be faster than creating the database from scratch. Regardless of which method you use, you can always modify the database later, tailoring it to meet your specific needs. Samantha Hooper reasons that the best way for you to learn Access is to start a new database from scratch, so she asks you to create a database that will track customer communication.

STEPS

1. **Start Access**

2. **Click the Browse folder button 📁 to the right of the File Name box, navigate to the drive and folder where you store your Data Files, type Quest in the File name box, click OK, then click the Create button**

   A new, blank database file with a single table named Table1 is created as shown in Figure A-5. While you might be tempted to start entering data into the table, a better way to build a table is to first define the columns, or **fields**, of data that the table will store. **Table Design View** provides the most options for defining fields.

3. **Click the View button 📐 on the Fields tab to switch to Design View, type Customers as the table name, then click OK**

   The table name changes from Table1 to Customers, and you are positioned in Table Design View, a window you use to name and define the fields of a table. Access created a field named ID with an AutoNumber data type. The **data type** is a significant characteristic of a field because it determines what type of data the field can store, such as text, dates, or numbers. See Table A-3 for more information about data types.

4. **Type CustID to rename ID to CustID, press the [↓] to move to the first blank Field Name cell, type FirstName, press [↓], type LastName, press [↓], type Phone, press [↓], type Birthday, then press [↓]**

   Be sure to separate the first and last names so that you can easily sort, find, and filter on either part of the name later. The Birthday field will only contain dates, so you should change its data type from Text (the default data type) to Date/Time.

5. **Click Text in the Birthday row, click the list arrow, then click Date/Time**

   With these five fields properly defined for the new Customers table, as shown in Figure A-6, you're ready to enter data. You switch back to Datasheet View to enter or edit data. **Datasheet View** is a spreadsheet-like view of the data in a table. A **datasheet** is a grid that displays fields as columns and records as rows. The new **field names** you just defined are listed at the top of each column.

6. **Click the View button 📋 to switch to Datasheet View, click Yes when prompted to save the table, press [Tab] to move to the FirstName field, type your first name, press [Tab] to move to the LastName field, type your last name, press [Tab] to move to the Phone field, type 111-222-3333, press [Tab], type 1/32/80, and press [Tab]**

   Because 1/32/80 is not a valid date, Access does not allow you to make that entry and displays an error message as shown in Figure A-7. This shows that setting the best data type for each field before entering data helps prevent data entry errors.

TROUBLE
Tab through the CustID field rather than typing a value. The CustID value automatically increments to the next number.

7. **Edit the Birthday entry for the first record to 1/31/80, press [Tab], enter two more sample records containing reasonable data, right-click the Customers table tab, then click Close to close the Customers table**

FIGURE A-5: Creating a database with a new table

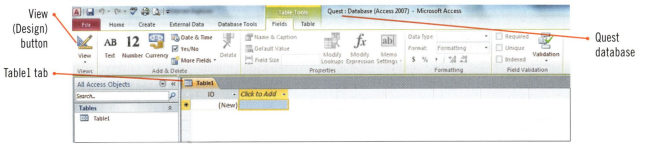

View (Design) button

Table1 tab

Quest database

FIGURE A-6: Defining field names and data types for the Customers table in Table Design View

View (Datasheet) button

New field names

Customers table tab

Data type changed to Date/Time for the Birthday field

Field Name	Data Type
CustID	AutoNumber
FirstName	Text
LastName	Text
Phone	Text
Birthday	Date/Time

FIGURE A-7: Entering your first record in the Customers table

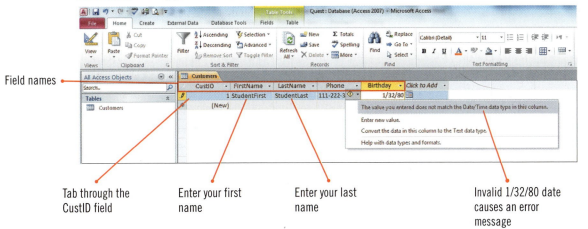

Field names

Tab through the CustID field

Enter your first name

Enter your last name

Invalid 1/32/80 date causes an error message

TABLE A-3: Data types

data type	description of data
Text	Text or numbers not used in calculations such as a name, zip code, or phone number
Memo	Lengthy text greater than 255 characters, such as comments or notes
Number	Numeric data that can be used in calculations, such as quantities
Date/Time	Dates and times
Currency	Monetary values
AutoNumber	Sequential integers controlled by Access
Yes/No	Only two values: Yes or No
Attachment	External files such as .jpg images, spreadsheets, and documents
Hyperlink	Web and e-mail addresses

Creating a Table

After creating your database and first table, you need to create new, related tables to build a relational database. Creating a table consists of these essential tasks: determining how the table will participate in the relational database, meaningful naming of each field in the table, selecting an appropriate data type for each field, and naming the table. Samantha Hooper asks you to create another table to store customer comments. The new table will be related to the Customers table so each customer's comments are linked to each customer.

1. **Click the Create tab on the Ribbon, then click the Table Design button in the Tables group**

   Design View is a view in which you create and manipulate the structure of an object.

2. **Enter the field names and data types as shown in Figure A-8**

   The Comments table will contain four fields. CommentID is set with an AutoNumber data type so each record is automatically numbered by Access. The Comment field has a Memo data type so a large comment can be recorded. CommentDate is a Date/Time field to identify the date of the comment. CustID has a Number data type and will be used to link the Comments table to the Customers table later.

3. **Click the Home tab, click the View button [icon] to switch to Datasheet View, click Yes when prompted to save the table, type Comments as the table name, click OK, then click No when prompted to create a primary key**

   A **primary key field** contains unique data for each record. You'll identify a primary key field for the Comments table later. For now, you'll enter the first record in the Comments table in Datasheet View. A **record** is a row of data in a table. Refer to Table A-4 for a summary of important database terminology.

4. **Press [Tab] to move to the Comment field, type Interested in future tours to Australia, press [Tab], type 1/7/13 in the CommentDate field, press [Tab], then type 1 in the CustID field**

   As shown in Figure A-9, you entered 1 in the CustID field to connect this comment with the customer in the Customers table that has a CustID value of 1. Knowing which CustID value to enter for each comment is difficult. After you properly relate the tables (a task you have not yet performed), Access can make it easier to associate comments and customers.

5. **Right-click the Comments table tab, then click Close**

Creating a table in Datasheet View

In Access 2010, you can create a new table in Datasheet View using commands on the Fields tab of the Ribbon. You can also enter data in Datasheet View. Entering data in Datasheet View *before* finishing field design activities can introduce a wide variety of data entry errors, such as entering textual data in what should be defined as a Number or Date/Time field. If you design your tables using Table Design View, you avoid the temptation of entering data before you finish defining fields, which helps minimize many types of common data entry errors.

FIGURE A-8: Creating the Comments table

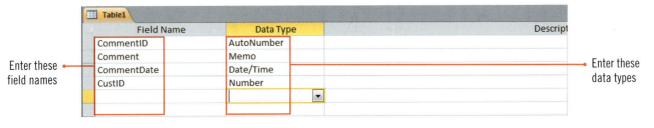

Enter these field names

Enter these data types

FIGURE A-9: Entering the first record in the Comments table

Comments table tab

First record in the Comments table

TABLE A-4: Important database terminology

term	description
Field	A specific piece or category of data such as a first name, last name, city, state, or phone number
Record	A group of related fields that describes a person, place, thing, or transaction such as a customer, location, product, or sale
Key field	A field that contains unique information for each record, such as a customer number for a customer
Table	A collection of records for a single subject such as Customers, Products, or Sales
Relational database	Multiple tables that are linked together to address a business process such as managing tours, sales, and customers at Quest Specialty Travel
Objects	The parts of an Access database that help you view, edit, manage, and analyze the data: **tables**, **queries**, **forms**, **reports**, **macros**, and **modules**

Creating Primary Keys

The primary key field of a table serves two important purposes. First, it contains data that uniquely identifies each record. No two records can have the exact same entry in the field designated as the primary key field. Secondly, the primary key field helps relate one table to another in a **one-to-many relationship**, where one record from one table is related to many records in the second table. For example, one record in the Customers table can be related to many records in the Comments table. (One customer can have many comments.) The primary key field is always on the "one" side of a one-to-many relationship between two tables. Samantha Hooper asks you to check that a primary key field has been appropriately identified for each table in the new Quest database.

1. **Right-click the Comments table in the Navigation Pane, then click Design View**
    Table Design View for the Comments table opens. The field with the AutoNumber data type is generally the best candidate for the primary key field in a table because it automatically contains a unique number for each record.

> **TROUBLE**
> Make sure the Design tab is selected on the Ribbon.

2. **Click the CommentID field if it is not already selected, then click the Primary Key button in the Tools group on the Design tab**
    The CommentID field is now set as the primary key field for the Comments table as shown in Figure A-10.

> **QUICK TIP**
> You can also click the Save button on the Quick Access toolbar to save a table.

3. **Right-click the Comments table tab, click Close, then click Yes to save the table**
    Any time you must save design changes to an Access object such as a table, Access displays a dialog box to remind you to save the object.

4. **Right-click the Customers table in the Navigation Pane, then click Design View**
    Access has already set CustID as the primary key field for the Customers table as shown in Figure A-11.

5. **Right-click the Customers table tab, then click Close**
    You were not prompted to save the Customers table because you made no design changes. Now that you're sure that each table in the Quest database has an appropriate primary key field, you're ready to link the tables. The primary key field plays a critical role in this relationship.

FIGURE A-10: Creating a primary key field for the Comments table

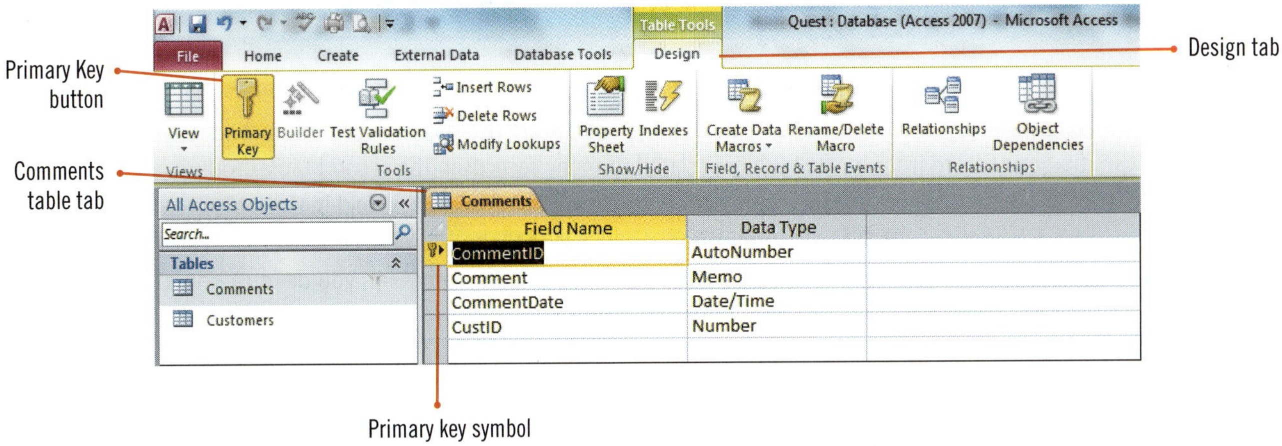

FIGURE A-11: Confirming the primary key field for the Customers table

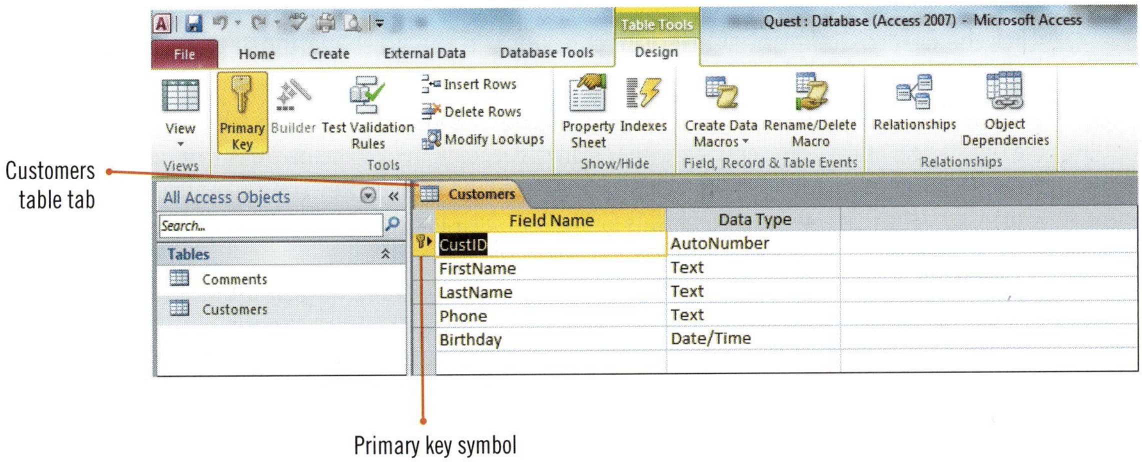

Learning about field properties

Properties are the characteristics that define the field. Two properties are required for every field: Field Name and Data Type. Many other properties, such as Field Size, Format, Caption, and Default Value, are defined in the Field Properties pane in the lower half of a table's Design View. As you add more property entries, you are generally restricting the amount or type of data that can be entered in the field, which increases data entry accuracy. For example, you might change the Field Size property for a State field to 2 to eliminate an incorrect entry such as FLL. Field properties change depending on the data type of the selected field. For example, date fields do not have a Field Size property because Access controls the size of fields with a Date/Time data type.

Relating Two Tables

After you create tables and set primary key fields, you must link the tables together in one-to-many relationships to enjoy the benefits of a relational database. A one-to-many relationship between two tables means that one record from the first table is related to many records in the second table. You use a common field to make this connection. The common field is always the primary key field in the table on the "one" side of the relationship. Samantha Hooper explains that she has new comments to enter into the Quest database. To easily identify which customer is related to each comment, you define a one-to-many relationship between the Customers and Comments tables.

STEPS

1. **Click the Database Tools tab on the Ribbon, then click the Relationships button**

TROUBLE

If the Show Table dialog box doesn't appear, click the Show Table button on the Design tab.

2. **In the Show Table dialog box, double-click Customers, double-click Comments, then click Close**

    Each table is represented by a small **field list** window that displays the table's field names. A key symbol identifies the primary key field in each table. To relate the two tables in a one-to-many relationship, you connect them using the common field, which is always the primary key field on the "one" side of the relationship.

QUICK TIP

Drag a table's title bar to move the field list.

3. **Drag CustID in the Customers field list to the CustID field in the Comments field list**

    The Edit Relationships dialog box opens as shown in Figure A-12. **Referential integrity**, a set of Access rules that governs data entry, helps ensure data accuracy.

TROUBLE

If you need to delete an incorrect relationship, right-click a relationship line, then click Delete.

4. **Click the Enforce Referential Integrity check box in the Edit Relationships dialog box, then click Create**

    The **one-to-many line** shows the link between the CustID field of the Customers table (the "one" side) and the CustID field of the Comments table (the "many" side, indicated by the **infinity symbol**), as shown in Figure A-13. The linking field on the "many" side is called the **foreign key field**. Now that these tables are related, it is much easier to enter comments for the correct customer.

QUICK TIP

To print the Relationships window, click the Relationship Report button on the Design tab, then click Print.

5. **Click the Close button on the Design tab, click Yes to save changes, then double-click the Customers table in the Navigation Pane to open it in Datasheet View**

    When you relate two tables in a one-to-many relationship, expand buttons ⊞ appear to the left of each record in the table on the "one" side of the relationship. In this case, this is the Customers table.

6. **Click the expand button ⊞ to the left of the first record, then drag the ↔ pointer to widen the Comment field**

    A **subdatasheet** shows the related comment records for each customer. In other words, the subdatasheet shows the records on the "many" side of a one-to-many relationship. The expand button ⊞ also changed to the collapse button ⊟ for the first customer. Widening the Comment field allows you to see the entire entry in the Comments subdatasheet. Now the task of entering comments for the right customer is much more straightforward.

7. **Enter two more comments as shown in Figure A-14**

    Interestingly, the CustID field in the Comments table (the foreign key field) is not displayed in the subdatasheet. Behind the scenes, Access is entering the correct CustID value in the Comments table, which is the glue that ties each comment to the right customer.

8. **Close the Customers table, then click Yes if prompted to save changes**

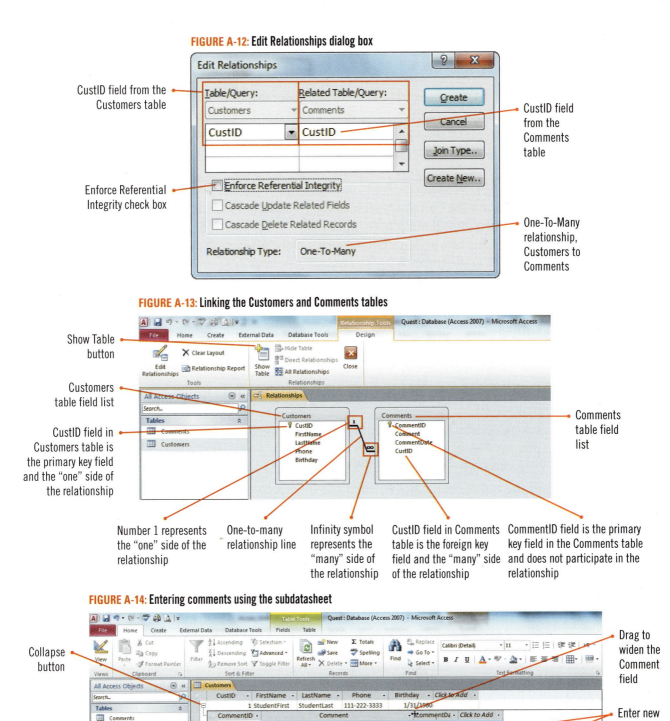

FIGURE A-12: Edit Relationships dialog box

- CustID field from the Customers table
- CustID field from the Comments table
- Enforce Referential Integrity check box
- One-To-Many relationship, Customers to Comments

FIGURE A-13: Linking the Customers and Comments tables

- Show Table button
- Customers table field list
- CustID field in Customers table is the primary key field and the "one" side of the relationship
- Comments table field list
- Number 1 represents the "one" side of the relationship
- One-to-many relationship line
- Infinity symbol represents the "many" side of the relationship
- CustID field in Comments table is the foreign key field and the "many" side of the relationship
- CommentID field is the primary key field in the Comments table and does not participate in the relationship

FIGURE A-14: Entering comments using the subdatasheet

- Collapse button
- Expand button
- Drag to widen the Comment field
- Enter new comments
- Your customers will be different

Enforcing referential integrity

Referential integrity is a set of rules that helps reduce invalid entries and orphan records. An **orphan record** is a record in the "many" table that doesn't have a matching entry in the linking field of the "one" table. With referential integrity enforced on a one-to-many relationship, you cannot enter a value in a foreign key field of the "many" table that does not have a match in the linking field of the "one" table. Referential integrity also prevents you from deleting a record in the "one" table if a matching entry exists in the foreign key field of the "many" table. You should enforce referential integrity on all one-to-many relationships if possible. If you are working with a database that already contains orphan records, you cannot enforce referential integrity on that relationship.

Access 2010

Entering Data

Your skill in navigating and entering data is a key to your success with a relational database. You use either mouse or keystroke techniques to navigate the data in the table's datasheet. Even though you have already successfully entered some data, Samantha Hooper asks you to master this essential skill by entering several more customers in the Quest database.

STEPS

1. **Double-click the Customers table in the Navigation Pane to open it, press [Tab] three times, then press [Enter] three times**

   The Customers table reopens. The Comments subdatasheets are collapsed. Both the [Tab] and [Enter] keys move the focus to the next field. The **focus** refers to which data you would edit if you started typing. The record that has the focus is highlighted in light blue. The field name that has the focus is highlighted in light orange. When you navigate to the last field of the record, pressing [Tab] or [Enter] advances the focus to the first field of the next record. You can also use the Next record ▶ and Previous record ◀ **navigation buttons** on the navigation bar in the lower-left corner of the datasheet to navigate the records. The **Current record** text box on the navigation bar tells you the number of the current record as well as the total number of records in the datasheet.

2. **Click the FirstName field of the fourth record to position the insertion point to enter a new record**

   You can also use the New (blank) record button ▶ on the navigation bar to move to a new record. You enter new records at the end of the datasheet. You learn how to sort and reorder records later. A complete list of navigation keystrokes is shown in Table A-5.

QUICK TIP

Access databases are multiuser with one important limitation: two users cannot edit the same *record* at the same time. In that case, a message explains that the second user must wait until the first user moves to a different record.

3. **At the end of the datasheet, enter the three records shown in Figure A-15**

   The **edit record symbol** 🖉 shown in Figure A-16 appears to the left of the record you are currently editing. When you move to a different record, Access saves the data. Therefore, Access never prompts you to save *data* because it performs that task automatically. Saving data automatically allows Access databases to be **multiuser** databases, which means that more than one person can enter and edit data in the same database at the same time.

   Your CustID values might differ from those in Figure A-16. Because the CustID field is an **AutoNumber** field, Access automatically enters the next consecutive number into the field as it creates the record. If you delete a record or are interrupted when entering a record, Access discards the value in the AutoNumber field and does not reuse it. AutoNumber values do not represent the number of records in your table. Instead, they provide a unique value per record, similar to check numbers. Each check number is unique, and does not represent the number of checks you have written.

Changing from Navigation mode to Edit mode

If you navigate to another area of the datasheet by clicking with the mouse pointer instead of pressing [Tab] or [Enter], you change from **Navigation mode** to Edit mode. In **Edit mode**, Access assumes that you are trying to make changes to the current field value, so keystrokes such as [Ctrl][End], [Ctrl][Home], [◀], and [▶] move the insertion point within the field. To return to Navigation mode, press [Tab] or [Enter] (thus moving the focus to the next field), or press [▲] or [▼] (thus moving the focus to a different record).

FIGURE A-15: Three records to add to the Customers table

CustID	FirstName	LastName	Phone	Birthday
[Tab]	Nicolas	McNeil	444-555-6666	4/1/1983
[Tab]	Toby	Stanton	555-666-7777	5/1/1984
[Tab]	Renada	Champ	666-777-8888	6/1/1985

FIGURE A-16: New records in the Customers table

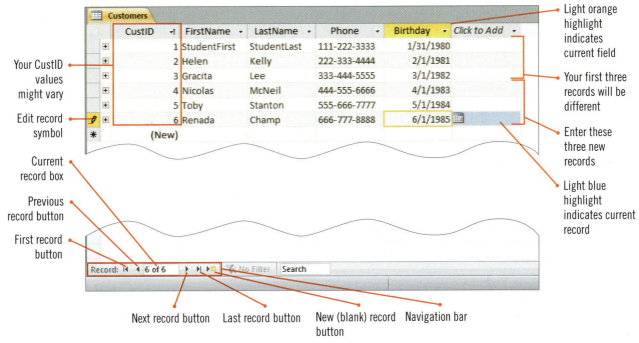

Your CustID values might vary

Edit record symbol

Current record box

Previous record button

First record button

Light orange highlight indicates current field

Your first three records will be different

Enter these three new records

Light blue highlight indicates current record

Next record button   Last record button   New (blank) record button   Navigation bar

TABLE A-5: Navigation mode keyboard shortcuts

shortcut key	moves to the
[Tab], [Enter], or [→]	Next field of the current record
[Shift][Tab] or [←]	Previous field of the current record
[Home]	First field of the current record
[End]	Last field of the current record
[Ctrl][Home] or [F5]	First field of the first record
[Ctrl][End]	Last field of the last record
[↑]	Current field of the previous record
[↓]	Current field of the next record

Windows Live

Using **cloud computing** (work done in a virtual environment), you can take advantage of Windows Live SkyDrive, a free service from Microsoft. Using Windows Live SkyDrive, you and your colleagues can store files in a "cloud" and retrieve them anytime you are connected to the Internet. That way, you can access files containing data whenever you need them. To use Windows Live SkyDrive, you need a free Windows Live ID, which you obtain at the Windows Live Web site. You can find more information and projects in the "Working with Windows Live and Microsoft Office Web Apps" appendix.

Editing Data

Updating information in a database is another critical data management task. To change the contents of an existing record, navigate to the field you want to change and type the new information. You can delete unwanted data by clicking the field and using [Backspace] or [Delete] to delete text to the left or right of the insertion point. Other data entry keystrokes are summarized in Table A-6. Samantha Hooper asks you to correct two records in the Customers table.

1. **Double-click the name in the FirstName field of the second record, type Jesse, press [Enter], type Siren, press [Enter], type 111-222-4444, press [Enter], type 2/15/81, then press [Enter]**

   You changed the name, telephone number, and birthdate of the second customer. You'll also change the third customer.

   > **QUICK TIP**
   > The ScreenTip for the Undo button 🔄 displays the action you can undo.

2. **Press [Enter] to move to the FirstName field of the third record, type Naresh, press [Enter], type Kast, press [Enter], type 111-222-5555, then press [Esc]**

   Pressing [Esc] once removes the current field's editing changes, so the Phone value changes back to the previous entry. Pressing [Esc] twice removes all changes to the current record. When you move to another record, Access saves your edits, so you can no longer use [Esc] to remove editing changes to the current record. You can, however, click the Undo button 🔄 on the Quick Access toolbar to undo changes to a previous record.

3. **Retype 111-222-5555, press [Enter], click the Calendar icon, then click March 15, 1982 as shown in Figure A-17**

   When you are working in the Birthday field, which has a Date/Time data type, you can enter a date from the keyboard or use the **Calendar Picker**, a pop-up calendar to find and select a date.

4. **Click the record selector for the last record (the one for Renada Champ), click the Delete button in the Records group on the Home tab, then click Yes**

   A message warns that you cannot undo a record deletion. The Undo button is dimmed, indicating that you cannot use it. The Customers table now has five records, as shown in Figure A-18. Keep in mind that your CustID values might differ from those in the figure because they are controlled by Access.

5. **Click the File tab, click Print, click Print Preview to review the printout of the Customers table before printing, click the Print button, click OK, then click the Close Print Preview button**

6. **Click the File tab, click Exit to close the Quest.accdb database and Access 2010, then click Yes if prompted to save design changes to the Customers table**

Resizing and moving datasheet columns

You can resize the width of a field in a datasheet by dragging the **column separator**, the thin line that separates the field names to the left or right. The pointer changes to ↔ as you make the field wider or narrower. Release the mouse button when you have resized the field. To adjust the column width to accommodate the widest entry in the field, double-click the column separator. To move a column, click the field name to select the entire column, then drag the field name left or right.

FIGURE A-17: Editing customer records

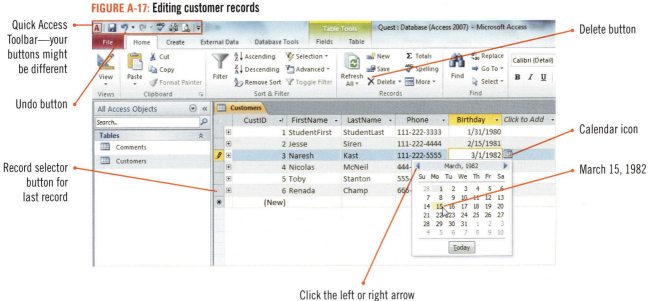

Quick Access Toolbar—your buttons might be different

Undo button

Record selector button for last record

Delete button

Calendar icon

March 15, 1982

Click the left or right arrow to change the month

FIGURE A-18: Final Customers datasheet

CustID	FirstName	LastName	Phone	Birthday	Click to Add
1	StudentFirst	StudentLast	111-222-3333	1/31/1980	
2	Jesse	Siren	111-222-4444	2/15/1981	
3	Naresh	Kast	111-222-5555	3/15/1982	
4	Nicolas	McNeil	444-555-6666	4/1/1983	
5	Toby	Stanton	555-666-7777	5/1/1984	
(New)					

Your name is entered here

TABLE A-6: Edit mode keyboard shortcuts

editing keystroke	action
[Backspace]	Deletes one character to the left of the insertion point
[Delete]	Deletes one character to the right of the insertion point
[F2]	Switches between Edit and Navigation mode
[Esc]	Undoes the change to the current field
[Esc][Esc]	Undoes all changes to the current record
[F7]	Starts the spell-check feature
[Ctrl][']	Inserts the value from the same field in the previous record into the current field
[Ctrl][;]	Inserts the current date in a Date field

Practice

Concepts Review

For current SAM information, including versions and content details, visit SAM Central (http://www.cengage.com/samcentral). If you have a SAM user profile, you may have access to hands-on instruction, practice, and assessment of the skills covered in this unit. Since various versions of SAM are supported throughout the life of this text, check with your instructor for the correct instructions and URL/Web site for accessing assignments.

Label each element of the Access window shown in Figure A-19.

FIGURE A-19

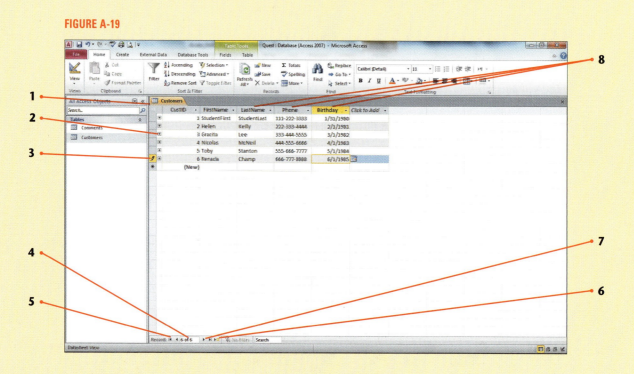

Match each term with the statement that best describes it.

9. **Table**
10. **Query**
11. **Field**
12. **Record**
13. **Datasheet**
14. **Form**
15. **Report**

a. A subset of data from one or more tables

b. A collection of records for a single subject, such as all the customer records

c. A professional printout of database information

d. A spreadsheet-like grid that displays fields as columns and records as rows

e. A group of related fields for one item, such as all of the information for one customer

f. A category of information in a table, such as a company name, city, or state

g. An easy-to-use data entry screen

Select the best answer from the list of choices.

16. Which of the following is *not* a typical benefit of relational databases?

a. More accurate data

b. Faster information retrieval

c. More common than spreadsheets

d. Minimized duplicate data entry

17. Which of the following is *not* an advantage of managing data with relational database software such as Access versus spreadsheet software such as Excel?

a. Allows multiple users to enter data simultaneously

b. Provides data entry forms

c. Reduces duplicate data entry

d. Uses a single table to store all data

18. The object that creates a professional printout of data that includes headers, footers, and graphics is the:

a. Query.

b. Report.

c. Table.

d. Form.

19. The object that contains all of the database data is the:

a. Report.

b. Page.

c. Form.

d. Table.

20. When you create a new database, which object is created first?

a. Query

b. Module

c. Table

d. Form

Skills Review

1. Understand relational databases.

    a. Identify five advantages of managing database information in Access versus using a spreadsheet.

    b. Create a sentence to explain how the terms *field*, *record*, *table*, and *relational database* relate to one another.

2. Explore a database.

    a. Start Access.

    b. Open the RealEstate-A.accdb database from the drive and folder where you store your Data Files. Enable content if a Security Warning message appears.

    c. Open each of the three tables to study the data they contain. On a sheet of paper, complete Table A-7.

    d. Double-click the ListingsByRealtor query in the Navigation Pane to open it. Change any occurrence of Gordon Matusek to your name. Move to another record to save your changes.

TABLE A-7

table name	number of records	number of fields

    e. Double-click the RealtorsMainForm in the Navigation Pane to open it. Use the navigation buttons to navigate through the 11 realtors to observe each realtor's listings.

    f. Double-click the RealtorListingReport in the Navigation Pane to open it. Scroll through the report to make sure your name is positioned correctly. The report is currently sorted in ascending order by realtor first names.

    g. Close the RealEstate-A database, and then close Access 2010.

3. Create a database.

    a. Start Access, use the Browse folder button to navigate to the drive and folder where you store your Data Files, type **RealEstateMarketing** as the File Name, click OK, and then click Create to create a new database named RealEstateMarketing.accdb.

Skills Review (continued)

b. Switch to Table Design View, name the table **Prospects**, then enter the following fields and data types:

field name	data type
ProspectID	AutoNumber
ProspectFirst	Text
ProspectLast	Text
Phone	Text
Email	Hyperlink
Street	Text
City	Text
State	Text
Zip	Text

c. Save the table, switch to Datasheet View, and enter two records using your name in the first record and your professor's name in the second. Tab through the ProspectID field, an AutoNumber field.

d. Enter **OK** (Oklahoma) as the value in the State field for both records. Use school or fictitious (rather than personal) data for all other field data, and be sure to fill out each record completely.

e. Widen each column in the Prospects table so that all data is visible, then save and close the Prospects table.

4. Create a table.

a. Click the Create tab on the Ribbon, click Table Design, then create a new table with the following two fields and data types:

field name	data type
StateAbbrev	Text
StateName	Text

b. Save the table with the name **States**. Click No when asked if you want Access to create the primary key field.

5. Create primary keys.

a. In Table Design View of the States table, set the StateAbbrev as the primary key field.

b. Save the States table and open it in Datasheet View.

c. Enter one state record, using **OK** for the StateAbbrev value and **Oklahoma** for the StateName value to match the State value of OK that you entered for both records in the Prospects table.

d. Close the States table.

6. Relate two tables.

a. From the Database Tools tab, open the Relationships window.

b. Add the States then the Prospects table to the Relationships window.

c. Drag the bottom edge of the Prospects table to expand the field list to display all of the fields.

d. Drag the StateAbbrev field from the States table to the State field of the Prospects table.

e. In the Edit Relationships dialog box, click the Enforce Referential Integrity check box, then click Create. Your Relationships window should look similar to Figure A-20. If you connect the wrong fields by mistake, right-click the line connecting the two fields, click Delete, then try again.

f. Close the Relationships window, and save changes when prompted.

FIGURE A-20

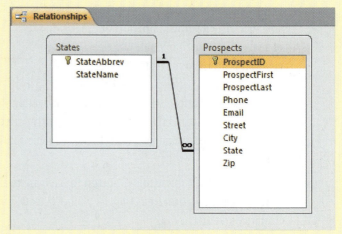

Skills Review (continued)

7. Enter data.

a. Open the States table and enter the following records:

StateAbbrev field	StateName field	StateAbbrev field	StateName field
CO	Colorado	NE	Nebraska
IA	Iowa	TX	Texas
KS	Kansas	WI	Wisconsin
MO	Missouri		

b. Add a few more state records using the correct two-character abbreviation for the state and the properly spelled state name.

c. Close and reopen the States table. Notice that Access sorts the records by the values in the primary key field, the StateAbbrev field.

8. Edit data.

a. Click the Expand button for the OK record to see the two related records from the Prospects table.

b. Enter two more prospects in the OK subdatasheet using any fictitious but realistic data as shown in Figure A-21. Notice that you are not required to enter a value for the State field, the foreign key field in the subdatasheet.

c. If required by your instructor, print the States datasheet and the Prospects datasheet.

d. Click the File tab, then click Exit to close all open objects as well as the RealEstateMarketing.accdb database and Access 2010. If prompted to save any design changes, click Yes.

FIGURE A-21

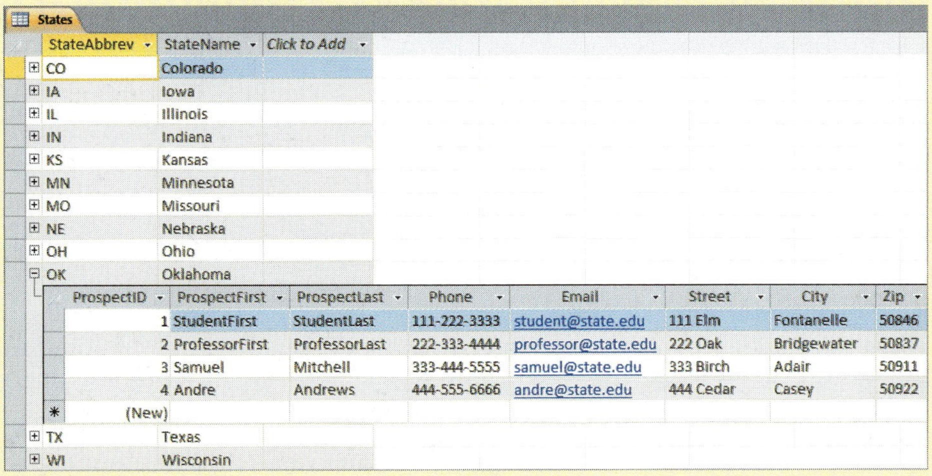

States

StateAbbrev	StateName	Click to Add
CO	Colorado	
IA	Iowa	
IL	Illinois	
IN	Indiana	
KS	Kansas	
MN	Minnesota	
MO	Missouri	
NE	Nebraska	
OH	Ohio	
OK	Oklahoma	

ProspectID	ProspectFirst	ProspectLast	Phone	Email	Street	City	Zip
1	StudentFirst	StudentLast	111-222-3333	student@state.edu	111 Elm	Fontanelle	50846
2	ProfessorFirst	ProfessorLast	222-333-4444	professor@state.edu	222 Oak	Bridgewater	50837
3	Samuel	Mitchell	333-444-5555	samuel@state.edu	333 Birch	Adair	50911
4	Andre	Andrews	444-555-6666	andre@state.edu	444 Cedar	Casey	50922
(New)							

StateAbbrev	StateName
TX	Texas
WI	Wisconsin

Independent Challenge 1

Review the following twelve examples of database tables:

- Telephone directory
- College course offerings
- Restaurant menu
- Cookbook
- Movie listing
- Islands of the Caribbean
- Encyclopedia
- Shopping catalog
- International product inventory
- Party guest list
- Members of the U.S. House of Representatives
- Ancient wonders of the world

In a Word document, complete the following tasks.

a. For each example, build a Word table with four to five columns. In the first row, identify four to five field names that you would expect to find in the table.

b. In the second and third rows of each table, enter two possible records. The first table, Telephone Directory, is completed in Figure A-22 as an example to follow.

FIGURE A-22

Table: Telephone Directory

FirstName	LastName	Street	Zip	Phone
Marco	Lopez	100 Main Street	88715	555-612-3312
Christopher	Stafford	253 Maple Lane	77824	555-612-1179

Independent Challenge 2

You are working with several civic groups to coordinate a community-wide cleanup effort. You have started a database called Recycle-A, which tracks the different clubs, their trash deposits, and the trash collection centers that are participating.

a. Start Access, then open the Recycle-A.accdb database from the drive and folder where you store your Data Files. Enable content if prompted.

b. Open each table's datasheet to study the number of fields and records per table. Notice that there are no expand buttons to the left of any records because relationships have not yet been established between these tables.

c. In a Word document, recreate and complete the table shown in Table A-8.

d. Close all table datasheets, then open the Relationships window and create the one-to-many relationships shown in Figure A-23. Click the Show Table button to add the field lists for each table to the Relationships window, and drag the title bars of the field lists to position them as shown in Figure A-23.

e. Be sure to enforce referential integrity on all relationships. If you create an incorrect relationship, right-click the line linking the fields, click Delete, and try again. Your final Relationships window should look like Figure A-23.

f. If required by your instructor, click the Relationship Report button on the Design tab, then click Print to print a copy of the Relationships for Recycle-A report. To close the report, right-click the Relationships for Recycle-A tab and click Close. Click No when prompted to save changes to the report.

g. Save your changes to the Relationships window, if necessary, close the Recycle-A.accdb database, then exit Access 2010.

TABLE A-8

table name	number of fields	number of records

FIGURE A-23

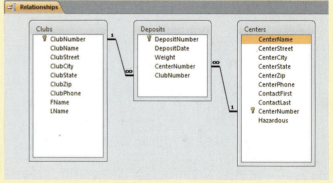

Independent Challenge 3

This Independent Challenge requires an Internet connection.

You are working for an advertising agency that provides advertising media for small and large businesses in the midwestern United States. You have started a database called BusinessContacts-A, which tracks your company's customers.

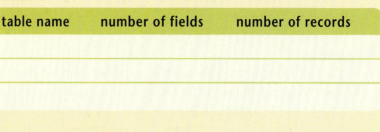

If you have a SAM 2010 user profile, an autogradable SAM version of this assignment may be available at http://www.cengage.com/sam2010. Check with your instructor to confirm that this assignment is available in SAM. To use the SAM version of this assignment, log into the SAM 2010 Web site and download the instruction and start files.

a. Start Access and open the BusinessContacts-A.accdb database from the drive and folder where you store your Data Files. Enable content if prompted.

b. Add a new record to the Customers table, using your own first and last names, $7,788.99 in the YTDSales field, and any reasonable entries for the rest of the fields.

c. Edit the Sprint Systems record (the first record). The Company name should be Embarq Corporation, and the Street value should be 2244 College St.

d. Delete the record for St Luke's Hospital (record 20), then close the Customers table.

e. Create a new table with two fields, State2 and StateName. Assign both fields a Text data type. The State2 field will contain the two-letter abbreviation for state names. The StateName field will contain the full state name.

f. Set the State2 field as the primary key field, then save the table as States.

Independent Challenge 3 (continued)

g. Enter at least three records into the States table, making sure that all of the states used in the Customers datasheet are entered in the States table. This includes *KS Kansas, MO Missouri,* and any other state you entered in Step b when you added a new record to the Customers table.

h. Close all open tables. Open the Relationships window, add both the States and Customers field lists to the window, then expand the size of the Customers field list so that all fields are visible.

i. Build a one-to-many relationship between the States and Customers tables by dragging the State2 field from the States table to the State field of the Customers table to create a one-to-many relationship between the two tables. Enforce referential integrity on the relationship. If you are unable to enforce referential integrity, it means that a value in the State field of the Customers table doesn't have a perfect match in the State2 field of the States table. Open both datasheets, making sure every state in the Customers table is also represented in the States table, close all datasheets, then reestablish the one-to-many relationship between the two tables with referential integrity.

j. Close the Relationships window and save your changes.

Advanced Challenge Exercise

- Use your favorite search engine to research the two-character abbreviations for the 13 provinces of Canada using the Web search criteria of **provinces of Canada postcodes**.
- Enter the 13 records into the States table, entering the two-character abbreviation in the State2 field and the province name in the StateName field. Note that all 13 entries are different from the 50 states in the United States. Close the States table.
- Right-click the States table in the Navigation Pane and click Rename. Enter **StatesProvinces** as the new table name.
- Reopen the Relationships window, click the Show Table button, double-click StatesProvinces, and click Close. The relationship between the StatesProvinces table and the Customers table has remained intact, but when you rename a table after establishing relationships, review the Relationships window to make sure all tables are visible.
- Click the Relationship Report button on the Design tab, then click Print to print the report.
- Right-click the Relationships for BusinessContacts-A tab, then click Close. Click Yes to save the report, then click OK to name the report Relationships for BusinessContacts-A.
- Close the Relationships window, saving changes as prompted.

k. Close the BusinessContacts-A.accdb database, and exit Access 2010.

Real Life Independent Challenge

This Independent Challenge requires an Internet connection.

Now that you've learned about Microsoft Access and relational databases, brainstorm how you might use an Access database in your daily life or career. Start by visiting the Microsoft Web site, and explore what's new about Access 2010.

a. Using your favorite search engine, look up the keywords *benefits of a relational database* or *benefits of Microsoft Access* to find articles that discuss the benefits of organizing data in a relational database.

b. Read several articles about the benefits of organizing data in a relational database such as Access, identifying three distinct benefits. Use a Word document to record those three benefits. Also, copy and paste the Web site address of the article you are referencing for each benefit you have identified.

c. In addition, as you read the articles that describe relational database benefits, list any terminology unfamiliar to you, identifying at least five new terms.

d. Using a search engine or a Web site that provides a computer glossary such as *www.whatis.com* or *www.webopedia.com*, look up the definition of the new terms, and enter both the term and the definition of the term in your document as well as the Web site address where your definition was found.

e. Finally, based on your research and growing understanding of Access 2010, list three ways you could use an Access database to organize, enhance, or support the activities and responsibilities of your daily life or career. Type your name at the top of the document, and submit it to your instructor as requested.

Visual Workshop

Open the Basketball-A.accdb database from the drive and folder where you store your Data Files, enable content if prompted, then open the Offense query datasheet, which lists offensive statistics by player by game. Modify any of the Kelsey Douglas records to contain your first and last names, then move to a new record, observing the power of a relational database to modify every occurrence of that name throughout the database. Close the Offense query, then open the Players table, shown in Figure A-24. Note that your name will be listed in alphabetical order based on the current sort field, PLast. Print the Players datasheet if requested by your instructor, then close the Players table, exit the Basketball-A.accdb database, and exit Access.

FIGURE A-24

PFirst	PLast	Height	PlayerNo	GradYear	Position	HomeTown	HomeState	Lettered
Kristen	Czyenski	73	35	2015	F	Omaha	NE	☐
Denise	Franco	72	42	2016	F	Antigua	WI	☑
Sydney	Freesen	68	4	2014	G	Panora	IA	☐
Theresa	Grant	73	22	2013	F	McKinney	TX	☐
Megan	Hile	74	45	2015	F	Cumberland	IA	☑
Amy	Hodel	72	21	2014	F	Oakbrook	IL	☑
Ellyse	Howard	70	12	2016	G	Osseo	MN	☑
Jamie	Johnson	75	52	2016	F	Belleville	IL	☐
Sandy	Robins	65	23	2013	G	Anita	IA	☐
StudentFirst	StudentLast	69	5	2015	G	Linden	IA	☑
Ashley	Sydnes	75	30	2013	F	Salina	KS	☐
Morgan	Tyler	71	51	2014	G	Roseau	MN	☐
Abbey	Walker	76	32	2014	C	Fargo	ND	☐
*		0	0					☐

UNIT B
Access 2010

Building and Using Queries

Files You Will Need:

QuestTravel-B.accdb
Recycle-B.accdb
Membership-B.accdb
Congress-B.accdb
Vet-B.accdb
Baseball-B.accdb

You build queries in an Access database to ask "questions" about data, such as which adventure tours are scheduled for July or what types of tours take place in Florida. Queries present the answer in a datasheet, which you can sort, filter, and format. Because queries are stored in the database, they can be used multiple times. Each time a query is opened, it displays a current view of the latest updates to the database.  Samantha Hooper, tour developer for U.S. group travel at Quest Specialty Travel, has several questions about the customer and tour information in the Quest database. You'll develop queries to provide Samantha with up-to-date answers.

OBJECTIVES

Use the Query Wizard

Work with data in a query

Use Query Design View

Sort and find data

Filter data

Apply AND criteria

Apply OR criteria

Format a datasheet

Using the Query Wizard

A **query** allows you to select a subset of fields and records from one or more tables and then present the selected data as a single datasheet. A major benefit of working with data through a query is that you can focus on only the information you need to answer your question, rather than navigating the fields and records from many large tables. You can enter, edit, and navigate data in a query datasheet just like a table datasheet. However, keep in mind that Access data is physically stored only in tables, even though you can view and edit it through other Access objects such as queries and forms. Because a query doesn't physically store the data, a query datasheet is sometimes called a **logical view** of the data. Technically, a query is a set of **SQL (Structured Query Language)** instructions, but because you can use Access query tools such as Query Design View, you are not required to know SQL to build or use Access queries. You use the Simple Query Wizard to build a query that displays a few fields from the Tours and Customers tables in one datasheet.

STEPS

1. **Start Access, open the QuestTravel-B.accdb database, enable content if prompted, then maximize the window**

   Access provides several tools to create a new query. One way is to use the **Simple Query Wizard**, which prompts you for information it needs to create a new query.

   > **TROUBLE**
   > If a Microsoft Access Security Notice dialog box opens, click the Open button.

2. **Click the Create tab on the Ribbon, click the Query Wizard button in the Queries group, then click OK to start the Simple Query Wizard**

   The first Simple Query Wizard dialog box opens, prompting you to select the fields you want to view in the new query.

3. **Click the Tables/Queries list arrow, click Table: Tours, double-click TourName, double-click City, double-click Category, then double-click Cost**

   So far, you've selected four fields from the Tours table to display basic tour information in this query. You also want to add the first and last name fields from the Customers table so you know which customers purchased each tour.

   > **TROUBLE**
   > Click the Remove Single Field button `<` if you need to remove a field from the Selected Fields list.

4. **Click the Tables/Queries list arrow, click Table: Customers, double-click FName, then double-click LName**

   You've selected four fields from the Tours table and two from the Customers table for your new query, as shown in Figure B-1.

5. **Click Next, click Next to select Detail, select Tours Query in the title text box, type TourCustomers as the name of the query, then click Finish**

   The TourCustomers datasheet opens, displaying four fields from the Tours table and two from the Customers table as shown in Figure B-2. The query can show which customers have purchased which tours because of the one-to-many table relationships established in the Relationships window.

FIGURE B-1: Selecting fields using the Simple Query Wizard

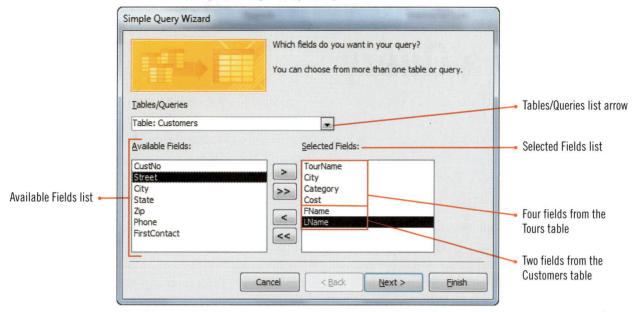

FIGURE B-2: TourCustomers datasheet

TourName	City	Category	Cost	FName	LName
Ames Ski Club	Breckenridge	Adventure	$850	Kristen	Collins
Stanley Bay Shelling	Captiva	Adventure	$750	Lisa	Wilson
Stanley Bay Shelling	Captiva	Adventure	$750	Kori	Yode
Yosemite National Park Great Cleanup	Sacramento	Service	$1,100	Kristen	Collins
American Heritage Tour	Philadelphia	Educational	$1,200	Kayla	Browning
American Heritage Tour	Philadelphia	Educational	$1,200	Mark	Custard
American Heritage Tour	Philadelphia	Educational	$1,200	Fritz	Garden
Bright Lights Expo	Branson	Site Seeing	$200	Kristen	Collins
Bright Lights Expo	Branson	Site Seeing	$200	Tom	Camel
Bright Lights Expo	Branson	Site Seeing	$200	Mark	Custard
Bright Lights Expo	Branson	Site Seeing	$200	Daniel	Cabriella
American Heritage Tour	Philadelphia	Educational	$1,200	Daniel	Cabriella
Red Reef Scuba	Islamadora	Adventure	$1,500	Gracita	Mayberry
Red Reef Scuba	Islamadora	Adventure	$1,500	Jacob	Alman
Red Reef Scuba	Islamadora	Adventure	$1,500	Julia	Bouchart
Bright Lights Expo	Branson	Site Seeing	$200	Samantha	Braven
Red Reef Scuba	Islamadora	Adventure	$1,500	Nancy	Diverman
Ames Ski Club	Breckenridge	Adventure	$850	Naresh	Hubert
Ames Ski Club	Breckenridge	Adventure	$850	Toby	Lang
Ames Ski Club	Breckenridge	Adventure	$850	Douglas	Margolis
Ames Ski Club	Breckenridge	Adventure	$850	Jenny	Nelson
Ames Ski Club	Breckenridge	Adventure	$850	Sharol	Olingback
Boy Scout Troop 274	Vail	Adventure	$1,900	Brad	Eahlie
Bridgewater Jaycees	Aspen	Adventure	$1,200	Nancy	Diverman
Bridgewater Jaycees	Aspen	Adventure	$1,200	Kathryn	Dotey

Record: I◄ ◄ 1 of 80 ► ►I ►▣   No Filter   Search

TourCustomers query

Four fields from the Tours table

Two fields from the Customers table

80 records

Working with Data in a Query

You enter and edit data in a query datasheet the same way you do in a table datasheet. Because all data is stored in tables, any edits you make in a query datasheet are permanently stored in the underlying tables, and are automatically updated in all views of the data in other queries, forms, and reports. You want to change the name of two tours and update one customer name. You can use the TourCustomers query datasheet to make these edits.

STEPS

1. **Double-click Stanley in the Stanley Bay Shelling tour name in either the second or third record, type Princess, then click any other record**

   All occurrences of Stanley Bay Shelling automatically update to Princess Bay Shelling because this tour name value is stored only once in the Tours table (see Figure B-3). The tour name is selected from the Tours table and displayed in the TourCustomers query for each customer who purchased this tour.

2. **Double-click Cabriella in the LName field, type Dodds, then click any other record**

   All occurrences of Cabriella automatically update to Dodds because this last name value is stored only once in the Customers table. This name is selected from the Customers table and displayed in the TourCustomers query for each tour this customer purchased.

3. **Click the record selector button to the left of the first record, click the Home tab, click the Delete button in the Records group, then click Yes**

   You can delete records from a query datasheet the same way you delete them from a table datasheet. Notice that the navigation bar now indicates you have 79 records in the datasheet as shown in Figure B-4.

4. **Right-click the TourCustomers query tab, then click Close**

Record selector
button for
first record

Updating to
Princess Bay
Shelling
in one record
updates
all records

TourName	City	Category	Cost	FName	LName
Ames Ski Club	Breckenridge	Adventure	$850	Kristen	Collins
Princess Bay Shelling	Captiva	Adventure	$750	Lisa	Wilson
Princess Bay Shelling	Captiva	Adventure	$750	Kori	Yode
Yosemite National Park Great Cleanup	Sacramento	Service	$1,100	Kristen	Collins
American Heritage Tour	Philadelphia	Educational	$1,200	Kayla	Browning
American Heritage Tour	Philadelphia	Educational	$1,200	Mark	Custard
American Heritage Tour	Philadelphia	Educational	$1,200	Fritz	Garden
Bright Lights Expo	Branson	Site Seeing	$200	Kristen	Collins
Bright Lights Expo	Branson	Site Seeing	$200	Tom	Camel
Bright Lights Expo	Branson	Site Seeing	$200	Mark	Custard
Bright Lights Expo	Branson	Site Seeing	$200	Daniel	Cabriella
American Heritage Tour	Philadelphia	Educational	$1,200	Daniel	Cabriella
Red Reef Scuba	Islamadora	Adventure	$1,500	Gracita	Mayberry

Change
Cabriella to
Dodds

TourCustomers
query tab

Delete button

79 records in
the datasheet

TourName	City	Category	Cost	FName	LName
Princess Bay Shelling	Captiva	Adventure	$750	Lisa	Wilson
Princess Bay Shelling	Captiva	Adventure	$750	Kori	Yode
Yosemite National Park Great Cleanup	Sacramento	Service	$1,100	Kristen	Collins
American Heritage Tour	Philadelphia	Educational	$1,200	Kayla	Browning
American Heritage Tour	Philadelphia	Educational	$1,200	Mark	Custard
American Heritage Tour	Philadelphia	Educational	$1,200	Fritz	Garden
Bright Lights Expo	Branson	Site Seeing	$200	Kristen	Collins
Bright Lights Expo	Branson	Site Seeing	$200	Tom	Camel
Bright Lights Expo	Branson	Site Seeing	$200	Mark	Custard
Bright Lights Expo	Branson	Site Seeing	$200	Daniel	Dodds
American Heritage Tour	Philadelphia	Educational	$1,200	Daniel	Dodds
Red Reef Scuba	Islamadora	Adventure	$1,500	Gracita	Mayberry
Red Reef Scuba	Islamadora	Adventure	$1,500	Jacob	Alman
Red Reef Scuba	Islamadora	Adventure	$1,500	Julia	Bouchart
Bright Lights Expo	Branson	Site Seeing	$200	Samantha	Braven
Red Reef Scuba	Islamadora	Adventure	$1,500	Nancy	Diverman
Ames Ski Club	Breckenridge	Adventure	$850	Naresh	Hubert
Ames Ski Club	Breckenridge	Adventure	$850	Toby	Lang
Ames Ski Club	Breckenridge	Adventure	$850	Douglas	Margolis
Ames Ski Club	Breckenridge	Adventure	$850	Jenny	Nelson
Ames Ski Club	Breckenridge	Adventure	$850	Sharol	Olingback
Boy Scout Troop 274	Vail	Adventure	$1,900	Brad	Eahlie
Bridgewater Jaycees	Aspen	Adventure	$1,200	Nancy	Diverman
Bridgewater Jaycees	Aspen	Adventure	$1,200	Kathryn	Dotey
Bridgewater Jaycees	Aspen	Adventure	$1,200	Anne	Duman

Record: 1 of 79   No Filter Search

Cabriella in
the LName
field
changed to
Dodds

Datasheet View

Using Query Design View

You use **Query Design View** to add, delete, or move the fields in an existing query, to specify sort orders, or to add **criteria** to limit the number of records shown in the resulting datasheet. You can also use Query Design View to create a new query from scratch. Query Design View presents the fields you can use for that query in small windows called field lists. If you use the fields of two or more related tables in the query, the relationship between two tables is displayed with a **join line** (also called a **link line**) identifying which fields are used to establish the relationship. Samantha Hooper asks you to print a list of Adventure tours in Colorado. You use Query Design View to modify the existing ToursByState query to meet her request.

STEPS

1. **Double-click the ToursByState query in the Navigation Pane to review the datasheet**

    The ToursByState query contains the StateName field from the States table, and the TourName, TourStartDate, and Cost fields from the Tours table.

2. **Click the View button ✎ in the Views group to switch to Query Design View**

    Query Design View displays the tables used in the query in the upper pane of the window. The link line shows that one record in the States table may be related to many records in the Tours table. The lower pane of the window, called the **query design grid** (or query grid for short) displays the field names, sort orders, and criteria used within the query.

3. **Click the first Criteria cell for the StateName field, then type Colorado as shown in Figure B-5**

    Criteria are limiting conditions you set in the query design grid. In this case, the condition limits the selected records to only those with "Colorado" in the StateName field.

4. **Click the View button ▦ in the Results group to switch to Datasheet View**

    Now only six records are selected, because only six of the tours have "Colorado" in the StateName field, as shown in Figure B-6. Remember that this query contains two ascending sort orders: StateName and TourName. Because all of the records have the same StateName, they are further sorted by the TourName values. You want to save this query with a different name.

5. **Click the File tab, click Save Object As, type ColoradoTours, click OK, then click the Home tab**

    In Access, the **Save command** on the File tab saves the current object, and the **Save Object As command** saves the current object with a new name. Recall that Access saves *data* automatically as you move from record to record.

6. **Right-click the ColoradoTours query tab, then click Close**

FIGURE B-5: ToursByState query in Design View

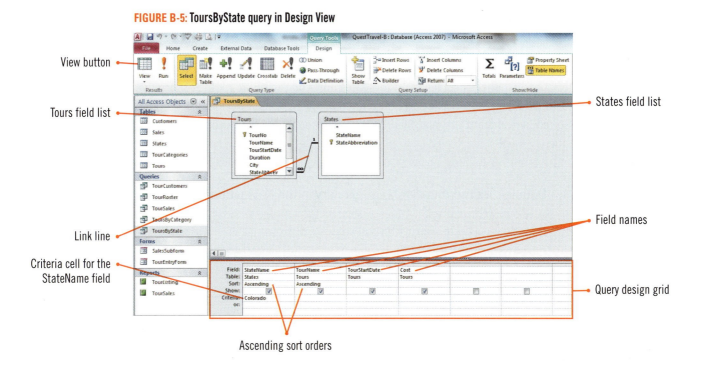

View button

Tours field list

Link line

Criteria cell for the
StateName field

States field list

Field names

Query design grid

Ascending sort orders

FIGURE B-6: ToursByState datasheet with Colorado criterion

Only six Colorado
records are
selected

TourName values
displayed in
ascending order

StateName	TourName	TourStartDate	Cost
Colorado	Ames Ski Club	01/20/2013	$850
Colorado	Boy Scout Troop 274	01/31/2013	$1,900
Colorado	Bridgewater Jaycees	03/05/2013	$1,200
Colorado	Eagle Hiking Club	07/07/2012	$695
Colorado	Franklin Family Reunion	03/29/2013	$700
Colorado	Team Discovery	07/17/2012	$550

Adding or deleting a table in a query

You might want to add a table's field list to the upper pane of Query Design View in order to select fields from that table for the query. To add a new table to Query Design View, click the Show Table button on the Design tab, then add the desired table(s). To delete an unneeded table from Query Design View, click its title bar, then press [Delete].

Sorting and Finding Data

The Access sort and find features are handy tools that help you quickly organize and find data in a table or query datasheet. Besides using these buttons, you can also click the list arrow on the field name in a datasheet, and then click a sorting option. ![watercolor] Samantha Hooper asks you to provide a list of tours sorted by TourStartDate, and then by Duration. You'll modify the ToursByCategory query to answer this query.

STEPS

1. **Double-click the ToursByCategory query in the Navigation Pane to open its datasheet**

    The ToursByCategory query currently sorts tours by Category, then by TourName. You'll add the Duration field to this query, then change the sort order for the records.

2. **Click the View button ![icon] in the Views group to switch to Design View, then double-click the Duration field in the Tours field list**

    When you double-click a field in a field list, Access inserts it in the next available position in the query design grid. You can also select a field, and then drag it to a specific column of the query grid. To select a field in the query grid, you click its field selector. The **field selector** is the thin gray bar above each field in the query grid. If you want to delete a field from a query, click its field selector, then press [Delete]. Deleting a field from a query does not delete it from the underlying table; the field is only deleted from the query's logical view of the data.

    Currently, the ToursByCategory query is sorted by Category and then by TourName. Access evaluates sort specifications from left to right. You want to sort this query first by TourStartDate then by Duration.

3. **Click Ascending in the Category Sort cell, click the list arrow, click (not sorted), click Ascending in the TourName Sort cell, click the list arrow, click (not sorted), double-click the TourStartDate Sort cell to specify an Ascending sort, then double-click the Duration Sort cell to specify an Ascending sort**

    The records are now set to be sorted in ascending order, first by TourStartDate, then by the values in the Duration field, as shown in Figure B-7. Because sort orders always work left to right, you sometimes need to rearrange the fields before applying a sort order that uses more than one field. To move a field in the query design grid, click its field selector, then drag it left or right.

4. **Click the View button ![icon] in the Results group to display the query datasheet**

    The new datasheet shows the Duration field in the fifth column. The records are now sorted in ascending order by the TourStartDate field. If two records have the same TourStartDate, they are further sorted by Duration. You can also sort directly in the datasheet using the Ascending and Descending buttons on the Home tab, but to specify multiple sort orders on nonconsecutive fields, it's best to use Query Design View. Your next task is to replace all occurrences of "Site Seeing" with "Cultural" in the Category field.

5. **Click the Find button on the Home tab, type Site Seeing in the Find What box, click the Replace tab, click in the Replace With box, then type Cultural**

    The Find and Replace dialog box is shown in Figure B-8.

    TROUBLE
    If your find-and-replace effort did not work correctly, click the Undo button ![icon] and repeat Steps 5 and 6.

6. **Click the Replace All button in the Find and Replace dialog box, click Yes to continue, then click Cancel to close the Find and Replace dialog box**

    Access replaced all occurrences of "Site Seeing" with "Cultural" in the Category field, as shown in Figure B-9.

7. **Right-click the ToursByCategory query tab, click Close, then click Yes if prompted to save changes**

FIGURE B-7: Changing sort orders for the ToursByCategory query

Duration field in the Tours table

Field selectors are thin gray bars above the field names

Sort orders for the Category and TourName fields are removed

Ascending sort orders for TourStartDate and Duration fields

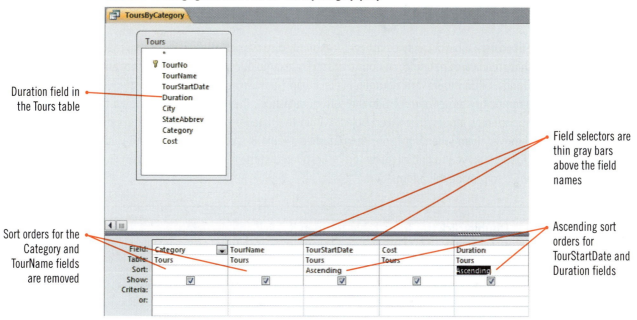

FIGURE B-8: Find and Replace dialog box

Site Seeing in the Find What text box

Cultural in the Replace With box

Additional Find and Replace options to fine-tune the search

Replace All button

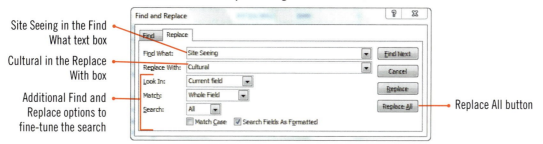

FIGURE B-9: Final ToursByCategory datasheet with new sort orders

Cultural replaces all occurrences of Site Seeing in the Category field

Replace button

Find button

TourStartDate is first sort order

Records with the same TourStartDate are further sorted by Duration values

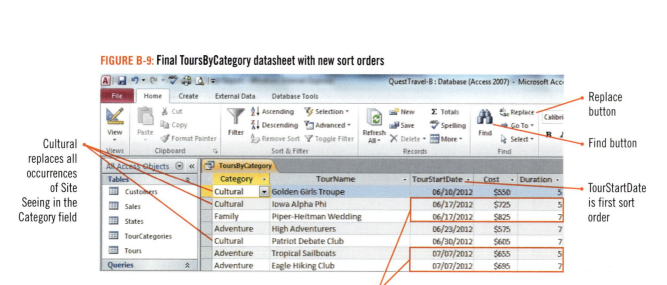

Filtering Data

Filtering a table or query datasheet temporarily displays only those records that match given criteria. Recall that criteria are limiting conditions you set. For example, you might want to show only tours in the state of Florida, or only tours with a duration of less than 7 days. While filters provide a quick and easy way to display a temporary subset of records in the current datasheet, they are not as powerful or flexible as queries. Most importantly, a query is a saved object within the database, whereas filters are temporary because Access removes them when you close the datasheet. Table B-1 compares filters and queries. Samantha Hooper asks you to find all Adventure tours offered in the month of July. You can filter the Tours table datasheet to provide this information.

STEPS

QUICK TIP

You can also apply a sort or filter by clicking the Sort and filter arrow to the right of the field name and choosing the sort order or filter values you want.

1. **Double-click the Tours table to open it, click any occurrence of Adventure in the Category field, click the Selection button in the Sort & Filter group, then click Equals "Adventure"**

   Eighteen records are selected, some of which are shown in Figure B-10. A filter icon appears to the right of the Category field. Filtering by the selected field value, called **Filter By Selection**, is a fast and easy way to filter the records for an exact match. To filter for comparative data (for example, where TourStartDate is *equal to* or *greater than* 7/1/2012), you must use the **Filter By Form** feature.

2. **Click the Advanced button in the Sort & Filter group, then click Filter By Form**

   The Filter by Form window opens. The previous Filter By Selection criterion, "Adventure" in the Category field, is still in the grid. Access distinguishes between text and numeric entries by placing "quotation marks" around text criteria.

QUICK TIP

If you need to clear previous criteria, click the Advanced button, then click Clear All Filters.

3. **Click the TourStartDate cell, then type 7/*/2012 as shown in Figure B-11**

   Filter by Form also allows you to apply two or more criteria at the same time. An asterisk (*) in the day position of the date criterion works as a wildcard, selecting any date in the month of July (the 7th month) in the year 2012.

QUICK TIP

Be sure to remove existing filters before applying a new filter, or the new filter will apply to the current subset of records instead of the entire datasheet.

4. **Click the Toggle Filter button in the Sort & Filter group**

   The datasheet selects nine records that match both filter criteria, as shown in Figure B-12. Note that filter icons appear next to the TourStartDate and Category field names as both fields are involved in the filter.

5. **Close the Tours datasheet, then click Yes when prompted to save the changes**

   Saving changes to the datasheet saves the last sort order and column width changes. Filters are not saved.

Using wildcard characters

To search for a pattern, you can use a **wildcard** character to represent any character in the condition entry. Use a question mark (?) to search for any single character, and an asterisk (*) to search for any number of characters. Wildcard characters are often used with the **Like operator**. For example, the criterion Like "12/*/13" would find all dates in December of 2013, and the criterion Like "F*" would find all entries that start with the letter F.

FIGURE B-10: Filtering the Tours table

Selection button

Toggle Filter button is selected, indicating the records are filtered

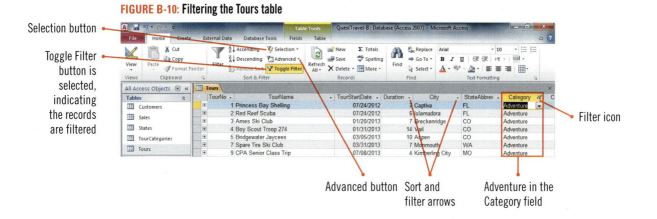

Filter icon

Advanced button   Sort and filter arrows   Adventure in the Category field

FIGURE B-11: Filtering by Form criteria

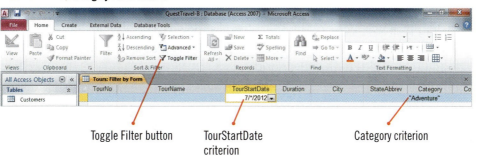

Toggle Filter button   TourStartDate criterion   Category criterion

FIGURE B-12: Results of filtering by form

Filter icons

TourNo	TourName	TourStartDate	Duration	City	StateAbbrev	Category	Cost
1	Princess Bay Shelling	07/24/2012	7	Captiva	FL	Adventure	$750
2	Red Reef Scuba	07/24/2012	6	Islamadora	FL	Adventure	$1,500
17	Tropical Sailboats	07/07/2012	5	Key West	FL	Adventure	$655
18	Eagle Hiking Club	07/07/2012	7	Aspen	CO	Adventure	$695
19	Paradise Water Club	07/14/2012	7	Hollister	MO	Adventure	$595
20	Team Discovery	07/17/2012	5	Breckenridge	CO	Adventure	$550
21	Gulfside Birdwatchers	07/17/2012	7	Tampa Bay	FL	Adventure	$700
22	Perfect Waves	07/15/2012	5	Huntington Beach	CA	Adventure	$500
46	Bigfoot Rafting Club	07/31/2012	4	Placerville	CA	Adventure	$455
(New)							

TourStartDate values are in July 2012

Category is equal to Adventure

TABLE B-1: Filters vs. queries

characteristics	filters	queries
Are saved as an object in the database	No	Yes
Can be used to select a subset of records in a datasheet	Yes	Yes
Can be used to select a subset of fields in a datasheet	No	Yes
Resulting datasheet used to enter and edit data	Yes	Yes
Resulting datasheet used to sort, filter, and find records	Yes	Yes
Commonly used as the source of data for a form or report	No	Yes
Can calculate sums, averages, counts, and other types of summary statistics across records	No	Yes
Can be used to create calculated fields	No	Yes

Applying AND Criteria

As you have seen, you can limit the number of records that appear on a query datasheet by entering criteria in Query Design View. Criteria are tests, or limiting conditions, for which the record must be true to be selected for the query datasheet. To create **AND criteria**, which means that all criteria must be true to select the record, enter two or more criteria on the same Criteria row of the query design grid. Samantha Hooper asks you to provide a list of all family tours in the state of Florida with a duration equal to or less than 7 days. Use Query Design View to create the query with AND criteria to meet her request.

STEPS

1. **Click the Create tab on the Ribbon, click the Query Design button in the Queries group, double-click Tours, then click Close in the Show Table dialog box**

   You want four fields from the Tours table in this query.

2. **Drag the lower edge of the Tours field list down to display all of the fields, double-click TourName, double-click Duration, double-click StateAbbrev, then double-click Category to add these fields to the query grid**

   First add criteria to select only those records in Florida. Because you are using the StateAbbrev field, you need to use the two-letter state abbreviation for Florida, FL, as the Criteria entry.

3. **Click the first Criteria cell for the StateAbbrev field, type FL, then click the View button 🔲 to display the results**

   Querying for only those tours in the state of Florida selects 11 records. Next, you add criteria to select only those records in the Family category.

4. **Click the View button 📊 to switch to Design View, click the first Criteria cell for the Category field, type Family, then click 🔲**

   Criteria added to the same line of the query design grid are AND criteria. When entered on the same line, each criterion must be true for the record to appear in the resulting datasheet. Querying for both FL and Family tours selects three records with durations of 8, 7, and 3 days. Every time you add AND criteria, you *narrow* the number of records that are selected because the record must be true for *all* criteria.

5. **Click 📊, click the first Criteria cell for the Duration field, then type <=7 as shown in Figure B-13**

   Access assists you with **criteria syntax**, rules that specify how to enter criteria. Access automatically adds "quotation marks" around text criteria in Text fields ("FL" and "Family") and pound signs (#) around date criteria in Date/Time fields. The criteria in Number, Currency, and Yes/No fields are not surrounded by any characters. See Table B-2 for more information about comparison operators such as > (greater than).

TROUBLE
If your datasheet doesn't match Figure B-14, return to Query Design View and compare your criteria to that of Figure B-13.

6. **Click 🔲 to display the query datasheet**

   The third AND criterion further narrows the number of records selected to two, as shown in Figure B-14.

7. **Click the Save button 💾 on the Quick Access toolbar, type FamilyFL as the query name, click OK, then close the query**

   The query is saved with the new name, FamilyFL, as a new object in the QuestTravel-B database.

Searching for blank fields

Is Null and Is Not Null are two other types of common criteria. The **Is Null** criterion finds all records where no entry has been made in the field. **Is Not Null** finds all records where there is any entry in the field, even if the entry is 0. Primary key fields cannot have a null entry.

FIGURE B-13: Query Design View with AND criteria

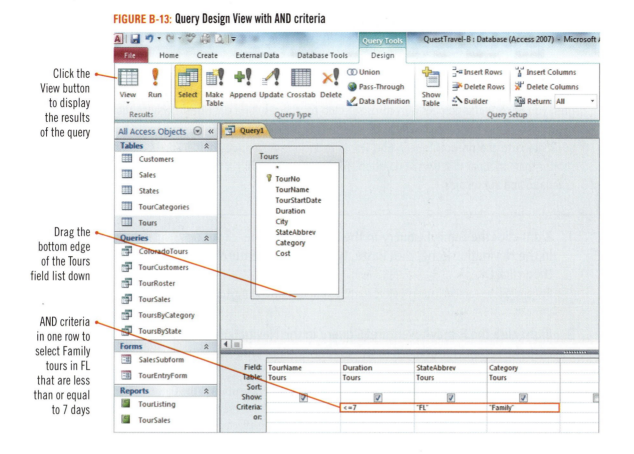

Click the View button to display the results of the query

Drag the bottom edge of the Tours field list down

AND criteria in one row to select Family tours in FL that are less than or equal to 7 days

FIGURE B-14: Final datasheet of FamilyFL query

Save button

All three criteria are true for these two records: <=7 duration, FL, and Family

TABLE B-2: Comparison operators

operator	description	expression	meaning
>	Greater than	>500	Numbers greater than 500
>=	Greater than or equal to	>=500	Numbers greater than or equal to 500
<	Less than	<"Braveheart"	Names from A to Braveheart, but not Braveheart
<=	Less than or equal to	<="Bridgewater"	Names from A through Bridgewater, inclusive
<>	Not equal to	<>"Fontanelle"	Any name except for Fontanelle

Applying OR Criteria

You use **OR criteria** when any one criterion must be true in order for the record to be selected. Enter OR criteria on *different* Criteria rows of the query design grid. As you add rows of OR criteria to the query design grid, you *increase* the number of records selected for the resulting datasheet because the record needs to match *only one* of the Criteria rows to be selected for the datasheet. Samantha Hooper asks you to add criteria to the previous query. She wants to include Adventure tours in the state of Florida that are shorter than or equal to 7 days in duration. To do this, you modify a copy of the FamilyFL query to use OR criteria to add the records.

1. **Right-click the FamilyFL query in the Navigation Pane, click Copy, right-click a blank spot in the Navigation Pane, click Paste, type FamilyAdventureFL in the Paste As dialog box, then click OK**

   By copying the FamilyFL query before starting your modifications, you avoid changing the FamilyFL query by mistake.

2. **Right-click the FamilyAdventureFL query in the Navigation Pane, click Design View, click the second Criteria cell in the Category field, type Adventure, then click the View button ⊞ to display the query datasheet**

   The query selected 20 records including all of the tours with Adventure in the Category field. Note that some of the Duration values are greater than 7 and some of the StateAbbrev values are not FL. Because each row of the query grid is evaluated separately, all Adventure tours are selected regardless of criteria in any other row. In other words, the criteria in one row have no effect on the criteria of other rows. To make sure that the Adventure tours are also in Florida and have a duration of less than or equal to 7 days, you need to modify the second row of the query grid (the "or" row) to specify that criteria.

   QUICK TIP
   The Datasheet, Design, and other view buttons are also located in the lower-right corner of the Access window.

3. **Click the View button ⊠, click the second Criteria cell in the Duration field, type <=7, click the second Criteria cell in the StateAbbrev field, then type FL**

   Query Design View should look like Figure B-15.

4. **Click ⊞ to display the query datasheet**

   Seven records are selected that meet all three criteria as entered in row one *or* row two of the query grid, as shown in Figure B-16.

5. **Right-click the FamilyAdventureFL query tab, click Close, then click Yes to save and close the query datasheet**

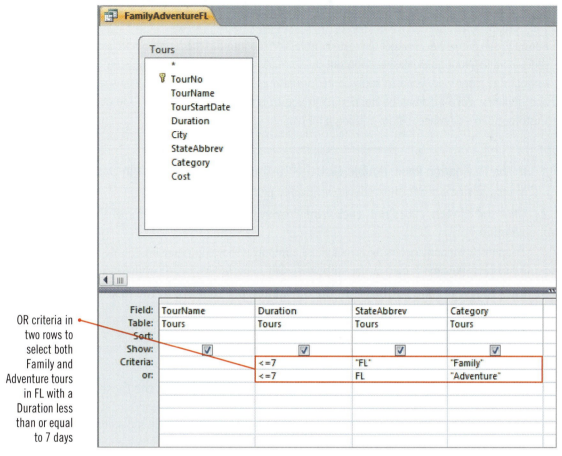

OR criteria in
two rows to
select both
Family and
Adventure tours
in FL with a
Duration less
than or equal
to 7 days

FIGURE B-16: Final datasheet of the FamilyAdventureFL query

TourName	Duration	StateAbbrev	Category
Princess Bay Shelling	7	FL	Adventure
Red Reef Scuba	6	FL	Adventure
Piper-Heitman Wedding	7	FL	Family
High Adventurers	7	FL	Adventure
Tropical Sailboats	5	FL	Adventure
Gulfside Birdwatchers	7	FL	Adventure
Harper Reunion	3	FL	Family

All three criteria are true for either row:
<=7 duration, FL, and Family
or
<=7 duration, FL, and Adventure

Formatting a Datasheet

Although the primary Access tool to create a professional printout is the report object, you can print a data-sheet as well. Although a datasheet printout does not allow you to add custom headers, footers, images, or subtotals as reports do, you can apply some formatting, such as changing the font size, font face, colors, and gridlines. Samantha Hooper asked you to print a list of customers. You decide to format the Customers table datasheet before printing it for her.

STEPS

1. **In the Navigation Pane, double-click the Customers table to open it in Datasheet View**

   Before applying new formatting enhancements, you preview the default printout.

2. **Click the File tab, click Print, click Print Preview, then click the header of the printout to zoom in**

   The preview window displays the layout of the printout, as shown in Figure B-17. By default, the printout of a datasheet contains the object name and current date in the header. The page number is in the footer.

3. **Click the Next Page button ▶ in the navigation bar to move to the next page of the printout**

   The last two fields print on the second page because the first is not wide enough to accommodate them. You decide to switch the report to landscape orientation so that all of the fields print on one page, and then increase the size of the font before printing to make the text easier to read.

4. **Click the Landscape button in the Page Layout group, then click the Close Print Preview button**

   You return to Datasheet View where you can make font face, font size, font color, gridline color, and background color choices.

5. **Click the Font list arrow** Calibri **in the Text Formatting group, click Times New Roman, click the Font Size list arrow** 11 **, then click 12**

   With the larger font size applied, you need to resize some columns to accommodate the widest entries.

6. **Use the ✛ pointer to double-click the field separator between the Street and City field names, then double-click the field separator between the Phone and FirstContact field names**

   Double-clicking the field separators widens the column as necessary to display every entry in that field, as shown in Figure B-18.

QUICK TIP
If you need a print-out of this data-sheet, click the Print button on the Print Preview tab, then click OK.

7. **Click the File tab, click Print, then click Print Preview**

   All of the fields now fit across a page in landscape orientation. The printout is still two pages, but with the larger font size, it is easier to read.

8. **Right-click the Customers table tab, click Close, click Yes when prompted to save changes, click the File tab, then click Exit to close the QuestTravel-B.accdb database and Access 2010**

FIGURE B-17: Preview of Customers datasheet

Landscape button

Header

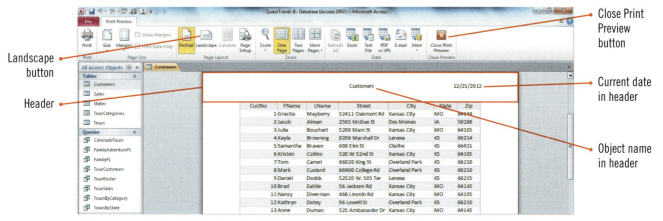

Close Print Preview button

Current date in header

Object name in header

FIGURE B-18: Formatting the Customers datasheet

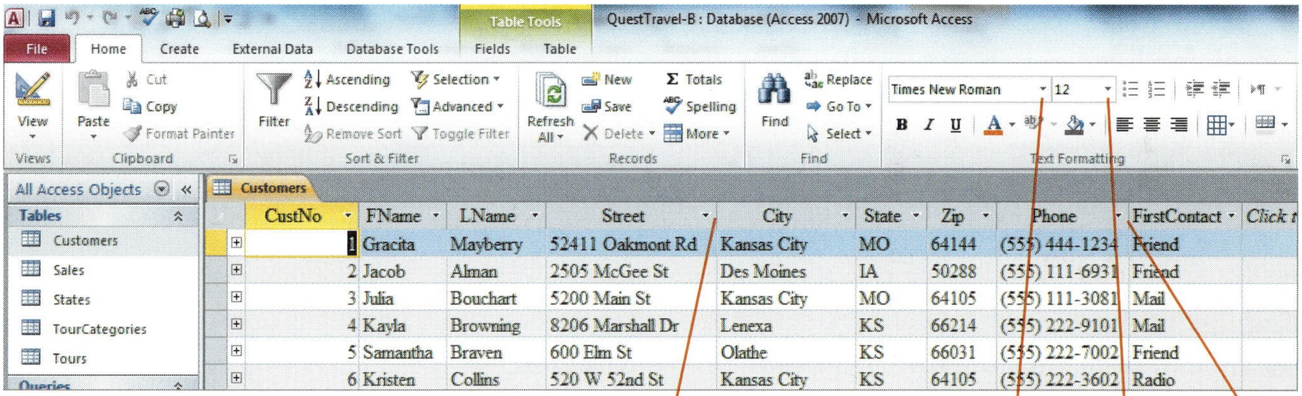

Field separator

Font list arrow

Font Size list arrow

Field separator

Access 2010

Practice

For current SAM information, including versions and content details, visit SAM Central (http://www.cengage.com/samcentral). If you have a SAM user profile, you may have access to hands-on instruction, practice, and assessment of the skills covered in this unit. Since various versions of SAM are supported throughout the life of this text, check with your instructor for the correct instructions and URL/Web site for accessing assignments.

Concepts Review

Label each element of the Access window shown in Figure B-19.

FIGURE B-19

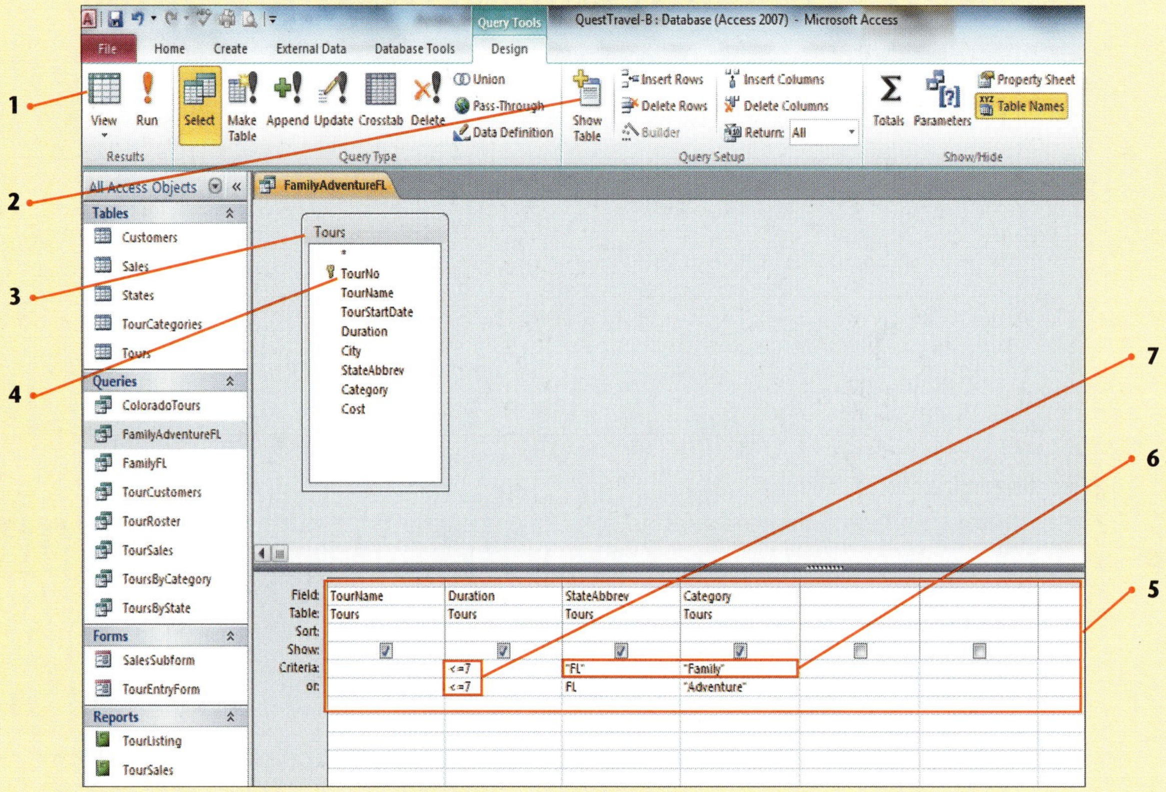

Match each term with the statement that best describes it.

8. **Query grid**
9. **Criteria**
10. **Filter**
11. **Syntax**
12. **Field lists**
13. **Sorting**
14. **Wildcard**
15. **Is Null**

a. Creates a temporary subset of records
b. Small windows that display field names
c. Rules that determine how criteria are entered
d. Limiting conditions used to restrict the number of records that are selected in a query
e. Used to search for a pattern of characters
f. Criterion that finds all records where no entry has been made in the field
g. The lower pane in Query Design View
h. Putting records in ascending or descending order based on the values of a field

Select the best answer from the list of choices.

16. **AND criteria:**
    a. Must all be true for the record to be selected.
    b. Determine sort orders.
    c. Determine fields selected for a query.
    d. Help set link lines between tables in a query.

17. **SQL stands for which of the following?**
    a. Standard Query Language
    b. Special Query Listing
    c. Structured Query Language
    d. Simple Query Listing

18. **A query is sometimes called a logical view of data because:**
    a. You can create queries with the Logical Query Wizard.
    b. Queries do not store data, they only display a view of data.
    c. Queries contain logical criteria.
    d. Query naming conventions are logical.

19. **Which of the following describes OR criteria?**
    a. Selecting a subset of fields and/or records to view as a datasheet from one or more tables
    b. Using two or more rows of the query grid to select only those records that meet given criteria
    c. Reorganizing the records in either ascending or descending order based on the contents of one or more fields
    d. Using multiple fields in the query design grid

20. **Which of the following is *not* true about a query?**
    a. A query can be used to create calculated fields.
    b. A query can be used to create summary statistics.
    c. A query can be used to enter and edit data.
    d. A query is the same thing as a filter.

Skills Review

1. **Use the Query Wizard.**
    a. Open the Recycle-B.accdb database from the drive and folder where you store your Data Files. Enable content if prompted.
    b. Create a new query using the Simple Query Wizard. Select the CenterName field from the Centers table, the DepositDate and Weight fields from the Deposits table, and the ClubName field from the Clubs table. Select Detail, and enter **CenterDeposits** as the name of the query.
    c. Open the query in Datasheet View, change any record with the Big Trash Can CenterName value to a center name that includes your last name.

2. **Work with data in a query.**
    a. Delete the first record.
    b. Change any occurrence of Lions in the ClubName field to **Lions of Okoboji**.
    c. Click any value in the DepositDate field, then click the Descending button in the Sort & Filter group on the Home tab to sort the records in descending order on the DepositDate field.
    d. Use the Calendar Picker to choose the date of **1/9/2013** for the first record.
    e. Save and close the CenterDeposits query.

3. **Use Query Design View.**
    a. Click the Create tab, click the Query Design button, double-click Clubs, double-click Deposits, and then click Close to add the Clubs and Deposits tables to Query Design View.
    b. Drag the bottom edge of the Clubs table down to display all of the field names.

c. Add the following fields from the Clubs table to the query design grid in the following order: FName, LName, ClubName. Add the following fields from the Deposits table in the following order: DepositNumber, DepositDate, Weight. View the results in Datasheet View observing the number of records that are selected.

d. In Design View, enter criteria to display only those records with a Weight value of **greater than or equal to 100**, then observe the number of records that are selected.

e. Save the query with the name **100PlusDeposits**, and close it.

4. Sort and find data.

a. Open the CenterDeposits query in Datasheet View to observe how the records are currently sorted (in descending order based on the DepositDate field).

b. In Query Design View, choose an ascending sort order for the CenterName and DepositDate fields. (*Note*: Queries that are created with the Query Wizard do not show the 1 and infinity symbols on the link lines between the tables. However, the one-to-many relationships between these tables are still intact.)

c. Display the query in Datasheet View noting how the records have been resorted.

d. Click any value in the ClubName field, then use the Find and Replace dialog box to find all occurrences of **Patriots**, and replace them with **Kansas City Patriots**.

5. Filter data.

a. Filter the CenterDeposits datasheet for only those records where the ClubName equals **Kansas City Patriots**.

b. Apply an advanced filter by form and use wildcard characters to further narrow the records so that only the deposits made in the year 2012 are selected.

c. If requested by your instructor, print the filtered CenterDeposits datasheet.

d. Save and close the CenterDeposits query.

6. Apply AND criteria.

a. Open the 100PlusDeposits query in Query Design View.

b. Modify the criteria to select all of the listings with a ClubName of **Ice Kings** and a Weight value of greater than or equal to 100.

c. In the results, edit Tara in any occurrence in the FName field to your initials.

d. If requested by your instructor, print the 100PlusDeposits query.

7. Apply OR criteria.

a. Open the 100PlusDeposits query in Query Design View.

b. Add criteria to include the records with **Jaycees** as the ClubName with a Weight value **greater than or equal to 100** to the existing selections so that both the Ice Kings and Jaycees large deposit records are selected.

c. Save the 100PlusDeposits query, then switch to Datasheet View.

8. Format a datasheet.

a. In the 100PlusDeposits datasheet, apply an Arial Narrow font and a 14-point font size.

b. Resize all columns so that all data and field names are visible. See Figure B-20.

c. Save the 100PlusDeposits query.

d. If requested by your instructor, print the datasheet.

e. Close the 100PlusDeposits query and the Recycle-B.accdb database, then exit Access 2010.

FIGURE B-20

FName	LName	ClubName	DepositNumber	DepositDate	Weight
Francis	Weaver	Jaycees	25	8/21/2012	105
Francis	Weaver	Jaycees	59	3/7/2011	200
Francis	Weaver	Jaycees	63	4/23/2011	105
Francis	Weaver	Jaycees	75	7/9/2011	200
Francis	Weaver	Jaycees	82	1/31/2010	100
Francis	Weaver	Jaycees	99	3/6/2010	200
SI	Block	Ice Kings	6	2/23/2012	100
SI	Block	Ice Kings	42	1/31/2011	100
SI	Block	Ice Kings	46	2/14/2011	185
SI	Block	Ice Kings	50	2/19/2011	185
SI	Block	Ice Kings	60	3/8/2011	145
SI	Block	Ice Kings	61	4/20/2011	115
SI	Block	Ice Kings	67	5/2/2011	105
SI	Block	Ice Kings	86	2/14/2010	200
SI	Block	Ice Kings	94	2/27/2010	100
*				(New)	

Independent Challenge 1

You have built an Access database to track member-ship in a community service club. The database tracks member names and addresses as well as their status in the club, which moves from rank to rank as the members contribute increased hours of service to the community.

a. Start Access, open the Membership-B.accdb database from the drive and folder where you store your Data Files, enable content if prompted, then open the Activities, Members, and Zips tables to review their datasheets.

b. In the Zips table, click the expand button to the left of the 64131, Overland Park, KS, record to display the two members linked to that zip code. Click the expand button to the left of the Gabriel Hammer record to display the two activity records linked to Gabriel.

c. Close all three datasheets, click the Database Tools tab, then click the Relationships button. The Relationships window also shows you that one record in the Zips table is related to many records in the Members table through the common ZipCode field, and that one record in the Members table is related to many records in the Activities table through the common MemberNo field.

FIGURE B-21

FirstName	LastName	ActivityDate	HoursWorked
StudentFirst	StudentLast	3/29/2012	4
Golga	Collins	3/31/2012	8
Martha	Duman	3/27/2012	4
Allie	Eahlie	3/29/2012	4
Jana	Eckert	3/29/2012	5
Quentin	Garden	3/29/2012	4
Quentin	Garden	3/30/2012	8
Loraine	Goode	3/29/2012	5
Gabriel	Hammer	3/29/2012	5
Jeremiah	Hopper	3/27/2012	4
Helen	Hubert	3/29/2012	5
Heidi	Kalvert	3/29/2012	4
Harvey	Mackintosh	3/30/2012	4
Jon	Maxim	3/30/2012	4
Micah	Mayberry	3/29/2012	4
Patch	Mullins	3/30/2012	8
Patch	Mullins	3/31/2012	8
Young	Nelson	3/30/2012	10
Mallory	Olson	3/31/2012	8
Su	Vogue	3/30/2012	8
Sherry	Walker	3/29/2012	4
Taney	Wilson	3/30/2012	8

March2012

d. Close the Relationships window.

e. In Query Design View, build a query with the following fields: FirstName and LastName from the Members table, and ActivityDate and HoursWorked from the Activities table.

f. View the datasheet, observe the number of records selected, then return to Query Design View.

g. Add criteria to select only those records where the ActivityDate is in March of 2012. (*Hint*: Use a wildcard character in the day position of the date criterion.) Apply an ascending sort order to the LastName and ActivityDate fields, then view the datasheet.

h. Enter your name in the first record, widen all columns so that all data and field names are visible, and save the query with the name **March2012** as shown in Figure B-21.

i. If requested by your instructor, print the datasheet.

j. Close the March2012 query and the Membership-B.accdb database, then exit Access 2010.

Independent Challenge 2

You work for a nonprofit agency that relies on grant money from the federal government. To keep in touch with elected members of Congress, you have developed an Access database with contact information for the House of Representatives. The director of the agency has asked you to create several state lists of representatives. You will use queries to extract this information.

If you have a SAM 2010 user profile, an autogradable SAM version of this assignment may be available at http://www.cengage.com/sam2010. Check with your instructor to confirm that this assignment is available in SAM. To use the SAM version of this assignment, log into the SAM 2010 Web site and download the instruction and start files.

a. Start Access, open the Congress-B.accdb database from the drive and folder where you store your Data Files, then enable content if prompted.

b. Open the Representatives and the States tables. Notice that one state is related to many representatives as evidenced by the expand buttons to the left of the records in the States tables.

Independent Challenge 2 (continued)

c. Close both datasheets, then using Query Design View, create a query with the StateAbbrev, StateName, and Capital fields from the States table (in that order) as well as the LName field from the Representatives table.

d. Sort the records in ascending order on the StateName field, then the LName field.

e. Add criteria to select the representatives from North Carolina or South Carolina. Use the StateAbbrev field to enter your criteria, using the two-character state abbreviations of NC and SC.

f. Save the query with the name **Carolinas**, view the results, then change the last name of Boehlert to your last name. Resize the columns as needed to view all the data and field names.

g. Print the datasheet if requested by your instructor, then save and close it.

h. Close the Congress-B.accdb database, then exit Access 2010.

Independent Challenge 3

You have built an Access database to track the veterinarians and clinics in your area.

a. Start Access, open the Vet-B.accdb database from the drive and folder where you store your Data Files, and enable content if prompted.

b. Open the Vets table and then the Clinics table to review the data in both datasheets.

c. Click the expand button next to the Veterinary Specialists record in the Clinics table, then add your name as a new record to the Vets subdatasheet.

d. Close both datasheets.

e. Using the Simple Query Wizard, select the VetLast and VetFirst fields from the Vets table, and select the ClinicName and Phone fields from the Clinics table. Title the query **ClinicListing**, then view the datasheet.

f. Find the single occurrence of Cooper in the VetLast field, and replace it with **Chen**.

g. Update any occurrence of Leawood Animal Clinic in the ClinicName field by changing Leawood to **Emergency**.

h. In Query Design View, add criteria to select only Emergency Animal Clinic or Veterinary Specialists in the ClinicName field, then view the results.

Advanced Challenge Exercise

- In Query Design View, move the ClinicName field to the first column, then add an ascending sort order on the ClinicName and VetLast fields.
- Display the ClinicListing query in Datasheet View, resize the fields as shown in Figure B-22, then print the datasheet if requested by your instructor.
- Return to Query Design View of the ClinicListing query. Notice the link line between the tables. This link line was created by the Simple Query Wizard.
- Save and close the ClinicListing query then open the Relationships window. Notice the link line between the tables. In a Word document, explain the difference in appearance and meaning of the link line between the Vets and Clinics tables in the Relationships window with that of Query Design View.

i. If you have not already done so, save and close the ClinicListing datasheet, then close the Vet-B.accdb database and exit Access 2010.

FIGURE B-22

ClinicName	VetLast	VetFirst	Phone
Emergency Animal Clinic	Ridwell	Kirk	(913) 555-1311
Emergency Animal Clinic	Rosenheim	Howard	(913) 555-1311
Emergency Animal Clinic	Salamander	Stephen	(913) 555-1311
Veterinary Specialists	Garver	Mark	(816) 555-4000
Veterinary Specialists	Major	Mark	(816) 555-4000
Veterinary Specialists	Manheim	Thomas	(816) 555-4000
Veterinary Specialists	Stewart	Frank	(816) 555-4000
Veterinary Specialists	StudentLast	StudentFirst	(816) 555-4000

Real Life Independent Challenge

An Access database is an excellent tool to help record and track job opportunities. For this exercise you'll create a database from scratch that you can use to enter, edit, and query data in pursuit of a new job or career.

a. Create a new database named **Jobs.accdb**.

b. Create a table named **Positions** with the following field names, data types, and descriptions:

field name	data type	description
PositionID	AutoNumber	Primary key field
Title	Text	Title of position such as Accountant, Assistant Court Clerk, or Director of Finance
CareerArea	Text	Area of the career field such as Accounting, Information Systems, Retail, or Landscaping
AnnualSalary	Currency	Annual salary
Desirability	Number	Desirability rating of 1 = low to 5 = high to show how desirable the position is to you
EmployerID	Number	Foreign key field to the Employers table

c. Create a table named **Employers** with the following field names, data types, and descriptions:

field name	data type	description
EmployerID	AutoNumber	Primary key field
CompanyName	Text	Company name of the employer
EmpStreet	Text	Employer's street address
EmpCity	Text	Employer's city
EmpState	Text	Employer's state
EmpZip	Text	Employer's zip code
EmpPhone	Text	Employer's phone, including area code

d. Be sure to set EmployerID as the primary key field in the Employers table and the PositionID as the primary key field in the Positions table.

e. Link the Employers and Positions table together in a one-to-many relationship using the common EmployerID field. One employer record will be linked to many position records. Be sure to enforce referential integrity.

f. Using any valid source of potential employer data, enter five records into the Employers table.

g. Using any valid source of job information, enter five records into the Positions table by using the subdatasheets from within the Employers datasheet. Because one employer may have many positions, all five of your Positions records may be linked to the same employer, you may have one position record per employer, or any other combination.

h. Build a query that selects CompanyName from the Employers table, and the Title, CareerArea, AnnualSalary, and Desirability fields from the Positions table. Sort the records in descending order based on Desirability. Save the query as **JobList**, and print it if requested by your instructor.

i. Close the JobList datasheet, then close the Jobs.accdb database and exit Access 2010.

Visual Workshop

Open the Baseball-B.accdb database from the drive and folder where you store your Data Files, and enable content if prompted. Create a query based on the Players and Teams tables as shown in Figure B-23. Criteria has been added to select only those records where the PlayerPosition field values are equal to 1 or 2 (representing pitchers and catchers). An ascending sort order has been added to the TeamName and PlayerPosition fields. Save the query with the name **PitchersAndCatchers**, then compare the results to Figure B-23, making changes as necessary. Change the name of Roy Campanella to your name before printing the datasheet if requested by your instructor. Close the query and the Baseball-B.accdb database, then exit Access 2010.

FIGURE B-23

PitchersAndCatchers

TeamName	PlayerLast	PlayerFirst	Position
Brooklyn Beetles	Campanella	Roy	1
Brooklyn Beetles	Young	Cycylie	2
Mayfair Monarchs	Durocher	Luis	1
Mayfair Monarchs	Mathewson	Carl	2
Rocky's Rockets	Spalding	Andrew	1
Rocky's Rockets	Koufax	Sanford	2
Snapping Turtles	Ford	Charles	1
Snapping Turtles	Perry	Greg	2

UNIT C
Access 2010

Using Forms

Although you can enter and edit data on datasheets, most database designers develop and build forms as the primary method for users to interact with a database. In a datasheet, sometimes you have to scroll left or right to see all of the fields, which is inconvenient and time consuming. A form solves these problems by allowing you to organize the fields on the screen in any arrangement. A form also supports graphical elements such as pictures, buttons, and tabs, which make data entry faster and more accurate. In addition, forms provide a layer of database security and make the database much easier to use. Samantha Hooper, a tour developer at Quest Specialty Travel, asks you to create forms to make tour information easier to access, enter, and update.

OBJECTIVES

Use the Form Wizard
Create a split form
Use Form Layout View
Add fields to a form
Modify form controls
Create calculations
Modify tab order
Insert an image

Using the Form Wizard

A **form** is an Access database object that allows you to arrange the fields of a record in any layout so you can enter, edit, and delete records. A form provides an easy-to-use data entry and navigation screen. Forms provide many productivity and security benefits for the **user**, who is primarily interested in entering, editing, and analyzing the data in the database. As the **database designer**, the person responsible for building and maintaining tables, queries, forms, and reports, you also need direct access to all database objects, and you use the Navigation Pane for this purpose. Not all users should be able to access all the objects in a database—imagine how disastrous it would be if someone accidentally deleted an entire table of data. You can add a layer of security to your database with well-designed forms. Samantha Hooper asks you to build a form to enter and maintain tour information.

STEPS

1. **Start Access, open the QuestTravel-C.accdb database from the drive and folder where you store your Data Files, then enable content if prompted**

   You can use many methods to create a new form, but the Form Wizard is a fast and popular tool to get started. The **Form Wizard** prompts you for information it needs to create a form, such as the fields, layout, and title for the form.

2. **Click the Create tab on the Ribbon, then click the Form Wizard button in the Forms group**

   The Form Wizard starts, prompting you to select the fields for this form. You want to create a form to enter and update data in the Tours table.

3. **Click the Tables/Queries list arrow, click Table: Tours, then click the Select All Fields button** >>

   You could now select fields from other tables, if necessary, but in this case, you have all of the fields you need.

4. **Click Next, click the Columnar option button, click Next, type Tours Entry Form as the title, then click Finish**

   The Tours Entry Form opens in **Form View**, as shown in Figure C-1. The three different form views are summarized in Table C-1. Each item on the form is called a **control**. Field names are shown as label controls in the first column of the form. A **label** displays fixed text that doesn't change as you navigate from record to record. Labels usually describe other controls on the form such as text boxes that show field values. A label control is also often used in headers or footers. Field values are displayed in text box and combo box controls in the second column of the form. A **text box** is the most common type of control used to display field values. You enter, edit, find, sort, and filter data by working with the data in a text box control. The Category field value is displayed in a combo box control. A **combo box** is a combination of two controls: a text box and a list. You click the arrow button on a combo box control to display a list of values, or you can edit data directly in the combo box itself.

   QUICK TIP
   Always click a value in a field to identify which field you want to sort or filter before clicking a sort or filter button.

5. **Click Princess Bay Shelling in the TourName text box, click the Ascending button in the Sort & Filter group, then click the Next record button** ▶ **in the navigation bar to move to the second record**

   The Ames Ski Club is the second record when the records are sorted in ascending order on the TourName field. Information about the current record number and total number of records appears in the navigation bar, just as it does in a datasheet.

6. **Edit Ames Ski Club to Story County Ski Club**

   Your screen should look like Figure C-2. Forms displayed in Form View are the primary tool used to enter, edit, and delete data in an Access database.

7. **Right-click the Tours Entry Form tab, then click Close**

   When a form is closed, Access automatically saves any edits made to the current record.

FIGURE C-1: Tours Entry Form in Form View

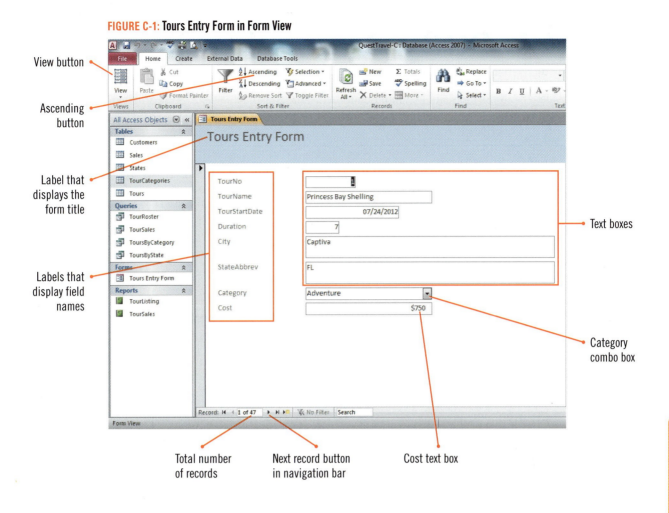

View button

Ascending button

Label that displays the form title

Labels that display field names

Text boxes

Category combo box

Total number of records

Next record button in navigation bar

Cost text box

FIGURE C-2: Editing data in a text box

Edit record symbol

Editing data in a text box

TABLE C-1: Form views

view	primary purpose
Form	To view, enter, edit, and delete data
Layout	To modify the size, position, or formatting of controls; shows data as you modify the form, making it the tool of choice when you want to change the appearance and usability of the form while viewing live data
Design	To modify the form header, detail, and footer section, or to access the complete range of controls and form properties; Design View does not display data

Creating a Split Form

In addition to the Form Wizard, you should be familiar with several other form creation tools. Table C-2 identifies those tools and the purpose for each. Samantha Hooper asks you to create another form to manage customer data. You'll work with the Split Form tool for this task.

STEPS

1. **Click the Customers table in the Navigation Pane, click the Create tab, click the More Forms button, then click Split Form**

   The Customers data appears in a split form as shown in Figure C-3. The benefit of a **split form** is that the upper pane allows you to display the fields of one record in any arrangement, and the lower pane maintains a datasheet view of the first few records, which you can navigate very quickly. The two panes of the split form are always synchronized. In other words, if you edit, sort, or filter records in the upper pane, the lower pane is automatically updated, and vice versa. The navigation bar shows that there are 37 total records.

2. **Click MO in the State text box in the upper pane, click the Home tab, click the Selection button in the Sort & Filter group, then click Does Not Equal "MO"**

   Twenty-six records are filtered where the State field is not equal to MO. You also need to change a value in the Jacob Alman record.

   > **TROUBLE**
   > Make sure you edit the record in the lower pane.

3. **In the lower pane, click Des Moines in the City field of the first record, edit the entry to read West Des Moines, click any other record in the lower pane, then click Jacob in the lower pane**

   Moving from record to record also automatically saves data, regardless of whether you are working in the upper or lower pane. Note that "West Des Moines" is the entry in the City field in both the upper and lower panes as shown in Figure C-4.

4. **Click the record selector for the Kristen Collins record in the lower pane, then click the Delete button in the Records group on the Home tab**

   A message appears indicating that you cannot delete this record because it contains related records in the Sales table. This is a benefit of referential integrity on the one-to-many relationships between the Customers, Sales, and Tours tables. Referential integrity prevents the creation of orphan records, records on the *many* side of a relationship (in this case, the Sales table), that do not have a match in the *one* side (in this case, the Customers table).

5. **Click OK, right-click the Customers form tab, click Close, click Yes when prompted to save changes, then click OK to save the form with the name Customers**

TABLE C-2: Form creation tools

tool	icon	creates a form:
Form		with one click based on the selected table or query
Form Design		from scratch with access to advanced design changes in Form Design View
Blank Form		with no controls starting in Form Layout View
Form Wizard		by answering a series of questions provided by the Form Wizard dialog boxes
Navigation		used to navigate or move between different areas of the database
More Forms		based on Multiple Items, Datasheet, Split Form, Modal Dialog, PivotChart, or PivotTable arrangements
Split Form		where the upper half displays data the fields of one record in any arrangement, and the lower half displays data as a datasheet

FIGURE C-3: Customers table in a split form

Record for CustNo 1 in the upper pane

MO in the State text box

Record for CustNo 1 in the lower pane

37 total records

Upper pane

Lower pane

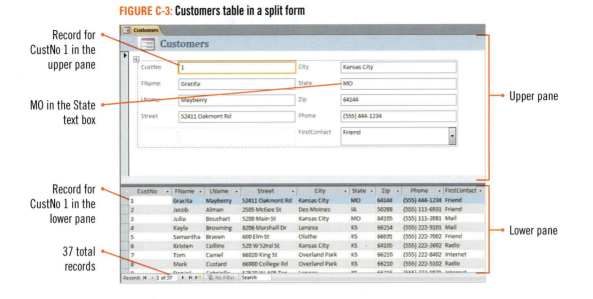

FIGURE C-4: Editing data in a split form

Selection button

Delete button

Record selector in upper pane

Record selector for Kristen Collins record

Filtered button

Des Moines changed to West Des Moines

First record in lower pane has been edited

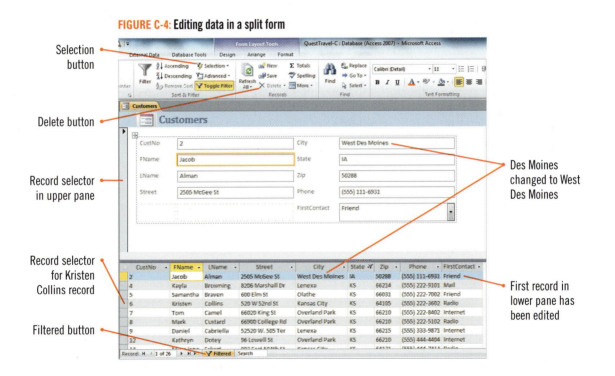

Using Form Layout View

Layout View lets you make some design changes to a form while you are browsing the data. For example, you can move and resize controls, add or delete a field in the form, or change formatting characteristics such as fonts and colors. Samantha Hooper asks you to make several design changes to the Tours Entry Form. You can make these changes in Layout View.

1. **Right-click the Tours Entry Form in the Navigation Pane, then click Layout View**

   In Layout View, you can move through the records, but you cannot enter or edit the data as you can in Form View.

   TROUBLE

   If your third record is not Bigfoot Rafting Club, sort the records in ascending order on the TourName field.
   ---

2. **Click the Next record button twice to move to the third record, Bigfoot Rafting Club**

   You often use Layout View to make minor design changes such as editing labels and changing formatting characteristics.

3. **Click the TourNo label to select it, click between the words Tour and No, then press [Spacebar]**

   You also want to edit a few more labels.

   TROUBLE

   Be sure to modify the *labels in the left column* instead of the text boxes on the right.
   ---

4. **Continue editing the labels as shown in Figure C-5**

   You also want to change the text color of the first two labels, Tour No and Tour Name, to red to make them more visible.

5. **Click the Tour No label, click the Home tab, click the Font Color button 🅰, click the Tour Name label, then click 🅰**

   Often, you want to apply the same formatting enhancement to multiple controls. For example, you decide to narrow the City and State Abbrev text boxes. Select the text boxes at the same time to make the same change to both.

   TROUBLE

   Be sure to modify the *text boxes in the right column* instead of the labels on the left.
   ---

6. **Click Placerville in the City text box, press and hold [Shift], click CA in the State Abbrev text box to select the two text boxes at the same time, release [Shift], then use the ↔ pointer to drag the right edge of the selection to the left to make the text boxes approximately half as wide**

   Layout View for the Tours Entry Form should look like Figure C-6. Mouse pointers in Form Layout and Form Design View are very important as they indicate what happens when you drag the mouse. Mouse pointers are described in Table C-3.

TABLE C-3: Mouse pointer shapes

shape	when does this shape appear?	action
⇖	When you point to any unselected control on the form (the default mouse pointer)	Single-clicking with this mouse pointer *selects* a control
✛	When you point to the upper-left corner or edge of a selected control in Form Design View or the middle of the control in Form Layout View	Dragging with this mouse pointer *moves* the selected control(s)
↕, ↔, ⤡, ⤢	When you point to any sizing handle (except the larger one in the upper-left corner in Form Design View)	Dragging with one of these mouse pointers *resizes* the control

FIGURE C-5: Using Layout View to modify form labels on the Tours Entry Form

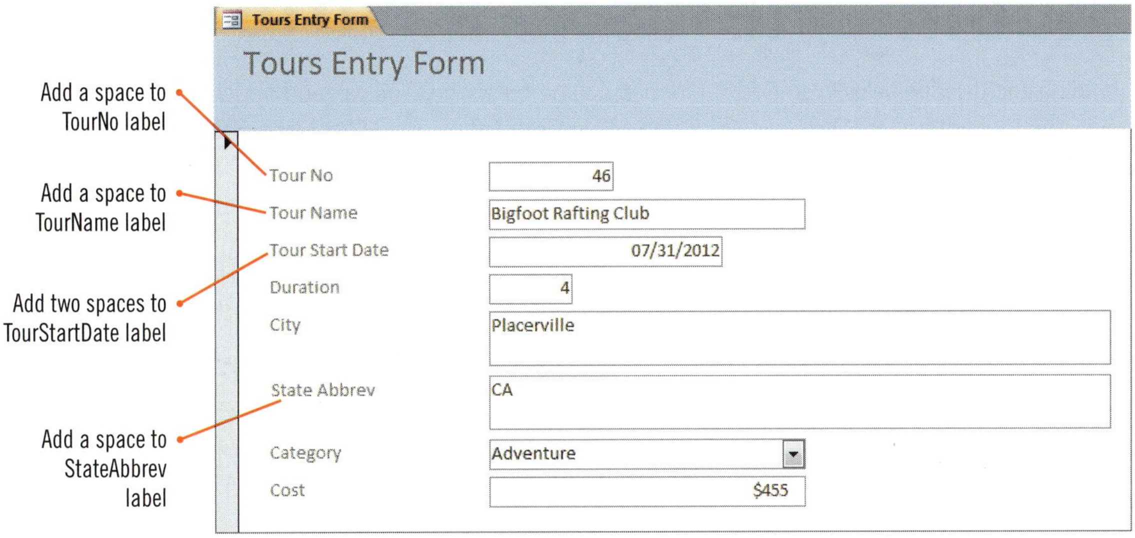

Add a space to TourNo label
Add a space to TourName label
Add two spaces to TourStartDate label
Add a space to StateAbbrev label
Tours Entry Form
Tours Entry Form
Tour No
46
Tour Name
Bigfoot Rafting Club
Tour Start Date
07/31/2012
Duration
4
City
Placerville
State Abbrev
CA
Category
Adventure
Cost
$455

FIGURE C-6: Layout View for the Tours Entry Form

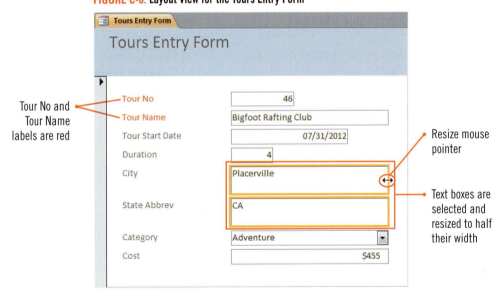

Tour No and Tour Name labels are red
Resize mouse pointer
Text boxes are selected and resized to half their width
Tours Entry Form
Tours Entry Form
Tour No
46
Tour Name
Bigfoot Rafting Club
Tour Start Date
07/31/2012
Duration
4
City
Placerville
State Abbrev
CA
Category
Adventure
Cost
$455

Access 2010

Adding Fields to a Form

Adding and deleting fields in an existing form is a common activity. You can add or delete fields in a form in either Layout View or Design View using the Field List window. The **Field List window** lists the database tables and the fields they contain. To add a field to the form, drag it from the Field List to the desired location on the form. To delete a field on a form, click the field to select it, then press the [Delete] key. Deleting a field from a form does not delete it from the underlying table nor does it have any effect on the data contained in the field. You can toggle the Field List on and off using the Add Existing Fields button on the Design tab. Samantha Hooper asks you to add the tour description from the TourCategories table to the Tours Entry Form. You can use Layout View and the Field List window to accomplish this goal.

1. **Click the Design tab on the Ribbon, click the Add Existing Fields button in the Tools group, then click the Show all tables link in the Field List window if the Field List window does not look like Figure C-7**

   The Field List window opens in Layout View, as shown in Figure C-7. Notice that the Field List is divided into sections. The upper section shows the tables currently used by the form, the middle section shows related tables, and the lower section shows other tables. The expand/collapse button to the left of the table names allows you to expand (show) the fields within the table or collapse (hide) them. The Description field is in the TourCategories table in the middle section.

   QUICK TIP
   If you make a mistake, click the Undo button and try again.

2. **Click the expand button ⊞ to the left of the TourCategories table, drag the Description field to the form, then use the ⌖ pointer to drag the new Description combo box and label below the Cost controls**

   When you add a new field to a form, two controls are usually generated: a label and a text box. The label contains the field name and the text box displays the contents of the field. The TourCategories table moved from the middle to the top section of the Field List. You also want to align and size the new controls with others already on the form. Form Design View works best for alignment activities.

3. **Right-click the Tours Entry Form tab, click Design View, click the Description label, press and hold [Shift], click the Cost label to select both labels, release [Shift], click the Arrange tab, click the Align button in the Sizing & Ordering group, then click Left**

   Now resize the labels.

4. **With the two labels still selected, click the Size/Space button in the Sizing & Ordering group, then click To Widest**

   With the new controls in position, you want to enter a new record. You must switch to Form View to edit, enter, or delete data.

   TROUBLE
   Don't worry if your Tour No value doesn't match Figure C-8. It is an AutoNumber value, controlled by Access.

5. **Click the Home tab, click the View button 🖳 to switch to Form View, click the New (blank) record button ▶⊞ in the navigation bar, click the TourName text box, then enter a new record in the updated form, as shown in Figure C-8**

   Note that when you select a value in the Category combo box, the Description automatically updates. This is due to the one-to-many relationship between the TourCategories and Tours tables in the Relationships window.

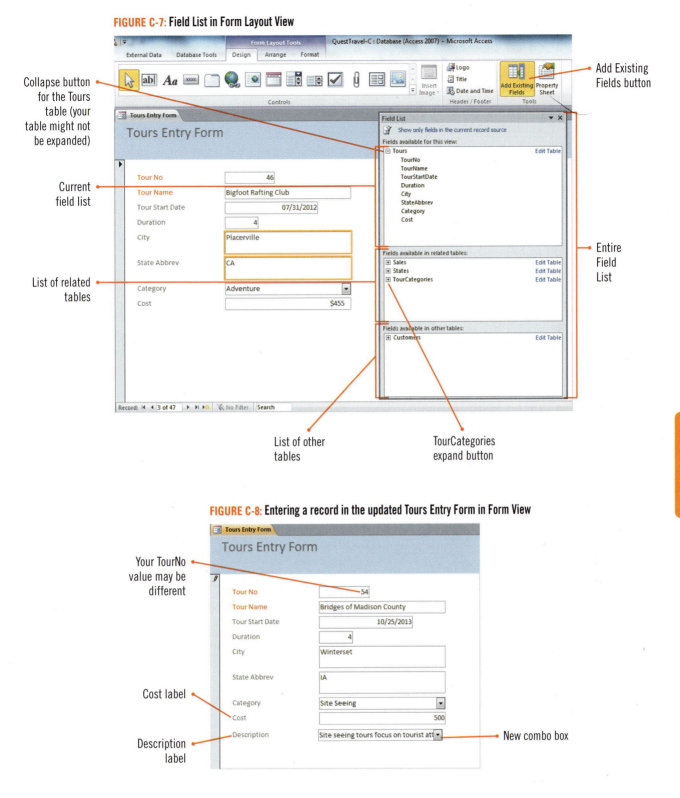

FIGURE C-7: Field List in Form Layout View

Collapse button for the Tours table (your table might not be expanded)

Current field list

List of related tables

Entire Field List

Add Existing Fields button

List of other tables

TourCategories expand button

FIGURE C-8: Entering a record in the updated Tours Entry Form in Form View

Your TourNo value may be different

Cost label

Description label

New combo box

Modifying Form Controls

You have already made many modifications to form controls such as changing the font color of labels and the size of text boxes. Labels and text boxes are the two most popular form controls. Other common controls are listed in Table C-4. When you modify controls, you change their **properties** (characteristics). All of the control characteristics you can modify are stored in the control's **Property Sheet**. Because Quest offers more adventure tours than any other type of tour, you decide to use the Property Sheet of the Category field to modify the default value to be "Adventure." You also use the Property Sheet to make other control modifications to better size and align the controls.

STEPS

1. **Click the Layout View button** 📋 **on the Home tab, then click the Property Sheet button in the Tools group**

   The Property Sheet window opens, showing you all of the properties for the selected item.

2. **Click the Category combo box, click the Data tab in the Property Sheet window (if it is not already selected), click the Default Value box, type Adventure, then press [Enter]**

   The Property Sheet should look like Figure C-9. Access often helps you with the **syntax** (rules) of entering property values. In this case, Access added quotation marks around "Adventure" to indicate that the default entry is text. Properties are categorized in the Property Sheet with the Format, Data, Event, and Other tabs. The All tab is a complete list of all the control's properties. You can use the Property Sheet to make all control modifications, although you'll probably find that some changes are easier to make using the Ribbon. The Property Sheet changes as you modify a control using the Ribbon.

TROUBLE
Be sure to click the Tour No label on the left, not the TourNo text box on the right.

3. **Click the Format tab of the Property Sheet, click the Tour No label in the form to select it, click the Home tab on the Ribbon, then click the Align Text Right button** 📑 **in the Text Formatting group**

   Notice that the **Text Align property** in the Property Sheet is automatically updated from Left to Right even though you changed the property using the Ribbon instead of directly in the Property Sheet.

4. **Click the Tour Name label, press and hold [Shift], then click every other label in the first column on the form**

   With all the labels selected, you can modify their Text Align property at the same time.

TROUBLE
You may need to click the Align Text Right button twice.

5. **Click the Align Text Right button** 📑 **in the Text Formatting group**

   Don't be overwhelmed by the number of properties available for each control on the form or the number of ways to modify each property. Over time, you will learn about most of these properties. At this point, it's only important to know the purpose of the Property Sheet and understand that properties are modified in various ways.

6. **Click the Save button** 💾 **on the Quick Access toolbar, click the Form View button** 📋 **on the Design tab, click the New (blank) record button** ▶ **in the navigation bar, then enter the record shown in Figure C-10**

   For new records, "Adventure" is provided as the default value for the Category combo box, but you can change it by typing a new value or selecting one from the list. With the labels right-aligned, they are much closer to the data in the text boxes that they describe.

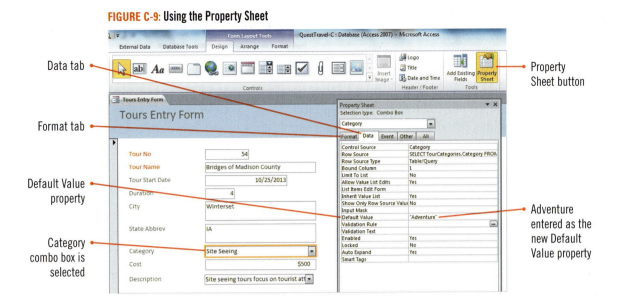

FIGURE C-9: Using the Property Sheet

Data tab
Format tab
Default Value property
Category combo box is selected
Property Sheet button
Adventure entered as the new Default Value property

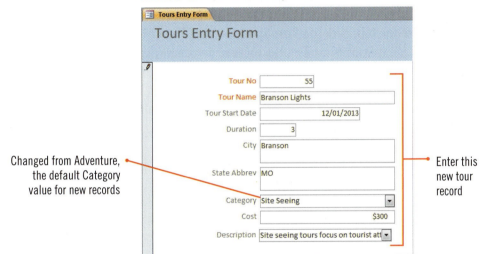

FIGURE C-10: Modified Tours Entry Form

Changed from Adventure, the default Category value for new records

Enter this new tour record

TABLE C-4: Common form controls

name	used to	bound	unbound
Label	Provide consistent descriptive text as you navigate from record to record; the label is the most common type of unbound control and can also be used as a hyperlink to another database object, external file, or Web page		X
Text box	Display, edit, or enter data for each record from an underlying record source; the text box is the most common type of bound control	X	
List box	Display a list of possible data entries	X	
Combo box	Display a list of possible data entries for a field, and provide a text box for an entry from the keyboard; combines the list box and text box controls	X	
Tab control	Create a three-dimensional aspect on a form		X
Check box	Display "yes" or "no" answers for a field; if the box is checked, it means "yes"	X	
Toggle button	Display "yes" or "no" answers for a field; if the button is pressed, it means "yes"	X	
Option button	Display a choice for a field	X	
Option group	Display and organize choices (usually presented as option buttons) for a field	X	
Line and Rectangle	Draw lines and rectangles on the form		X
Command button	Provide an easy way to initiate a command or run a macro		X

Creating Calculations

Text boxes are generally used to display data from underlying fields. The connection between the text box and field is defined by the **Control Source property** on the Data tab of the Property Sheet for that text box. A text box control can also display a calculation. To create a calculation in a text box, you enter an expression instead of a field name in the Control Source property. An **expression** is a combination of field names, operators (such as +, −, /, and *), and functions (such as Sum, Count, or Avg) that result in a single value. Sample expressions are shown in Table C-5. Samantha Hooper asks you to add a text box to the Tours Entry Form to calculate the tour end date. You can add a text box in Form Design View to accomplish this.

STEPS

1. **Right-click the Tours Entry Form tab, then click Design View**

   You want to add the tour end date calculation just below the Duration text box. First you'll resize the City and StateAbbrev fields.

2. **Click the City label, press and hold [Shift], click the City text box, click the StateAbbrev label, click the StateAbbrev text box to select the four controls together, release [Shift], click the Arrange tab, click the Size/Space button, then click To Shortest**

   With the City and StateAbbrev fields resized, you're ready to move them to make room for the new control to calculate the tour end date.

   > **QUICK TIP**
   > You can also press an arrow key to move a selected control.

3. **Click a blank spot on the form to deselect the four controls, click the StateAbbrev text box, use the ⬚ pointer to move it down, click the City text box, then use the ⬚ pointer to move it down**

   To add the calculation to determine the tour end date (the tour start date plus the duration), start by adding a new text box to the form between the Duration and City text boxes.

   > **TROUBLE**
   > If you position the new text box incorrectly, click Undo ↩ on the Quick Access toolbar and try again.

4. **Click the Design tab, click the Text Box button [ab] in the Controls group, then click between the Duration and City text boxes to insert the new text box**

   Adding a new text box automatically adds a new label to the left of the text box.

   > **TROUBLE**
   > The initial number in your label is based on previous work done to the form, so it might vary.

5. **Double-click the new Text22 label on the left, type Tour End Date, then press [Enter]**

   With the label updated to correctly identify the text box to the right, you're ready to enter the expression to calculate the tour end date.

6. **Click the new text box to select it, click the Data tab of the Property Sheet, click the Control Source property, type =[TourStartDate]+[Duration], then press [Enter] to update the form as shown in Figure C-11**

   All expressions entered in a control start with an equal sign (=). When referencing a field name within an expression, [square brackets]—(not parentheses) and not {curly braces}—surround the field name. In an expression, you must type the field name exactly as it was created in Table Design View, but you do not need to match the capitalization.

7. **Click the View button ▦ to switch to Form View, click the value in the Tour Name text box, click the Ascending button, select 7 in the Duration text box, type 5, then press [Enter]**

   Note that the tour end date, calculated by an expression, automatically changed to five days after the tour start date to reflect the new duration value. The updated Tours Entry Form with the tour date end calculation for the American Heritage Tour is shown in Figure C-12.

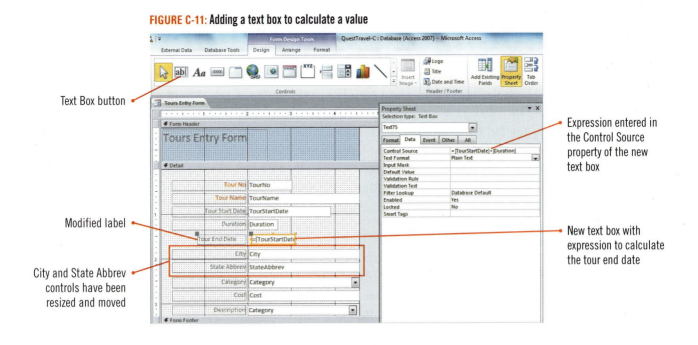

FIGURE C-11: Adding a text box to calculate a value

- Text Box button
- Modified label
- City and State Abbrev controls have been resized and moved
- Expression entered in the Control Source property of the new text box
- New text box with expression to calculate the tour end date

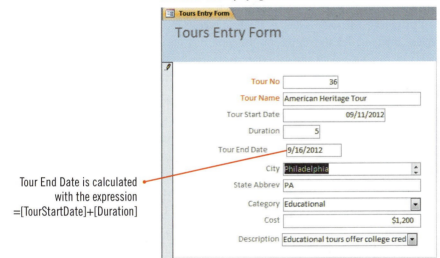

FIGURE C-12: Displaying the results of a calculation in Form View

Tour End Date is calculated with the expression =[TourStartDate]+[Duration]

TABLE C-5: Sample expressions

sample expression	description
=Sum([Salary])	Uses the **Sum function** to add the values in the Salary field
=[Price] * 1.05	Multiplies the Price field by 1.05 (adds 5% to the Price field)
=[Subtotal] + [Shipping]	Adds the value of the Subtotal field to the value of the Shipping field
=Avg([Freight])	Uses the **Avg function** to display an average of the values in the Freight field
=Date()	Uses the **Date function** to display the current date in the form of mm-dd-yy
="Page " &[Page]	Displays the word Page, a space, and the result of the [Page] field, an Access field that contains the current page number
=[FirstName]& " " &[LastName]	Displays the value of the FirstName and LastName fields in one control, separated by a space
=Left([ProductNumber],2)	Uses the **Left function** to display the first two characters in the ProductNumber field

Modifying Tab Order

After positioning all of the controls on the form, you should check the tab order and tab stops. **Tab order** is the order the focus moves as you press [Tab] in Form View. A **tab stop** refers to whether a control can receive the focus in the first place. By default, the tab stop property for all text boxes and combo boxes is set to Yes, but some text boxes, such as those that contain expressions, will not be used for data entry. Therefore, the tab stop property for a text box that contains a calculation should be set to No. Unbound controls such as labels and lines do not have a tab stop property because they cannot be used to enter or edit data. ▨▨▨ You plan to check the tab order of the Tours Entry Form, then change tab stops and tab order as necessary.

STEPS

1. **Press [Tab] enough times to move through several records, watching the focus move through the bound controls of the form**

   Because the tour end date text box is a calculated field, you don't want it to receive the focus. To prevent the Tour End Date text box from receiving the focus, you set its tab stop property to No using its Property Sheet. You can work with the Property Sheet in either Layout or Design View.

   > **QUICK TIP**
   > You can also switch between views using the View buttons in the lower-right corner of the window.

2. **Right-click the Tours Entry Form tab, click Design View, click the Tour End Date text box, click the Other tab in the Property Sheet, double-click the Tab Stop property to toggle it from Yes to No, then change the Name property to TourEndDate as shown in Figure C-13**

   The Other tab of the Property Sheet contains the properties you need to change the tab stop and tab order. The **Tab Stop property** determines whether the field accepts focus, and the **Tab Index property** indicates the numeric tab order for all controls on the form that have the Tab Stop property set to Yes. The **Name property** on the Other tab is also important as it identifies the name of the control, which is used in other areas of the database. To review your tab stop changes, return to Form View.

   > **QUICK TIP**
   > In Form Design View, press [Ctrl][.] to switch to Form View. In Form View, press [Ctrl][,] to switch to Form Design View.

3. **Click the View button ▦ on the Design tab to switch to Form View, then press [Tab] nine times to move to the next record**

   Now that the tab stop has been removed from the TourEndDate text box, the tab order flows correctly from the top to the bottom of the form, but skips the calculated field. To review the tab order for the entire form in one dialog box, you must switch to Form Design View.

   > **TROUBLE**
   > If the order of your fields does not match those in Figure C-14, move a field by clicking the field selector and then dragging the field.

4. **Right-click the Tours Entry Form tab, click Design View, then click the Tab Order button in the Tools group to open the Tab Order dialog box as shown in Figure C-14**

   The Tab Order dialog box allows you to view and change the tab order by dragging fields up or down using the field selectors to the left of the field names. Moving fields up and down in this list also renumbers the Tab Index property for the controls in their respective Property Sheets.

5. **Click OK to close the Tab Order dialog box, click the Property Sheet button to toggle it off, then click the Save button ▦ on the Quick Access toolbar to save your work**

FIGURE C-13: Using the Property Sheet to set tab properties

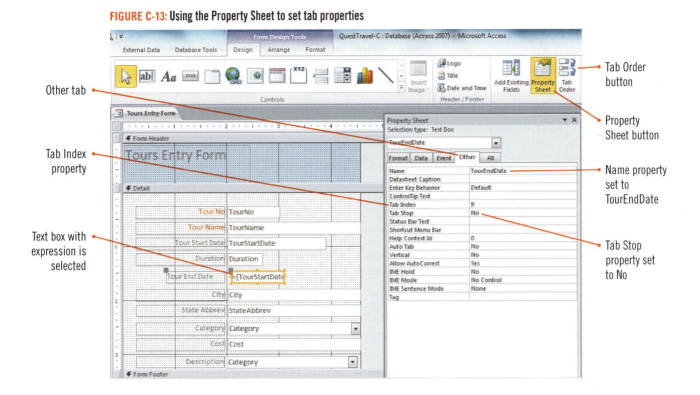

Other tab

Tab Index property

Text box with expression is selected

Tab Order button

Property Sheet button

Name property set to TourEndDate

Tab Stop property set to No

FIGURE C-14: Tab Order dialog box

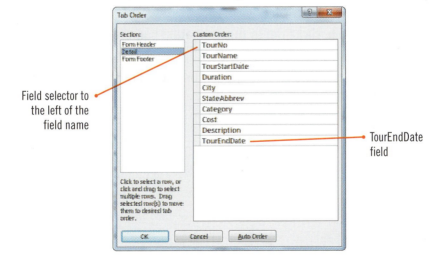

Field selector to the left of the field name

TourEndDate field

Inserting an Image

Graphic images, such as pictures, logos, or clip art, can add style and professionalism to a form. The form section in which you place the images is significant. **Form sections** determine where controls are displayed and printed; they are described in Table C-6. For example, if you add a company logo to the Form Header section, the image appears at the top of the form in Form View as well as at the top of a printout. If you add the same image to the Detail section, it prints next to each record in the printout because the Detail section is printed for every record. Samantha Hooper suggests that you add the Quest logo to the top of the Tours Entry Form. You can add the control in either Layout or Design View, but if you want to place it in the Form Header section, you have to work in Design View.

1. **Click the Form Header section bar, click the Insert Image button in the Controls group, click Browse, then navigate to the drive and folder where you store your Data Files**
   The Insert Picture dialog box opens, prompting you for the location of the image.

2. **Double-click QuestLogo.bmp, then click the right side of the Form Header section**
   The QuestLogo image is added to the right side of the Form Header. You want to resize it to about 1.5" × 1.5".

   > **TROUBLE**
   > The lower-right corner of the image touches the top edge of the Detail section. To resize the Quest logo, click it to select it.

3. **With the QuestLogo image still selected, use the ⬉ pointer to drag the lower-right corner of the image up and to the left so that it is about 1.5" × 1.5", then drag the top edge of the Detail section up using the ⬍ pointer as shown in Figure C-15**
   When an image or control is selected in Design View, you can use **sizing handles**, which are small squares at the corner of the selection box. Drag a handle to resize the image or control. With the form completed, you open it in Form View to observe the changes.

4. **Click the Save button 🖫 on the Quick Access toolbar, then click the View button ▦ to switch to Form View**
   You decide to add one more record with your final Tours Entry Form.

5. **Enter the new record shown in Figure C-16, using your last name in the TourName field**
   Now print only this single new record.

6. **Click the File tab, click Print in the navigation bar, click Print, click the Selected Record(s) option button, then click OK**

7. **Close the Tours Entry Form, click Yes if prompted to save it, close the QuestTravel-C.accdb database, then exit Access 2010**

TABLE C-6: Form sections

section	controls placed in this section print:
Form Header	Only once at the top of the first page of the printout
Detail	Once for every record
Form Footer	Only once at the end of the last page of the printout

FIGURE C-15: Adding an image to the Form Header section

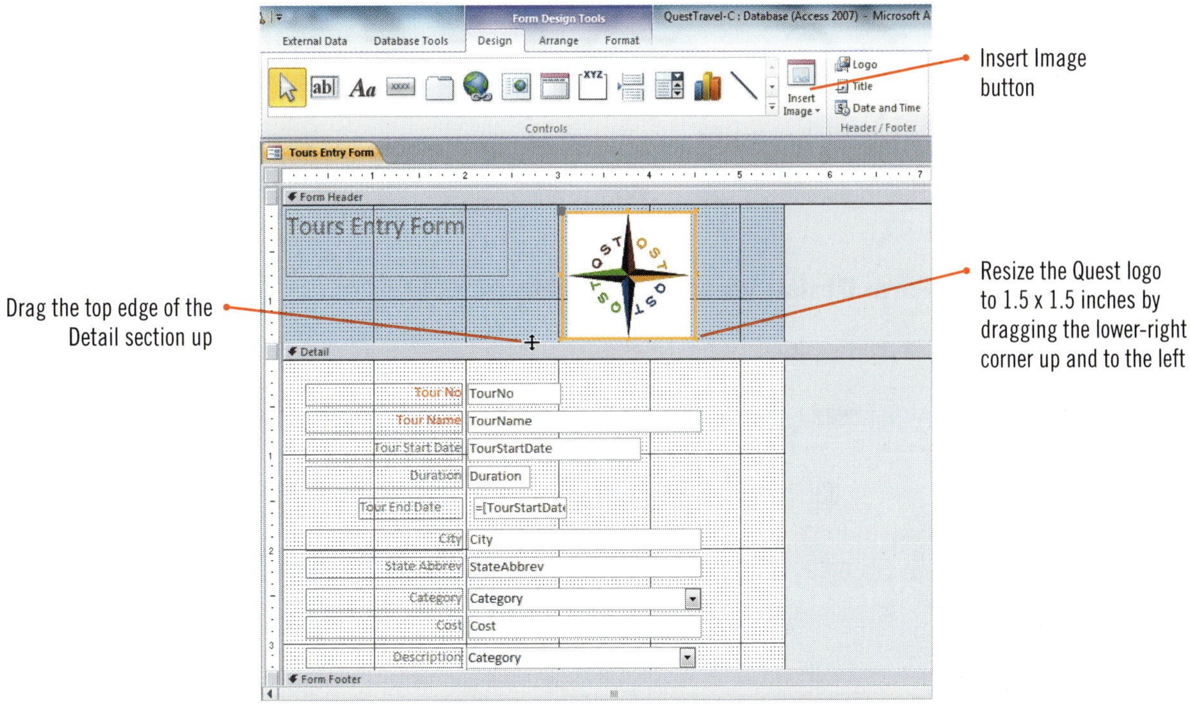

Insert Image button

Drag the top edge of the Detail section up

Resize the Quest logo to 1.5 x 1.5 inches by dragging the lower-right corner up and to the left

FIGURE C-16: Final Tours Entry Form with new record

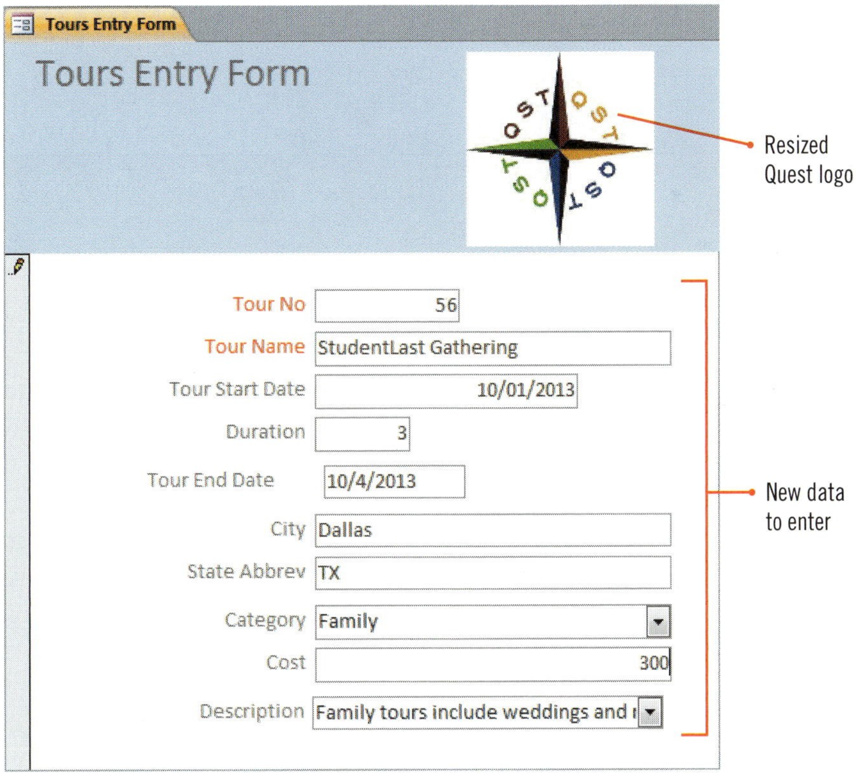

Resized Quest logo

New data to enter

Practice

For current SAM information, including versions and content details, visit SAM Central (http://www.cengage.com/samcentral). If you have a SAM user profile, you may have access to hands-on instruction, practice, and assessment of the skills covered in this unit. Since various versions of SAM are supported throughout the life of this text, check with your instructor for the correct instructions and URL/Web site for accessing assignments.

Concepts Review

Label each element of Form Design View shown in Figure C-17.

FIGURE C-17

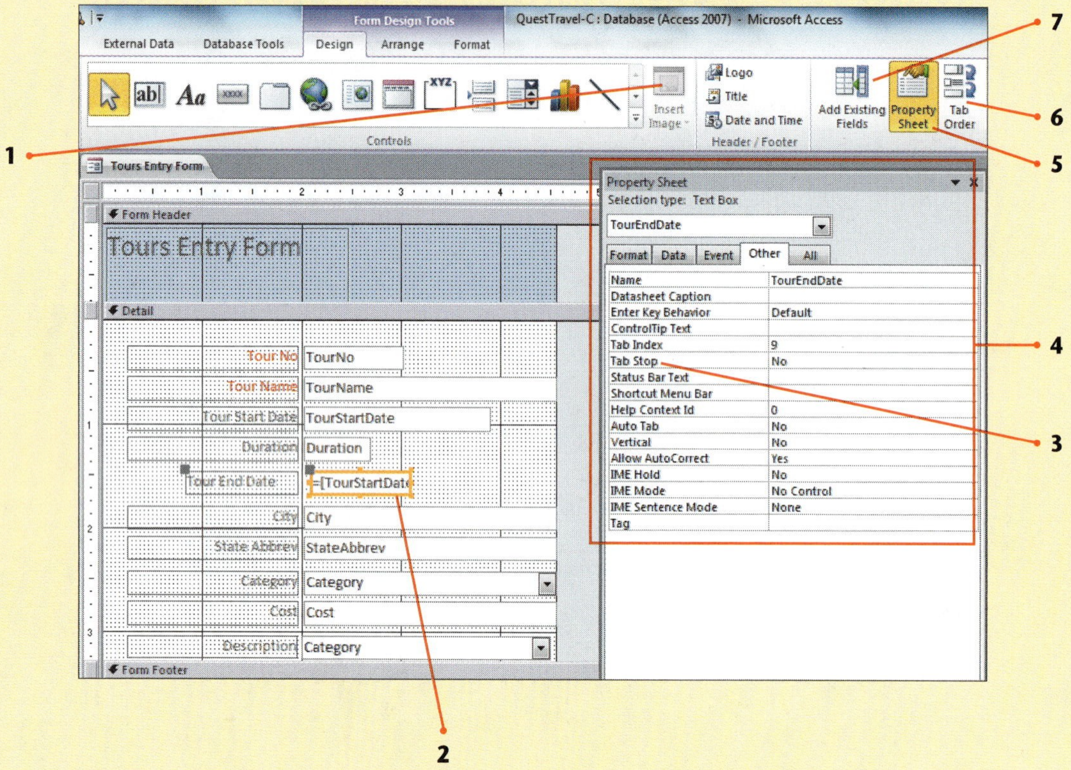

Match each term with the statement that best describes it.

8. Bound control
9. Calculated control
10. Detail section
11. Database designer
12. Tab order
13. Form Footer section

a. The way the focus moves from one bound control to the next in Form View
b. Created by entering an expression in a text box
c. Controls placed here print once for every record in the underlying record source
d. Used on a form to display data from a field
e. Controls placed here print only once at the end of the printout
f. Responsible for building and maintaining tables, queries, forms, and reports

Select the best answer from the list of choices.

14. Every element on a form is called a(n):
   a. Control.
   b. Item.
   c. Tool.
   d. Property.

15. Which of the following is probably *not* a graphic image?
   a. Logo
   b. Clip art
   c. Calculation
   d. Picture

16. The most common bound control is the:
  a. Label.
  b. Combo box.
  c. List box.
  d. Text box.

17. The most common unbound control is the:
  a. Command button.
  b. Label.
  c. Text box.
  d. Combo box.

18. Which form view *cannot* be used to view data?
  a. Layout
  b. Preview
  c. Design
  d. Datasheet

19. Which property helps you set tab order?
  a. Control Source
  b. Tab Index
  c. ControlTip
  d. Default

20. When you enter a calculation in a text box, the first character is a(n):
  a. Equal sign, =
  b. Left square bracket, [
  c. Left parenthesis, (
  d. Asterisk, *

Skills Review

1. Use the Form Wizard.
  a. Start Access and open the RealEstate-C.accdb database from the drive and folder where you store your Data Files. Enable content if prompted.
  b. Click the Create tab, then use the Form Wizard to create a form based on all of the fields in the Realtors table. Use a Columnar layout, and type **Realtor Entry Form** to title the form.
  c. Add a new record with your name. Note that the RealtorNo field is an AutoNumber field that is automatically incremented as you enter your first and last names. Enter your school's telephone number for the RPhone field value, and enter **4** as the AgencyNo field value.
  d. Save and close the Realtor Entry Form.

2. Create a split form.
  a. Click the Realtors table in the Navigation Pane, click the Create tab, click the More Forms button, then click Split Form.
  b. Switch to Form View, then navigate to the RealtorNo 11 (Rob Zacharias) record in either the upper or lower pane of the split form.
  c. Click the record selector in either the upper or lower pane for RealtorNo 11 (Rob Zacharias) and click the Delete button in the Records group to delete this realtor. Click Yes when prompted.
  d. Navigate to the RealtorNo 5 (Jane Ann Welch) record in either the upper or lower pane of the split form. Change Welch to **Rockaway**.
  e. Click the record selector in either the upper or lower pane for RealtorNo 5, Jane Ann Rockaway, and click the Delete button in the Records group. A message appears explaining why this record cannot be deleted. In a written document, explain the concept of an "orphan record" and how it applies to this situation. Click OK.
  f. Right-click the Realtors form tab, click Close, click Yes when prompted to save changes, and type **Realtors Split Form** as the name of the form.

3. Use Form Layout View.
  a. Open the Realtor Entry Form in Layout View.
  b. Modify the labels on the left to read: **Realtor Number**, **Realtor First Name**, **Realtor Last Name**, **Realtor Phone**, and **Agency Number**.
  c. Modify the text color of the labels to black.
  d. Resize the RFirst, RLast, and RPhone text boxes on the right to be the same width as the RealtorNo and AgencyNo text boxes.
  e. Save the Realtor Entry Form.

Skills Review (continued)

4. Add fields to a form.

a. Open the Field List window, show all the tables, then expand the field list for the Agencies table.

b. Drag the AgencyName field to the form, then move the AgencyName label and combo box to below the Agency Number controls.

c. Modify the AgencyName label to read **Agency Name**.

d. Modify the text color of the Agency Name label to black.

e. Save the form and close the Field List window.

5. Modify form controls.

a. In Layout View, use the Align Text Right button on the Home tab to right-align each of the labels in the left column.

b. Switch to Form View, then use the Agency Name combo box to change the Agency Name to **Marvin and Pam Realtors** for Realtor Number 1.

c. If the combo box is not wide enough to display the entire entry for Marvin and Pam Realtors, switch back to Layout View and widen the combo box as much as needed to display the entire entry in the combo box.

6. Create calculations.

a. Switch to Form Design View, then add a text box below the Realtor Entry Form label in the Form Header section. Delete the extra label that is created when you add a new text box.

b. Widen the text box to be almost as wide as the entire form, then enter the following expression into the text box, which will add the words **Information for** to the realtor's first name, a space, and then the realtor's last name. **="Information for "&[RFirst]&" "&[RLast]**

c. Save the form, then view it in Form View. Be sure the new text box correctly displays spaces in the text. Return to Design View to edit the expression as needed.

d. In Form View, change the Realtor Last Name in the first record from Matusek to **King**.

e. Tab to the Realtor Phone text box, observing the automatic change to the expression in the Form Header section.

7. Modify tab order.

a. Switch to Form Design View, then open the Property Sheet window.

b. Select the new text box with the expression in the Form Header section, then change the Tab Stop property from Yes to No.

c. Select the RealtorNo text box in the Detail section, then change the Tab Stop property from Yes to No. (AutoNumber fields cannot be edited, so they do not need to be in the tab order.)

d. Close the Property Sheet.

e. Save the form and view it in Form View. Tab through the form to make sure that the tab order is sequential. Use the Tab Order button on the Design tab in Form Design View to modify tab order, if necessary.

8. Insert an image.

a. Switch to Design View, and click the Form Header section bar.

b. Add the ForSale.bmp image to the right side of the Form Header, then resize the image to be about 1.5" × 1.5".

c. Remove extra blank area in the Form Header section by dragging the top edge of the Detail section up as far as possible.

FIGURE C-18

d. Save the form, then switch to Form View. Move through the records, observing the calculated field from record to record to make sure it is calculating correctly.

e. Find the record with your name as shown in Figure C-18, and then print only that record if requested by your instructor.

f. Close the Realtor Entry Form, close the RealEstate-C. accdb database, then exit Access.

Independent Challenge 1

As the manager of the scuba divers branch of the Quest Specialty Travel tour company, you have developed a database to help manage scuba dives. In this exercise, you'll create a data entry form to manage the dive trips.

If you have a SAM 2010 user profile, an autogradable SAM version of this assignment may be available at http://www.cengage.com/sam2010. Check with your instructor to confirm that this assignment is available in SAM. To use the SAM version of this assignment, log into the SAM 2010 Web site and download the instruction and start files.

a. Start Access, then open the QuestDives-C.accdb database from the drive and folder where you store your Data Files. Enable content if prompted.

b. Using the Form Wizard, create a form that includes all the fields in the DiveTrips table and uses the Columnar layout, then type **Dive Trip Entry** as the title of the form.

c. Switch to Layout View, then delete the ID text box and label.

d. Using Form Design View, select all of the text boxes except the last one for TripReport, and resize them to the shortest size using the To Shortest option on the Size/Space button on the Arrange tab.

e. Using Form Design View, resize the Location, City, State/Province, Country, Lodging, and TripReport text boxes to be no wider than the Rating text box.

f. Using Form Design View and Form Layout View, move, edit, format, and align the labels and text boxes as shown in Figure C-19. Note that there are spaces between the words in the labels, the labels are right-aligned, and the text boxes are left-aligned. Use a Light Blue color for the labels and a Dark Blue for the text in the text boxes.

g. In Form View, enter the Trip Report record as shown in Figure C-19, using your own name instead of Enter Your Name.

h. Save the form, then print only the first record with your name, if requested by your instructor.

i. Close the Dive Trip Entry form, close the QuestDives-C.accdb database, then exit Access 2010.

FIGURE C-19

> **Dive Trip Entry**
>
> ## Dive Trip Entry
>
> | Dive Master ID | 1 |
> | Location | Great Barrier Reef |
> | City | Cairns |
> | State/Province | QLD |
> | Country | Australia |
> | Trip Start Date | 5/14/2013 |
> | Lodging | Turtle Beach Resort |
> | Rating | 5 |
> | Certification Diving | ☐ |
> | Participants | 5 |
> | Trip Report | Great trip, wonderful weather. Enter Your Name |

Independent Challenge 2

You have built an Access database to track membership in a community service club. The database tracks member names and addresses as well as their status in the club, which moves from rank to rank as the members contribute increased hours of service to the community.

a. Start Access, then open the Membership-C.accdb database from the drive and folder where you store your Data Files. Enable content if prompted.

b. Using the Form Wizard, create a form based on all of the fields of the Members table and only the DuesOwed field in the Status table.

c. View the data by Members, use a Columnar layout, then enter **Member Information** as the title of the form.

d. Enter a new record with your name and the school name, address, and phone number of your school. Give yourself a StatusNo entry of **1**. In the DuesPaid field, enter **75**. DuesOwed automatically displays 100 because that value is pulled from the Status table and is based on the entry in the StatusNo field, which links the Members table to the Status table.

e. In Layout View, add a text box to the form and move it below the DuesOwed text box.

f. Open the Property Sheet for the new text box, and in the Control Source property of the new text box, enter the expression that calculates the balance between DuesOwed and DuesPaid: **=[DuesOwed]-[DuesPaid]**.

g. Open the Property Sheet for the new label, and change the Caption property for the new label to **Balance**.

Independent Challenge 2 (continued)

h. Right-align all of the labels in the first column.

i. Set the Tab Stop property for the text box that contains the calculated Balance to **No**, then close the Property Sheet.

Advanced Challenge Exercise

- Switch to Form Design View, then drag the right edge of the form to the 7" mark on the horizontal ruler.
- Resize the last three text boxes that contain DuesPaid, DuesOwed, and the expression to calculate the Balance to be the same size as the new Balance text box, and right-align all data within the three text boxes.
- Open the Property Sheet for the text box that contains the expression, and change the Format property on the Format tab to Currency. Close the Property Sheet.

FIGURE C-20

- Click a blank spot to the right of the text boxes, click the Insert Image button, browse for the PeoplePower.bmp image, then insert it to the right of the Company text box.
- Move and resize the controls as necessary to accommodate the picture, save the form, find the record with your name, and change the DuesPaid value to **85** as shown in Figure C-20.

Member Information

FName	StudentFirst
LName	StudentLast
Company	JCCC
Street	12345 College Blvd.
City	Overland Park
State	KS
Zip	66213
Phone	555-4444
StatusNo	1
DuesPaid	$85.00
DuesOwed	$100.00
Balance	$15.00

j. Print only the record with your name, if requested by your instructor.

k. Save and close the Member Information form, then close the Membership-C.accdb database and exit Access 2010.

Independent Challenge 3

You have built an Access database to organize the deposits at a recycling center. Various clubs regularly deposit recyclable material, which is measured in pounds when the deposits are made.

a. Open the Recycle-C.accdb database from the drive and folder where you store your Data Files. Enable content if prompted.

b. Using the Form Wizard, create a form based on all of the fields in the DepositList query. View the data by Deposits, use the Columnar layout, and title the form **Deposit Listing**.

c. Switch to Layout View, then make each label bold.

d. Switch to Form Design View and resize the CenterName and ClubName text boxes so they are the same height and width as the Weight text box.

e. Switch to Layout View and modify the DepositNumber and DepositDate labels so they read **Deposit Number** and **Deposit Date**. Modify the CenterName and ClubName labels so they read **Center Name** and **Club Name** as shown in Figure C-21.

FIGURE C-21

Deposit Listing

Deposit Number	1
Deposit Date	1/5/2012
Weight	60
Center Name	Trash Can
Club Name	Boy Scouts #11

Independent Challenge 3 (continued)

f. Switch to Form View, find and change any entry of Jaycees in the ClubName field to your last name, then print a deposit record with your name if requested by your instructor.

Advanced Challenge Exercise

- Using Form View of the Deposit Listing form, filter for all records with your last name in the ClubName field.
- Using Form View of the Deposit Listing form, sort the filtered records in descending order on the DepositDate field.
- Preview, then print the first record of the filtered and sorted records, if requested by your instructor.

g. Save and close the Deposit Listing form, close the Recycle-C.accdb database, then exit Access.

Real Life Independent Challenge

One way you can use an Access database on your own is to record and track your job search efforts. In this exercise, you will develop a form to help you enter data into your job-tracking database.

a. Open the JobSearch-C.accdb database from the drive and folder where you store your Data Files. Enable content if prompted.

b. Click the Create tab, then use the Form Wizard to create a new form based on all the fields of both the Employers and Positions tables.

c. View the data by Employers, use a Datasheet layout, accept the default names for the form and subform, then open the form to view information.

d. Use Layout View and Design View to modify the form labels, text box positions, and sizes as shown in Figure C-22. Note that the columns within the subform have been resized to display all of the data in the subform.

e. Change the CompanyName of IBM in the first record to **Your Last Name's Software**, and if instructed to create a printout, print only that record.

f. Save and close the Employers form, close the JobSearch-C.accdb database, then exit Access.

FIGURE C-22

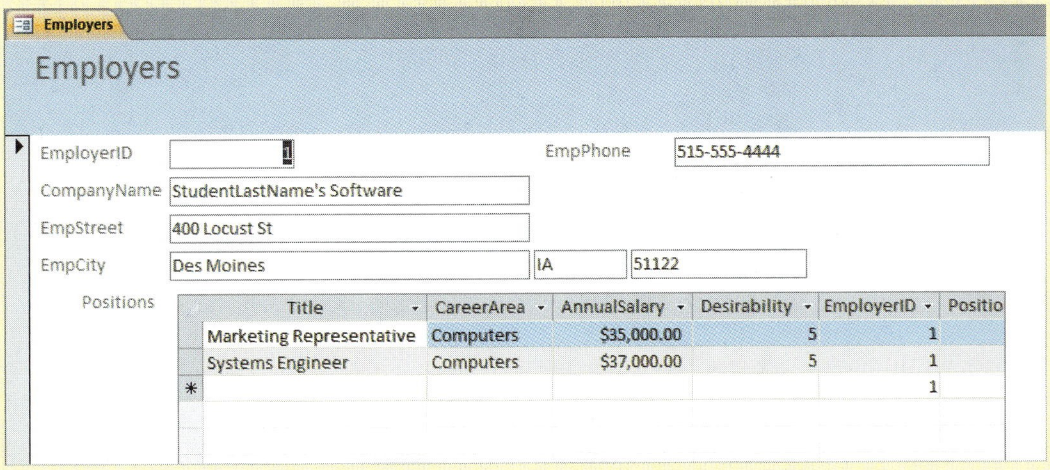

Visual Workshop

Open the Baseball-C.accdb database, enable content if prompted, then use the Split Form tool to create the form as shown in Figure C-23 based on the Players table. Resize the PlayerLast text box as shown. Modify the labels as shown. View the data in Form View, and sort the records in ascending order by last name. Change the name of Henry Aaron in the first record to **Your Name**, and if instructed to create a printout, print only that record. Save and close the Players form, close the Baseball-C.accdb database, then exit Access.

FIGURE C-23

Players

Players

Number	10013		Phone	(816) 927-4638
First Name	Student First Name		Position	7
Last Name	Student Last Name		Insurance	☑
Nickname	Henry		Uniform	☑
			Team Number	5

Number ▾	First Name ▾	Last Name ▾	Nicknan ▾	PlayerPhone ▾	Player ▾	Insuran ▾	Unifo ▾	TeamNumb ▾
10013	Student First Name	Student Last Na	Henry	(816) 927-4638	7	☑	☑	5
10022	John	Bench	Johnny	(913) 285-7451	6	☑	☑	3
10023	Louise	Brock	Lou	(913) 445-6543	4	☐	☑	5
10010	Roy	Campanella	Roy	(913) 252-1321	1	☑	☑	1
10024	Abner	Chandler	Abby	(816) 456-2098	6	☑	☑	7
10033	Roberta	Clemente	Bob	(913) 864-2725	9	☐	☐	5
10011	Tyrus	Cobb	Ty	(816) 919-2343	8	☑	☑	3
10034	Jeffrey	Dean	Speedy	(816) 660-2748	5	☑	☐	1
10014	Joey	DiMaggio	Joe	(913) 828-3848	5	☑	☑	3
10006	Abner	Doubleday	Abby	(913) 121-3212	3	☑	☑	5
10035	Luis	Durocher	Pop	(913) 765-2845	1	☐	☐	5
10015	Charles	Ford	Whitey	(913) 243-5667	1	☑	☑	3

Record: I◀ ◀ 1 of 36 ▶ ▶I ▶✳ | 🅧 No Filter | Search

Using Reports

A **report** is an Access object used to create professional-looking printouts. Although you can print a datasheet or form, reports are the primary object you use to print database content because they provide the most formatting, layout, and summary options. For example, a report might include formatting embellishments such as multiple fonts and colors, extra graphical elements such as clip art and lines, and multiple headers and footers. Reports are also very powerful data analysis tools. A report can calculate subtotals, averages, counts, or other statistics for groups of records. Samantha Hooper, a tour developer at Quest Specialty Travel, asks you to produce some reports to help her share and analyze data.

OBJECTIVES

Use the Report Wizard

Use Report Layout View

Review report sections

Apply group and sort orders

Add subtotals and counts

Resize and align controls

Format a report

Create mailing labels

Using the Report Wizard

You can create reports in Access by using the **Report Wizard**, a tool that asks questions to guide you through the initial development of the report, similar to the Form Wizard. Your responses to the Report Wizard determine the record source, style, and layout of the report. The **record source** is the table or query that defines the fields and records displayed on the report. The Report Wizard also helps you sort, group, and analyze the records. You use the Report Wizard to create a report to display the tours within each state.

STEPS

1. **Start Access, open the QuestTravel-D.accdb database, enable content if prompted, click the Create tab on the Ribbon, then click the Report Wizard button in the Reports group**

   The Report Wizard starts, prompting you to select the fields you want on the report. You can select fields from one or more tables or queries.

TROUBLE

If you select a field by mistake, click the unwanted field in the Selected Fields list, then click the Remove Field button <.

2. **Click the Tables/Queries list arrow, click Table: States, double-click the StateName field, click the Tables/Queries list arrow, click Table: Tours, click the Select All Fields button >> , click StateAbbrev in the Selected Fields list, then click the Remove Field button <**

   By selecting the StateName field from the States table, and all fields from the Tours table except the StateAbbrev field, you have all of the fields you need for the report as shown in Figure D-1. You selected the full state name stored in the States table instead of the two-letter state abbreviation used in the Tours table.

3. **Click Next, then click by States if it is not already selected**

   Choosing "by States" groups together the records for each state. In addition to record-grouping options, the Report Wizard later asks if you want to sort the records within each group. You can use the Report Wizard to specify up to four fields to sort in either ascending or descending order.

QUICK TIP

Click Back to review previous dialog boxes within a wizard.

4. **Click Next, click Next again to include no additional grouping levels, click the first sort list arrow, click TourStartDate, then click Next**

   The last questions in the Report Wizard deal with report appearance and creating a report title.

5. **Click the Stepped option button, click the Landscape option button, click Next, type Tours by State for the report title, then click Finish**

   The Tours by State report opens in **Print Preview**, which displays the report as it appears when printed, as shown in Figure D-2. The records are grouped by state, the first state being California, and then sorted in ascending order by the TourStartDate field within each state. Reports are **read-only** objects, meaning that they read and display data but cannot be used to change (write to) data. As you change data using tables, queries, or forms, reports constantly display those up-to-date edits just like all of the other Access objects.

6. **Scroll down to see the second grouping section on the report for the state of Colorado, then click the Next Page button ▶ in the navigation bar to see the second page of the report**

   Even in **landscape orientation** (11" wide by 8.5" tall as opposed to **portrait orientation**, which is 8.5" wide by 11" tall), the fields on the Tours by State report may not neatly fit on one sheet of paper. The labels in the column headings and the data in the columns need to be resized to improve the layout. Depending on your monitor, you might need to scroll to the right to display all the fields on this page.

FIGURE D-1: Selecting fields for a report using the Report Wizard

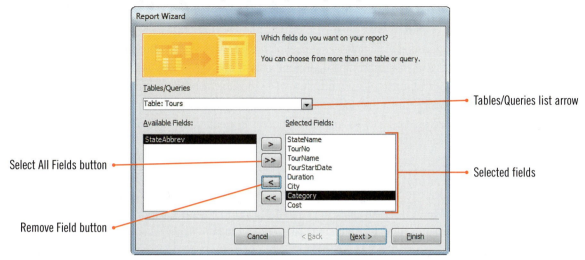

Select All Fields button

Remove Field button

Tables/Queries list arrow

Selected fields

FIGURE D-2: Tours by State report in Print Preview

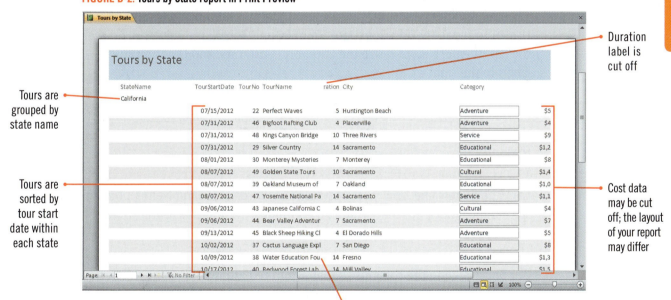

Tours are grouped by state name

Tours are sorted by tour start date within each state

Duration label is cut off

Cost data may be cut off; the layout of your report may differ

TourName data is cut off

Using Report Layout View

Like forms, reports have multiple views that you use for various report-building and report-viewing activities. While some tasks can be accomplished in more than one view, each view has a primary purpose to make your work with reports as easy and efficient as possible. The different report views are summarized in Table D-1. Samantha Hooper asks you to modify the Tours by State report so that all of the fields fit comfortably across one piece of paper in landscape orientation. You'll use Report Layout View to achieve this goal.

STEPS

1. **Right-click the Tours by State report tab, then click Layout View**

   Layout View opens and applies a grid to the report that helps you resize, move, and position controls. You decide to narrow the City column to make room for the Cost data.

2. **Click Sacramento (or any City value), then use the ↔ pointer to drag the right edge of the City column to the left to narrow it to about half of its current size as shown in Figure D-3**

   By narrowing the City column, you create extra space in the report.

3. **Click any value in the Cost column, use the ⁺̬ pointer to drag the Cost values to the left of the Category column, click the Cost label, then use ⁺̬ to move the Cost label to the left of the Category label**

   All the columns are now within the boundaries of a single piece of paper in landscape orientation. You also notice that centering some data would make it easier to read.

4. **Click any value in the TourNo column, click the Home tab, click the Center button ☰ in the Text Formatting group, click the TourNo label, then click ☰ again**

   The TourName column and Duration label could use a little more space.

   QUICK TIP

   Resizing with ↔ instead of moving with ⁺̬ maintains the vertical alignment of the controls.

5. **Use ↔ to resize the TourStartDate, TourNo, and TourName columns and their labels to the left, then use ↔ to resize the Category, Cost, City, and Duration columns and their labels to the right**

   Now the report has enough room to resize the TourName column and the Duration label.

   QUICK TIP

   Using the Undo button arrow ↺ ▾, you can undo many actions in Layout View.

6. **Resize the TourName column so that all of the data is visible, paying special attention to the longest value, Yosemite National Park Great Cleanup, then resize the Duration label to display the complete text**

   You can also rename labels in Report Layout View.

7. **Click the StateName label, click between the words State and Name, press the [Spacebar] so that the label reads State Name, then modify the TourStartDate, TourNo, and TourName labels to contain spaces as well**

   Modifying labels in this way helps make a report more readable and professional.

8. **Continue resizing the columns so that all of the data is visible, paying special attention to the longest value so your report looks like Figure D-4**

   All of the labels are positioned in the Page Header section so that they appear only once per page. The text box controls are positioned in the Detail section. Depending on your monitor, you might need to scroll to display all the columns in Report Layout View.

FIGURE D-3: Modifying the column width in Report Layout View

Right edge of report; yours may differ

Resizing the City field

FIGURE D-4: Final Tours by State report in Report Layout View

Report fits within width of the paper

Label is clearly displayed

Labels contain spaces

Data and label are centered in column

Longest value is clearly displayed

Cost column is moved

TABLE D-1: Report views

view	primary purpose
Report View	To quickly review the report without page breaks
Print Preview	To review each page of an entire report as it will appear if printed
Layout View	To modify the size, position, or formatting of controls; shows live data as you modify the report, making it the tool of choice when you want to change the appearance and positioning of controls on a report while also reviewing live data
Design View	To work with report sections or to access the complete range of controls and report properties; Design View does not display data

Reviewing Report Sections

Report **sections** determine where and how often controls in that section print in the final report. For example, controls in the Report Header section print only once at the beginning of the report, but controls in the Detail section print once for every record the report displays. Table D-2 describes report sections. You and Samantha Hooper preview the Tours by State report to review and understand report sections.

TROUBLE
You may need to zoom in and out several times by clicking the report to position it where you want.

1. **Right-click the Tours by State tab, click Print Preview, click the First Page button** ◄ **in the navigation bar if you need to see the first page of the report, then click in the middle of the top edge of the report to zoom in to 100% if needed as shown in Figure D-5**

   The first page contains four sections: Report Header, Page Header, StateAbbreviation Header, and Detail section.

2. **Click the Next Page button** ► **on the navigation bar to move to the second page**

   The second page of the report may not contain data. The report may be too wide to fit on a single sheet of paper. You'll fix the report width in Report Design View.

QUICK TIP
Pointing to the error indicator ◇ displays a message about the error.

3. **Right-click the Tours by State tab, click Design View, scroll to the far right using the bottom horizontal scroll bar, drag the right edge of the report to the 11" mark on the horizontal ruler, point to the error indicator in the upper-left corner of the report, then drag the right edge of the report as far as you can to the left as shown in Figure D-6**

   In Report Design View, you can work with the report sections and make modifications to the report that you cannot make in other views, such as narrowing the width. Report Design View does not display any data, though. For your report to fit on one page in landscape orientation, you need to move all of the controls within the 10.5" mark on the horizontal **ruler** to allow for 0.25" left and right margins. The **error indicator** in the upper-left corner of the report indicates that the report is too wide to fit on one piece of paper.

4. **Drag the text box with the page expression in the Page Footer section to the left about 1", then drag the right edge of the report to the left so that the report is less than 10.5" wide**

   The error indicator automatically disappears now that the report fits within the margins of a single piece of paper. To review your modifications, show the report in Print Preview.

QUICK TIP
You can also use the View buttons in the lower-right corner of a report to switch views.

5. **Right-click the Tours by State tab, click Print Preview, click the report to zoom in and out to examine the page, then click** ► **twice on the navigation bar to navigate to the last page as shown in Figure D-7**

   The last page of the report, page 3, shows how the Page Header and Page Footer sections border all pages (except the first page where the Report Header is at the top of the page). It also shows how the Group Header, tied to the StateName field, prints once per state, and how the tours within each state are created by the Detail section. Previewing each page of the report also helps you confirm that no blank pages are created.

TABLE D-2: Report sections

section	where does this section print?
Report Header	At the top of the first page
Page Header	At the top of every page (but below the Report Header on the first page)
Group Header	Before every group of records
Detail	Once for every record
Group Footer	After every group of records
Page Footer	At the bottom of every page
Report Footer	At the end of the report

FIGURE D-5: Tours by State report in Report View

Report Header

Page Header

StateAbbreviation Header

Detail section prints
once per record

FIGURE D-6: Tours by State report in Design View

Green error
indicator

Error
indicator
icon

Report
Header

Page
Header

Page
Footer

10.5"
mark on
horizontal
ruler

Resizing
the right
edge of
the report

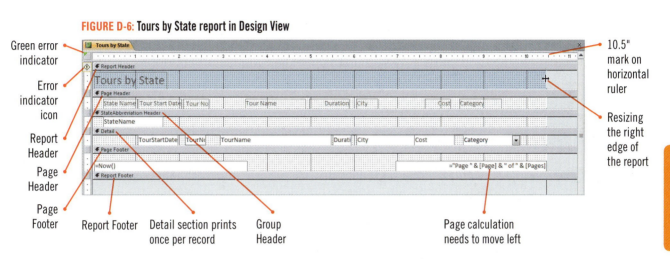

Report Footer   Detail section prints
once per record

Group
Header

Page calculation
needs to move left

FIGURE D-7: Tours by State report in Print Preview

Page Header

Group Header tied
to state data

Detail section
prints once for
every record in
that state

Your final page
might contain
more or less data,
depending on how
you moved and
resized fields

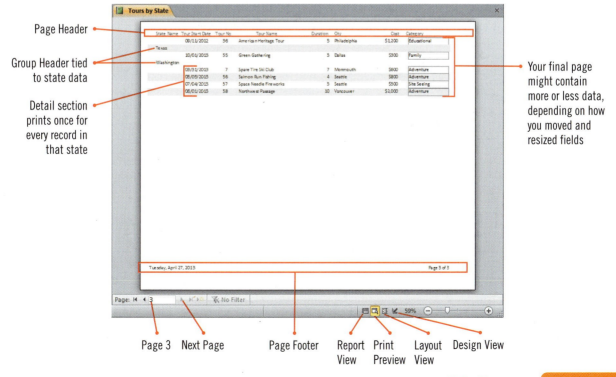

Page 3   Next Page   Page Footer   Report   Print   Layout   Design View
View   Preview   View

Access 2010

Applying Group and Sort Orders

Grouping means to sort records by a particular field *plus* provide a header and/or footer section before or after each group of sorted records. For example, if you group records by the StateName field, the Group Header is called the StateName Header and the Group Footer is called the StateName Footer. The StateName Header section appears once for each state in the report, immediately before the records in that state. The StateName Footer section also appears once for each state in the report, immediately after the records for that state. The records in the Tours by State report are currently grouped by the StateAbbreviation field. Samantha Hooper asks you to further group the records by the Category field (Adventure, Educational, and Family, for example) within each state.

1. **Close Print Preview to return to Report Design View, then click the Group & Sort button in the Grouping & Totals group to open the Group, Sort, and Total pane as shown in Figure D-8**

   To change sorting or grouping options for a report, you need to work in Report Design View. Currently, the records are grouped by the StateAbbreviation field and further sorted by the TourStartDate field. To add the Category field as a grouping field within each state, you work with the Group, Sort, and Total pane. Depending on your monitor, you might need to scroll to the right to display all the controls in Report Design View.

2. **Click the Add a group button in the Group, Sort, and Total pane, click Category, click the Move up button ⬆ so that Category is positioned between StateAbbreviation and TourStartDate, then click the More Options button to display the Category group options**

   A Category Header section is added to Report Design View just below the StateAbbreviation Header section. To print category information only once within each state, you move the Category control from the Detail section to the Category Header section.

3. **Right-click the Category combo box in the Detail section, click Cut on the shortcut menu, right-click the Category Header section, click Paste, then drag the Category combo box to the right to position it as shown in Figure D-9**

   Now that you've moved the Category combo box to the Category Header, it will print only once per category within each state. You no longer need the Category label in the Page Header section.

4. **Right-click the Category label in the Page Header section, click Cut, then switch to Print Preview and zoom to 100% as needed**

   The Tours by State report should look similar to Figure D-10. Notice that the values in the Category field now appear once per category, before the records in each category are listed.

FIGURE D-8: Group, Sort, and Total pane

Group & Sort button

Group, Sort, and Total pane

Add a group button

More Options button for StateAbbreviation

Category control

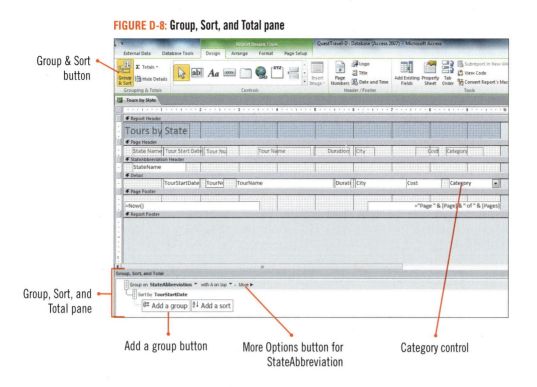

FIGURE D-9: Tours by State report with new Category Header section

Category combo box moved from Detail to Category Header section

Category group

Category label

Less Options button

with a header section

Move up button

Move down button

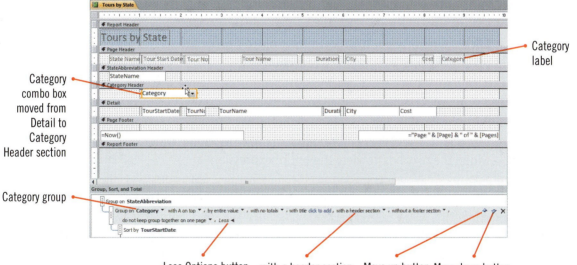

FIGURE D-10: Tours by State report grouped by state and category

Records are further grouped by category within each state

Within each category, records are sorted by tour start date

Adding Subtotals and Counts

In a report, you create a **calculation** by entering an expression into a text box. When a report is previewed or printed, the expression is evaluated and the resulting calculation is placed on the report. An **expression** is a combination of field names, operators (such as +, –, /, and *), and functions that result in a single value. A **function** is a built-in formula, such as Sum or Count, that helps you quickly create a calculation. Notice that every expression starts with an equal sign (=), and when it uses a function, the arguments for the function are placed in (parentheses). **Arguments** are the pieces of information that the function needs to create the final answer. When an argument is a field name, the field name must be surrounded by [square brackets]. Samantha Hooper asks you to add a calculation to the Tours by State report to sum the total number of tour days within each category and within each state.

STEPS

1. **Switch to Report Design View**

   A logical place to add subtotals for each group is immediately after the group in the Group Footer section. You need to use the Group, Sort, and Total pane to open the Group Footer sections for both the Category and StateAbbreviation fields.

   > **TROUBLE**
   >
   > Click Category in the Group, Sort, and Total pane to display the grouping options.

2. **Click the More Options button for the StateAbbreviation field in the Group, Sort, and Total pane, click the without a footer section list arrow, click with a footer section, then do the same for the Category field as shown in Figure D-11**

   With the StateAbbreviation and Category Footer sections open, you're ready to add controls to calculate the total number of tour days within each category and state. You can use a text box control with an expression to make this calculation.

3. **Click the Text Box button [ab] in the Controls group, then click just below the Duration text box in the Category Footer section**

   Adding a new text box automatically adds a new label to its left. First, you modify the label to identify the information, then you modify the text box to contain the correct expression to sum the number of tour days.

   > **TROUBLE**
   >
   > Depending on your activity in Report Design View, you may see a different number in the Text##: label.

4. **Click the Text19 label to select it, double-click Text19, type Total days:, click the Unbound text box to select it, click Unbound again, type =Sum([Duration]), press [Enter], then widen the text box to view the entire expression**

   The expression =Sum([Duration]) uses the Sum function to add up the days in the Duration field. Because the expression is entered in the Category Footer section, it will sum all Duration values for that category. To sum the Duration values for each state, the expression needs to be inserted in the StateAbbreviation Footer.

   > **QUICK TIP**
   >
   > Pasting the expression in the Report Footer section would subtotal the duration values for the entire report.

5. **Right-click the =Sum([Duration]) text box, click Copy, right-click the StateAbbreviation Footer section, click Paste, then press [→] enough times to position the controls in the StateAbbreviation Footer section just below those in the Category Footer section as shown in Figure D-12**

   With the expression in the StateAbbreviation Footer section, you're ready to preview your work.

6. **Switch to Print Preview, then position the report so you can see all of the Colorado tours on the second page**

   As shown in Figure D-13, 43 tour days are totaled for the Adventure category, and 7 for the Family category, which is a total of 50 tour days for the state of Colorado. The summary data would look better if it were aligned more directly under the individual Duration values. You resize and align controls in the next lesson.

FIGURE D-11: Opening group footer sections

Tours by State
Report Header
Tours by State
Page Header
State Name
Tour Start Date
Tour No
Tour Name
Duration
City
Cost
StateAbbreviation Header
StateName
Category Header
Category
Detail
TourStartDate
TourNo
TourName
Durati
City
Cost
Category Footer
StateAbbreviation Footer
Page Footer
=Now()
="Page " & [Page] & " of " & [Pages]
Group, Sort, and Total
Group on StateAbbreviation
Group on Category ▾ with A on top ▾, by entire value ▾, with no totals ▾, with title click to add, with a header section ▾, with a footer section ▾,
do not keep group together on one page ▾, Less ◂
Sort by TourStartDate
Category Footer section
StateAbbreviation Footer section
Category group within each state
Footer section added for the Category field

FIGURE D-12: Adding subtotals to group footer sections

Tours by State
Report Header
Tours by State
Page Header
State Name
Tour Start Date
Tour No
Tour Name
Duration
City
Cost
StateAbbreviation Header
StateName
Category Header
Category
Detail
TourStartDate
TourNo
TourName
Durati
City
Cost
Category Footer
Total days:
=Sum([Duration])
StateAbbreviation Footer
Total days:
=Sum([Duration])
Page Footer
=Now()
="Page " & [Page] & " of " & [Pages]
Category Footer
StateAbbreviation Footer
New labels to describe information
New text boxes to calculate total number of tour days

FIGURE D-13: Previewing the new group footer calculations

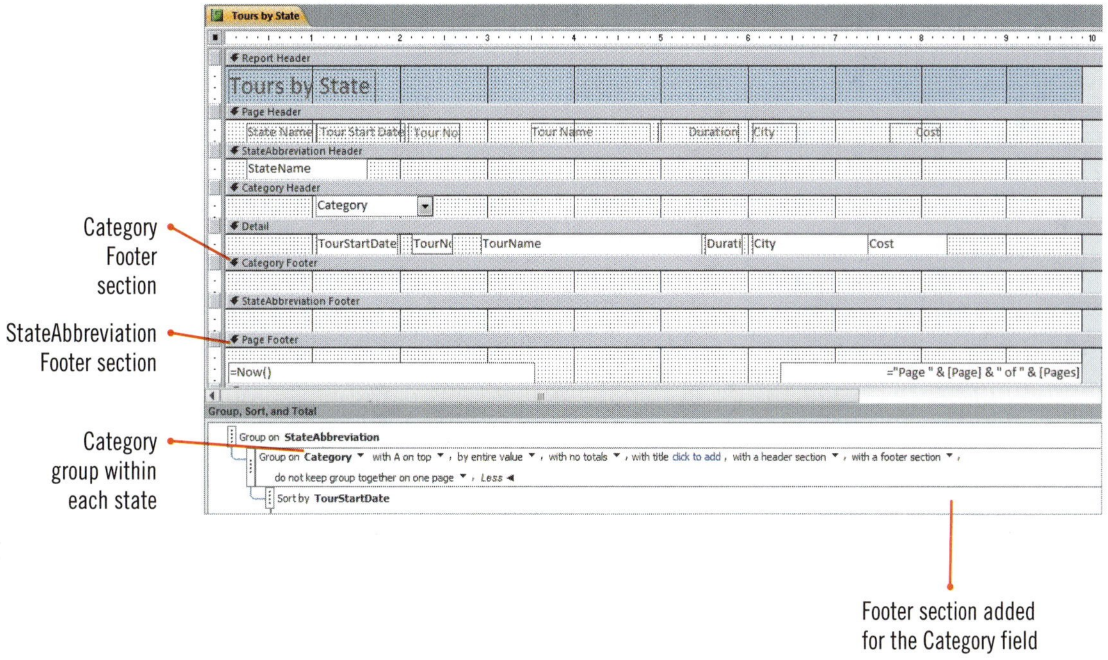

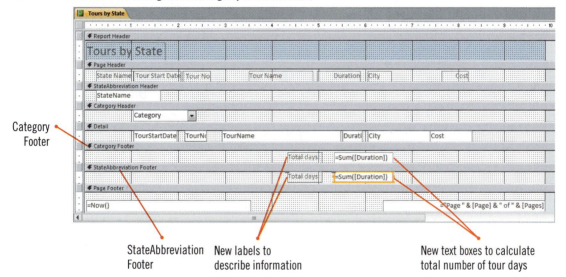

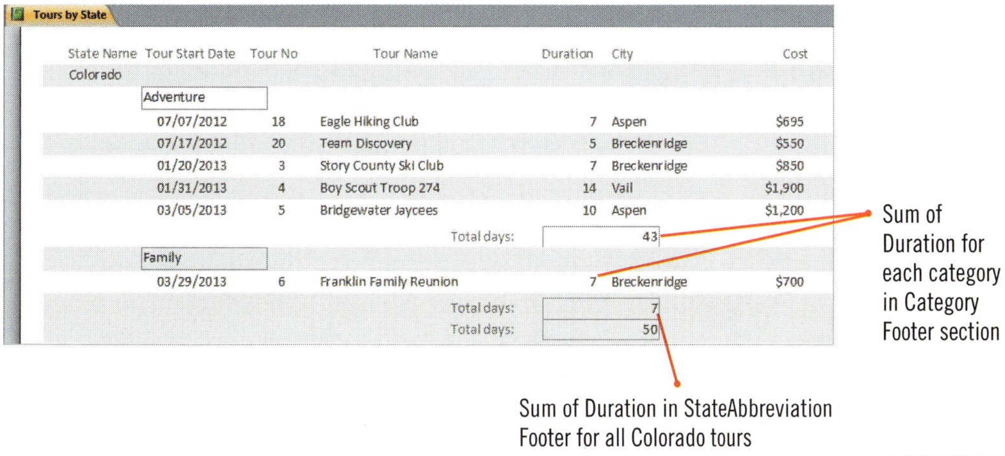

Tours by State
State Name
Tour Start Date
Tour No
Tour Name
Duration
City
Cost
Colorado
Adventure
07/07/2012 18 Eagle Hiking Club 7 Aspen $695
07/17/2012 20 Team Discovery 5 Breckenridge $550
01/20/2013 3 Story County Ski Club 7 Breckenridge $850
01/31/2013 4 Boy Scout Troop 274 14 Vail $1,900
03/05/2013 5 Bridgewater Jaycees 10 Aspen $1,200
Total days: 43
Family
03/29/2013 6 Franklin Family Reunion 7 Breckenridge $700
Total days: 7
Total days: 50
Sum of Duration for each category in Category Footer section
Sum of Duration in StateAbbreviation Footer for all Colorado tours

Resizing and Aligning Controls

After you add information to the appropriate section of a report, you might also want to align the data in precise columns and rows to make the information easier to read. There are two different types of **alignment** commands. You can left-, right-, or center-align a control *within its own border* using the Align Text Left ☰, Center ☰, and Align Text Right ☰ buttons on the Home tab. You can also align the edges of controls *with respect to one another* using the Left, Right, Top, and Bottom commands on the Align button of the Arrange tab in Report Design View. 🎨 You decide to resize and align several controls in the report to improve the readability of the Tours by State report. Layout View is a good choice for these tasks.

STEPS

1. **Switch to Layout View, then click the Group & Sort button to toggle off the Group, Sort, and Total pane**

   You decide to align the expressions that subtotal the number of tour days for each category within the Duration column.

2. **Click the Total days text box in the Category Footer, click the Home tab, click the Center button ☰ in the Text Formatting group, then use the ↔ pointer to resize the text box so that the data is aligned in the Duration column as shown in Figure D-14**

   With the calculation formatted as desired in the Category Footer, you can quickly apply those modifications to the calculation in the StateAbbreviation Footer as well.

   TROUBLE
   If you make a mistake, click the Undo button ↺ on the Quick Access toolbar.

3. **Scroll down the report far enough to find the StateAbbreviation Footer section, click the Total days text box in the StateAbbreviation Footer, click ☰, then use the ↔ pointer to resize the text box so that it is the same width as the text box in the Category Footer section**

   With both expressions centered and aligned, they are easier to read on the report. For longer or more complex numbers, you can right-align the values so that they align on the decimal point.

4. **Scroll the report so you can see all of the Colorado tours as shown in Figure D-15**

   You can apply resize, alignment, or formatting commands to more than one control at a time. Table D-3 provides techniques for selecting more than one control at a time in Report Design View.

Precisely moving and resizing controls

You can move and resize controls using the mouse, but you can move controls more precisely using the keyboard. Pressing the arrow keys while holding [Ctrl] moves selected controls one **pixel** (**picture element**) at a time in the direction of the arrow. Pressing the arrow keys while holding [Shift] resizes selected controls one pixel at a time.

Total days text box   Resize pointer

FIGURE D-15: Reviewing the widened and aligned controls

Widened and
resized text boxes

TABLE D-3: Selecting more than one control at a time in Report Design View

technique	description
Click, [Shift]+click	Click a control, then press and hold [Shift] while clicking other controls; each one is selected
Drag a selection box	Drag a selection box (an outline box you create by dragging the pointer in Report Design View); every control that is in or is touched by the edges of the box is selected
Click in the ruler	Click in either the horizontal or vertical ruler to select all controls that intersect the selection line
Drag in the ruler	Drag through either the horizontal or vertical ruler to select all controls that intersect the selection line as it is dragged through the ruler

Formatting a Report

Formatting refers to enhancing the appearance of the information. Table D-4 lists several of the most popular formatting commands found on the Format tab when you are working in Report Design View. Although the Report Wizard automatically applies many formatting embellishments, you often want to improve the appearance of the report to fit your particular needs. When reviewing the Tours by State report with Samantha, you decide to change the background color of some of the report sections to make the data easier to read. Your first change will be to shade each StateAbbreviation Header and Footer section (rather than alternating sections, the format initially provided by the Report Wizard). To make changes to entire report sections, you must work in Report Design View.

1. **Switch to Design View, click the StateAbbreviation Header section bar, click the Format tab, click the Alternate Row Color button arrow, click No Color, click the Shape Fill button, then click the Maroon 2 color square as shown in Figure D-16**

   Make a similar modification by applying a different fill color to the Category Header section.

2. **Click the Category Header section bar, click the Alternate Row Color button arrow, click No Color, click the Shape Fill button, click the Green 2 color square (just to the right of Maroon 2 in the Standard Colors section)**

   When you use the Alternate Row Color and Shape Fill buttons, you're actually modifying the **Back Color** and **Alternate Back Color** properties in the Property Sheet of the section or control you selected. Background shades can help differentiate parts of the report, but be careful with dark colors as they may print as solid black on some printers and fax machines.

3. **Switch to Layout View to review your modifications**

   The state and category sections are much clearer, but you decide to make one more modification to emphasize the report title.

4. **Click the Tours by State label in the Report Header section, click the Home tab, then click the Bold button B in the Text Formatting group**

   The report in Layout View should look like Figure D-17. You also want to add a label to the Report Footer section to identify yourself.

5. **Switch to Report Design View, drag the bottom edge of the Report Footer down about 0.5", click the Label button Aa in the Controls group, click at the 1" mark in the Report Footer, type Created by your name, press [Enter], click the Home tab, then click B in the Text Formatting group**

6. **Save, preview, and print the Tours by State report if required, then close it**

FIGURE D-16: Formatting section backgrounds

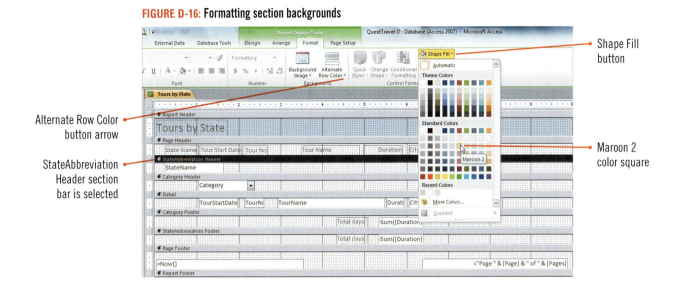

Shape Fill button

Maroon 2 color square

Alternate Row Color button arrow

StateAbbreviation Header section bar is selected

FIGURE D-17: Final formatted Tours by State report

Bold the Tours by State title

StateAbbreviation Header has Maroon 2 shade

Category Header has Green 2 shade

TABLE D-4: Useful formatting commands

button	button name	description
B	Bold	Toggles bold on or off for the selected control(s)
I	Italic	Toggles italics on or off for the selected control(s)
U	Underline	Toggles underline on or off for the selected control(s)
☰	Align Text Left	Left-aligns the selected control(s) within its own border
☰	Center	Centers the selected control(s) within its own border
☰	Align Text Right	Right-aligns the selected control(s) within its own border
Shape Fill ▾	Shape Fill	Changes the background color of the selected control(s)
Alternate Row Color	Alternate Row Color	Changes the background color of alternate records in the selected section
A	Font Color	Changes the text color of the selected control(s)
Shape Outline ▾	Shape Outline Line Thickness option Line Type option	Changes the border color of the selected control(s) Changes the border style of the selected control(s) Changes the special visual effect of the selected control(s)

Creating Mailing Labels

Mailing labels are often created to apply to envelopes, postcards, or letters when assembling a mass mailing. They have many other business purposes too, such as using them on paper file folders or name tags. Any data in your Access database can be converted into labels using the **Label Wizard**, a special report wizard that precisely positions and sizes information for hundreds of standard business labels. Samantha Hooper asks you to create mailing labels for all of the addresses in the Customers table. You use the Label Wizard to handle this request.

STEPS

1. **Click the Customers table in the Navigation Pane, click the Create tab, then click the Labels button in the Reports group**

   The first Label Wizard dialog box opens. The Filter by manufacturer list box provides over 30 manufacturers of labels. Because Avery is the most common, it is the default choice. With the manufacturer selected, your next task is to choose the product number of the labels you will feed through the printer. The label list box is the best source for this information. In this case, you'll be using Avery 5160 labels, a common type of sheet labels used for mailings and other purposes.

2. **Scroll through the Product numbers, then click 5160 as shown in Figure D-18**

   Note that by selecting a product number, you also specify the dimensions of the label and number of columns.

3. **Click Next, then click Next again to accept the default font and color choices**

   The third question of the Label Wizard asks how you want to construct your label. You'll add the fields from the Customers table in a standard mailing format.

4. **Double-click FName, press [Spacebar], double-click LName, press [Enter], double-click Street, press [Enter], double-click City, type comma and press [Spacebar], double-click State, press [Spacebar], then double-click Zip**

   If your prototype label doesn't look exactly like Figure D-19, delete the fields and try again. Be careful to put a space between the FName and LName fields in the first row, a comma and a space between the City and State fields, and a space between the State and Zip fields.

5. **Click Next, double-click LName to select it as a sorting field, click Next, click Finish to accept the name Labels Customers for the new report, then click OK if prompted**

   A portion of the new report is shown in Figure D-20. It is generally a good idea to print the first page of the report on standard paper to make sure everything is aligned correctly before printing on labels.

QUICK TIP
To include your name on the print-out, first change Jacob Alman's name to your own in the Customers table, then close and open the report again.

6. **Click the Print button on the Print Preview tab, click the From box, type 1, click the To box, type 1, then click OK if a printout is desired**

7. **Close the Labels Customers report, close the QuestTravel-D.accdb database, then exit Access 2010**

FIGURE D-18: Label Wizard dialog box

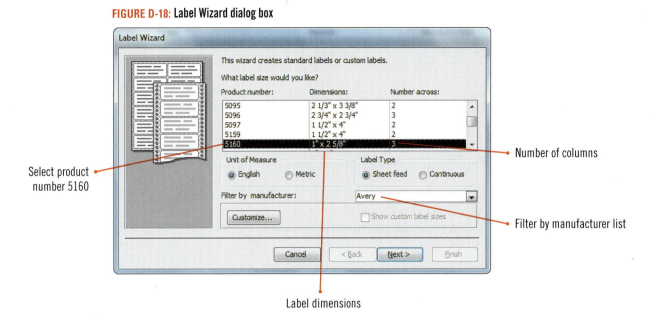

Label Wizard
This wizard creates standard labels or custom labels.
What label size would you like?
Product number: Dimensions: Number across:
5095 2 1/3" x 3 3/8" 2
5096 2 3/4" x 2 3/4" 3
5097 1 1/2" x 4" 2
5159 1 1/2" x 4" 2
5160 1" x 2 5/8" 3
Unit of Measure
English
Metric
Label Type
Sheet feed
Continuous
Filter by manufacturer:
Avery
Customize...
Show custom label sizes
Cancel
< Back
Next >
Finish
Select product number 5160
Number of columns
Filter by manufacturer list
Label dimensions

FIGURE D-19: Building a prototype label

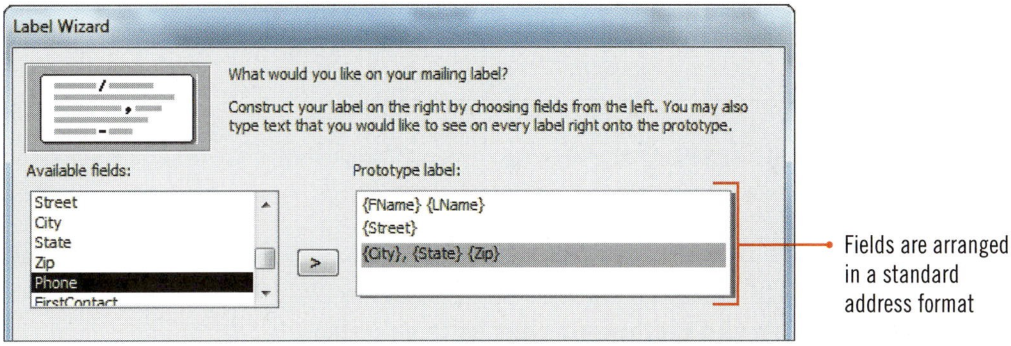

Label Wizard
What would you like on your mailing label?
Construct your label on the right by choosing fields from the left. You may also type text that you would like to see on every label right onto the prototype.
Available fields:
Street
City
State
Zip
Phone
FirstContact
Prototype label:
{FName} {LName}
{Street}
{City}, {State} {Zip}
Fields are arranged in a standard address format

FIGURE D-20: Labels Customers report

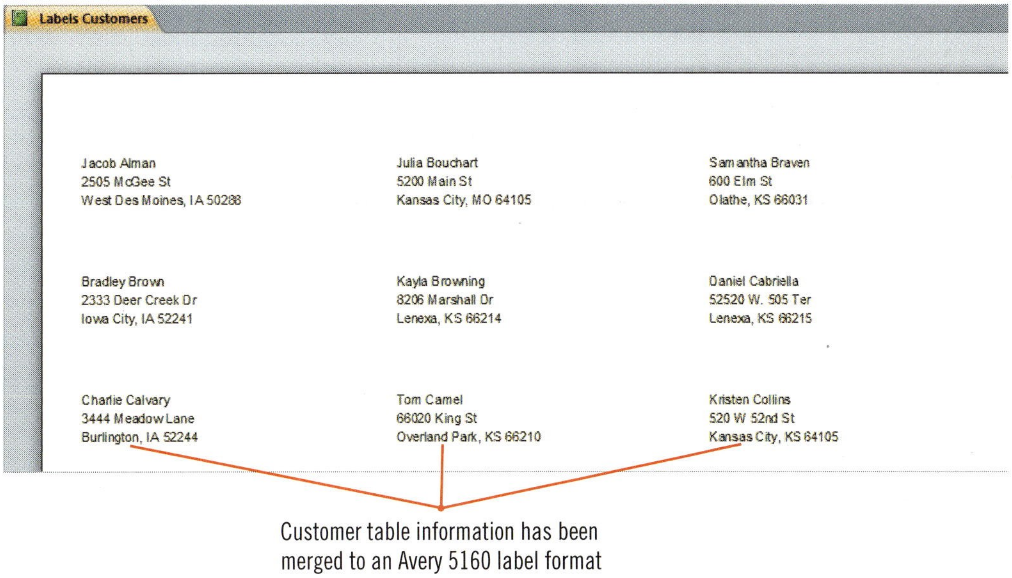

Labels Customers
Jacob Alman
2505 McGee St
West Des Moines, IA 50288
Julia Bouchart
5200 Main St
Kansas City, MO 64105
Samantha Braven
600 Elm St
Olathe, KS 66031
Bradley Brown
2333 Deer Creek Dr
Iowa City, IA 52241
Kayla Browning
8206 Marshall Dr
Lenexa, KS 66214
Daniel Cabriella
52520 W. 505 Ter
Lenexa, KS 66215
Charlie Calvary
3444 Meadow Lane
Burlington, IA 52244
Tom Camel
66020 King St
Overland Park, KS 66210
Kristen Collins
520 W 52nd St
Kansas City, KS 64105
Customer table information has been merged to an Avery 5160 label format

Access 2010

Practice

For current SAM information, including versions and content details, visit SAM Central (http://www.cengage.com/samcentral). If you have a SAM user profile, you may have access to hands-on instruction, practice, and assessment of the skills covered in this unit. Since various versions of SAM are supported throughout the life of this text, check with your instructor for the correct instructions and URL/Web site for accessing assignments.

Concepts Review

Label each element of the Report Design View window shown in Figure D-21.

FIGURE D-21

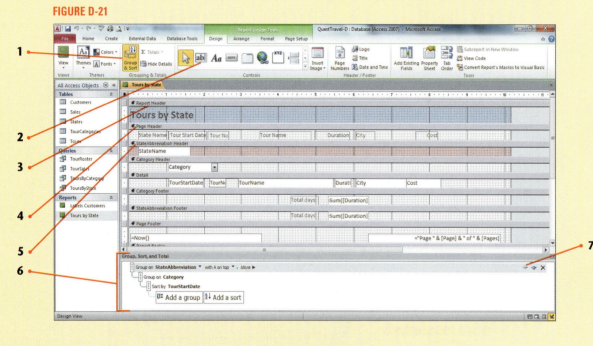

Match each term with the statement that best describes it.

8. Expression
9. Section
10. Detail section
11. Record source
12. Formatting
13. Grouping
14. Alignment

a. Left, center, or right are common choices
b. Prints once for every record
c. Used to identify which fields and records are passed to the report
d. Sorting records *plus* providing a header or footer section
e. Determines how controls are positioned on the report
f. A combination of field names, operators, and functions that results in a single value
g. Enhancing the appearance of information displayed in the report

Select the best answer from the list of choices.

15. Which of the following is *not* a valid report view?
   a. Print Preview
   b. Design View
   c. Layout View
   d. Section View

16. **Which type of control is most commonly placed in the Detail section?**
   - **a.** Image
   - **b.** Line
   - **c.** Label
   - **d.** Text box

17. **A title for a report would most commonly be placed in which report section?**
   - **a.** Report Header
   - **b.** Detail
   - **c.** Group Footer
   - **d.** Report Footer

18. **A calculated expression that presents page numbering information would probably be placed in which report section?**
   - **a.** Report Header
   - **b.** Group Footer
   - **c.** Detail
   - **d.** Page Footer

19. **Which of the following expressions counts the number of records using the FirstName field?**
   - **a.** =Count([FirstName])
   - **b.** =Count(FirstName)
   - **c.** =Count[FirstName]
   - **d.** =Count{FirstName}

20. **To align the edges of several controls with each other, you use the alignment commands on the:**
   - **a.** Formatting tab.
   - **b.** Print Preview tab.
   - **c.** Design tab.
   - **d.** Arrange tab.

Skills Review

1. **Use the Report Wizard.**
   - **a.** Start Access and open the RealEstate-D.accdb database from the drive and folder where you store your Data Files. Enable content if prompted.
   - **b.** Use the Report Wizard to create a report based on the RLast and RPhone fields from the Realtors table, and the Type, SqFt, BR, Bath, and Asking fields from the Listings table.
   - **c.** View the data by Realtors, do not add any more grouping levels, and sort the records in descending order by the Asking field.
   - **d.** Use a Stepped layout and a Landscape orientation. Title the report **Realtor Listings**.
   - **e.** Preview the first page of the new report. Notice whether any fields or field names need more space.

2. **Use Report Layout View.**
   - **a.** Switch to Layout View.
   - **b.** Narrow the RLast and RPhone columns enough so they are only as wide as necessary.
   - **c.** Modify the RLast label to read **Realtor**, the RPhone label to read **Phone**, the SqFt label to read **Square Feet**, the BR label to read **Bedrooms**, and the Bath label to read **Baths**.
   - **d.** Switch to Print Preview, and view each page of the report.

3. **Review report sections.**
   - **a.** Switch to Report Design View.
   - **b.** Drag the text box that contains the Page calculation in the lower-right corner of the Page Footer section to the left so that it is to the left of the 9" mark on the horizontal ruler.
   - **c.** Drag the right edge of the entire report to the left so it ends within the 10.5" mark on the horizontal ruler.

4. **Apply group and sort orders.**
   - **a.** Open the Group, Sort, and Total pane.
   - **b.** Add the Type field as a grouping field between the RealtorNo grouping field and Asking sort field.
   - **c.** Cut and paste the Type combo box from its current position in the Detail section to the Type Header section.
   - **d.** Move the Type combo box in the Type Header section so its left edge is at about the 1" mark on the horizontal ruler.
   - **e.** Delete the Type label in the Page Header section.
   - **f.** Switch to Layout View, and move the Asking column—the data and label—closer to the Square Feet column.
   - **g.** Select the Type text box, and right-align the information in the text box.

Skills Review (continued)

5. Add subtotals and counts.

  a. Switch to Report Design View, then open the RealtorNo Footer section.

  b. Add a text box control to the RealtorNo Footer section, just below the Asking text box in the Detail section. Change the label to read **Subtotal:**, and enter the expression **=Sum([Asking])** in the text box.

  c. Drag the bottom edge of the Report Footer down about 0.25" to add space to the Report Footer.

  d. Copy and paste the new expression in the RealtorNo Footer section to the Report Footer section. Position the controls as directly under the controls in the RealtorNo Footer section as possible.

  e. Modify the label in the Report Footer section to read **Grand Total:**.

  f. Preview the last page of the report to view both the new subtotals in the RealtorNo Footer section as well as in the Report Footer section.

6. Resize and align controls.

  a. Switch to Layout View, close the Group, Sort, and Total pane if it is open, and move to the last page of the report to view the Subtotal and Grand Total calculations.

  b. Right-align the text within the Subtotal and Grand Total labels. Move the labels so that their right edges are aligned.

  c. Move the labels and text boxes as needed so that the calculations are positioned directly under the Asking column. Also make sure that the right edges of text boxes that contain the calculations are aligned with the right edge of the Asking column. (*Hint*: If you want to precisely align the right edges of two controls, you need to switch to Report Design View, select both controls at the same time, click the Align button on the Arrange tab, and then click Right to right-align the right edges of the selected controls. Or you can use your mouse or arrow keys to move the right edges of the controls in Layout View.)

  d. Save the report.

7. Format a report.

  a. Switch to Report Design View, and change the Alternate Row Color of the Detail section to No Color.

  b. Change the Alternate Row Color of the Type Header section to No Color.

  c. Change the Alternate Row Color of the RealtorNo Header section to No Color, and change the Shape Fill color of the RealtorNo Header section to Green 2.

  d. Select the RLast text box in the RealtorNo Header section, and change the Shape Fill color to Green 2 to match the RealtorNo Header section. Apply the same Green 2 background color to the RPhone text box.

  e. Bold the title of the report, the **Realtor Listings** label in the Report Header.

  f. Double-click a sizing handle on the label in the Report Header to expand it to accommodate the entire label. Be sure to double-click a sizing handle of the label, not the label itself, which opens the Property Sheet.

  g. Change the font color of each label in the Page Header section to black.

  h. Save and preview the report in Report View. It should look like Figure D-22.

  i. In Report Design View, add a label to the left side of the Report Footer section with your name.

  j. Return to Print Preview, print the report if requested by your instructor, then close the Realtor Listings report.

FIGURE D-22

Realtor	Phone		Asking	Square Feet	Bedrooms	Baths
King	555-222-8877					
		Cabin				
			222000	1900	3	1
		Mobile Home				
			129000	1200	3	2
		New				
			345000	2900	3	2.5
			305000	3000	2	3
		Ranch				
			475000	3400	4	4
			395000	2000	3	3.5
			375000	3000	3	2.5
			290000	2000	3	3
			220000	1215	3	2
		Subtotal:	2756000			

8. Create mailing labels.

  a. Click the Agencies table in the Navigation Pane, then start the Label Wizard.

  b. Choose Avery 5160 labels and the default text appearance choices.

  c. Build a prototype label with the AgencyName on the first line, Street on the second line, and City, State, and Zip on the third line with a comma and space between City and State, and a space between State and Zip.

  d. Sort by AgencyName, and name the report **Labels Agencies**.

Skills Review (continued)

e. Preview then close the report. Click OK if a warning dialog box appears regarding horizontal space.

f. If your instructor asks you to print the Labels Agencies report, open the Agencies table and change the name of Four Lakes Realtors to **YourLastName Realtors**. Close the Agencies table, reopen the Labels Agencies report, then print it.

g. Close the Labels Agencies report, close the RealEstate-D.accdb database, then exit Access 2010.

Independent Challenge 1

As the office manager of an international convention planning company, you have created a database to track convention, enrollment, and company data. Your goal is to create a report of up-to-date attendee enrollments.

If you have a SAM 2010 user profile, an autogradable SAM version of this assignment may be available at http://www.cengage.com/sam2010. Check with your instructor to confirm that this assignment is available in SAM. To use the SAM version of this assignment, log into the SAM 2010 Web site and download the instruction and start files.

a. Start Access, then open the Conventions-D.accdb database from the drive and folder where you store your Data Files. Enable content if prompted.

b. Use the Report Wizard to create a report with the AttendeeFirst and AttendeeLast fields from the Attendees table, the CompanyName field from the Companies table, and the ConventionName and CountryName from the Conventions table.

c. View your data by Conventions, do not add any more grouping levels, and sort in ascending order by CompanyName, then AttendeeLast.

d. Use the Block layout and Portrait orientation, then name the report **Convention Listing**.

e. In Layout View, change the labels in the Page Header section from ConventionName to **Convention**, CountryName to **Country**, CompanyName to **Company**, and AttendeeLast to **Attendee**. Delete the AttendeeFirst label.

f. Open the Group, Sort, and Total pane, then use the More Options button to open the CompanyName field's Group Header and Group Footer sections.

g. In Report Design View, expand the ConventionNo Header section about 0.5", then use Cut and Paste to move the ConventionName text box from the Detail section to the ConventionNo Header section. Left-align the ConventionName text box with the Convention label in the Page Header section. Drag the top edge of the CompanyName Header section up to close the extra space in the ConventionNo Header.

h. Expand the CompanyName Header section about 0.25". Drag the CompanyName text box to the bottom of the CompanyName Header section. Use Cut and Paste to move the CountryName text box from the Detail section to the ConventionNo Header section and position it directly above the CompanyName text box in the CompanyName Header section.

i. Delete the Country and CompanyName labels in the Page Header section.

j. In Layout View, scroll through the entire report and widen the ConventionName and CompanyName text boxes as necessary to show all of the data. Be careful, however, to not expand the report beyond the width of the portrait orientation of the report.

k. In Design View, expand the CompanyName Footer, and enter an expression in a new text box to count the values in the AttendeeLast field, **=Count([AttendeeLast])**. Position the new text box directly below the AttendeeLast text box.

l. Modify the new label in the Company Name Footer to read **Count:**. Format the text color of the label to black.

m. Change the color of the report title and the labels in the Page Header section to black. Preview the report. The subtotal count for the first convention should be 21.

n. If required to print the report, switch to Report Design View, add your name as a label to the Report Header section, then print the first page.

o. Save and close the Convention Listing report, close the Conventions-D.accdb database, then exit Access 2010.

Independent Challenge 2

You have built an Access database to track membership in a community service club. The database tracks member names and addresses as well as their status in the club, which moves from rank to rank as the members contribute increased hours of service to the community.

a. Start Access and open the Membership-D.accdb database from the drive and folder where you store your Data Files. Enable content if prompted.

b. Open the Members table, find and change the name of Traci Kalvert to your name, then close the Members table.

c. Use the Report Wizard to create a report using the Status and DuesOwed fields from the Status table, and the FName, LName, and DuesPaid fields from the Members table.

d. View the data by Status. Do not add any more grouping fields, and sort the records in ascending order by LName.

e. Use a Stepped layout and Portrait orientation, title the report **Dues Report**, then preview the report.

f. Switch to Report Design View, then use the Group, Sort, and Total pane to open the StatusNo Footer section.

g. Add a text box to the StatusNo Footer section, just below the DuesPaid text box. Change the label to **Count:** and the expression in the text box to **=Count([DuesPaid])**.

h. Expand the StatusNo Footer section as necessary, and add a second text box to the StatusNo Footer section, just below the first. Change the label to **Subtotal:** and the expression in the text box to **=Sum([DuesPaid])**.

i. Move, resize, and align the controls in the StatusNo Footer section as needed so they are positioned directly under the DuesPaid text box in the Detail section.

Advanced Challenge Exercise

- Open the Property Sheet for the =Sum([DuesPaid]) text box. On the Format tab, set the Format property to Currency and the Decimal Places property to 2.
- Expand the StatusNo Footer section as necessary, and add a third text box to the StatusNo Footer section, just below the second. Change the label to **Balance:**.
- Change the text box expression to **=Count([LName])*[DuesOwed]–Sum([DuesPaid])**. This expression counts the number of values in the LName field, and multiplies it by the DuesOwed field. From that value, the sum of the DuesPaid field is subtracted. This calculates the balance between dues owed and dues paid.
- Open the Property Sheet for the text box with the balance calculation. On the Format tab, set the Format property to Currency and the Decimal Places property to 2.

j. Align the right edges of the DuesPaid text box in the Detail section and all text boxes in the StatusNo Footer section.

k. Save, then preview the Dues Report, print the first page of the Dues Report if requested by your instructor, then close it.

l. Close the Membership-D.accdb database, then exit Access.

Independent Challenge 3

You have built an Access database to organize the deposits at a recycling center. Various clubs regularly deposit recyclable material, which is measured in pounds when the deposits are made.

a. Start Access and open the Recycle-D.accdb database from the drive and folder where you store your Data Files. Enable content if prompted.

b. Open the Centers table, change **Trash Can** to **YourLastName Recycling**, then close the table.

c. Use the Report Wizard to create a report with the CenterName field from the Centers table, the Deposit Date and Weight from the Deposits table, and the ClubName field from the Clubs table.

d. View the data by Centers, do not add any more grouping levels, and sort the records in ascending order by DepositDate.

e. Use a Stepped layout and a Portrait orientation, then title the report **Deposit Listing**.

f. In Layout View, center the Weight label and Weight data. Resize any other labels to display all of their text.

g. Add spaces to the labels so that CenterName becomes **Center Name**, DepositDate becomes **Deposit Date**, and ClubName becomes **Club Name**.

Independent Challenge 3 (continued)

h. In Report Design View, open the Group, Sort, and Total pane and add a CenterNumber Footer section.

i. Add a text box to the CenterNumber Footer section just below the Weight text box with the expression **=Sum([Weight])**.

j. Rename the new label to be **Total Center Weight:** and move it to the left as needed so that it doesn't overlap the text box.

k. Resize and align the edges of the =Sum([Weight]) text box in the CenterNumber Footer section with the Weight text box in the Detail section. Center the data in the =Sum([Weight]) text box.

l. Expand the Report Footer section, then copy and paste the =Sum([Weight]) text box from the CenterNumber Footer section to the Report Footer section.

m. Move and align the controls in the Report Footer section with their counterparts in the CenterNumber Footer section.

n. Change the label in the Report Footer section to **Grand Total Weight:**.

o. Drag the top edges of every section bar up as far as possible to remove extra blank space in the report, then preview the last page of the report as shown in Figure D-23. Your spacing may be a bit different, but the Center subtotals and grand total should match.

p. Save and close the Deposit Listing report, close the Recycle-D.accdb database, then exit Access.

FIGURE D-23

4/23/2013	90	Boy Scouts #11
5/1/2013	105	Girl Scouts #11
6/4/2013	90	Lions
6/20/2013	85	Junior League
8/31/2013	50	Girl Scouts #11
10/2/2013	90	Lions
Total Center Weight:	2720	
Grand Total Weight:	9365	

Real Life Independent Challenge

One way you can use an Access database on your own is to record and track your job search efforts. In this exercise, you create a report to help read and analyze data into your job-tracking database.

a. Start Access and open the JobSearch-D.accdb database from the drive and folder where you store your Data Files. Enable content if prompted.

b. Open the Employers table, and enter five more records to identify five more potential employers.

c. Use subdatasheets in the Employers table to enter five more potential jobs. You may enter all five jobs for one employer, one job for five different employers, or any combination thereof. Be sure to check the spelling of all data entered.

d. Use the Report Wizard to create a report that lists all fields from the Employers table except for EmployerID, and all fields from the Positions table except for the Desirability, EmployerID, and PositionID fields.

e. View the data by Employers, do not add any more grouping levels, and do not add any sort orders.

f. Use a Block layout and a Landscape orientation, then title the report **Job Openings**.

g. In Layout View, revise the labels in the Page Header section from CompanyName to **Company**, EmpStreet to **Street**, EmpCity to **City**, EmpState to **State**, EmpZip to **Zip**, EmpPhone to **Phone**, CareerArea to **Area**, and AnnualSalary to **Salary**.

h. In Layout View, resize the columns so that all data fits on one landscape piece of paper.

i. In Report Design View, move the Page expression in the Page Footer section and the right edge of the report to the left, within the 10.5" mark on the horizontal ruler.

j. Preview and save the Job Openings report, then print it if requested by your instructor.

k. Close the Job Openings report, close the JobSearch-D.accdb database, then exit Access 2010.

Visual Workshop

Open the Basketball-D.accdb database from the drive and folder where you store your Data Files and enable content if prompted. Open the Players table, enter your own name instead of Kelsey Douglas, then close the table. Your goal is to create the report shown in Figure D-24. Use the Report Wizard, and select the PFirst, PLast, HomeTown, and HomeState fields from the Players table. Select the FieldGoals, 3Pointers, and FreeThrows fields from the Stats table. View the data by Players, do not add any more grouping levels, and do not add any more sorting levels. Use a Block layout and a Portrait orientation, then title the report **Scoring Report**. In Layout View, resize all of the columns so that they fit on a single piece of portrait paper, and change the labels in the Page Header section as shown. In Report Design View, move the page calculation in the Page Footer section within the margins of the report, and drag the right edge of the report to the left to eliminate blank pages. Open the PlayerNo Footer section and add text boxes with expressions to sum the FieldGoals, 3Pointers, and FreeThrow fields. Move, modify, and resize all controls as needed.

FIGURE D-24

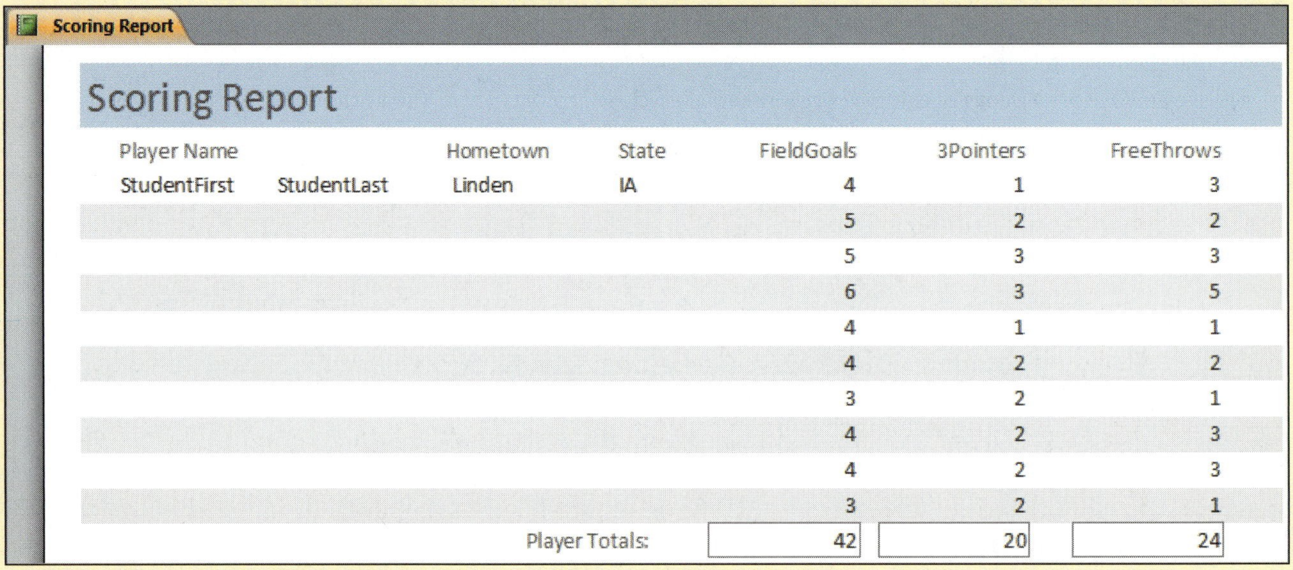

Player Name		Hometown	State	FieldGoals	3Pointers	FreeThrows
StudentFirst	StudentLast	Linden	IA	4	1	3
				5	2	2
				5	3	3
				6	3	5
				4	1	1
				4	2	2
				3	2	1
				4	2	3
				4	2	3
				3	2	1
		Player Totals:		42	20	24

Scoring Report

Modifying the Database Structure

In this unit, you refine a database by adding a new table to an existing database and then linking tables using one-to-many relationships to create a relational database. You work with fields that have different data types, including Text, Number, Currency, Date/Time, and Yes/No, to define the data stored in the database. You create and use Attachment fields to store images. You also modify table and field properties to format and validate data. Working with Samantha Hooper, the tour developer for U.S. group travel at Quest Specialty Travel, you are developing an Access database to track the tours, customers, sales, and payments for this division. The database consists of multiple tables that you link, modify, and enhance to create a relational database.

OBJECTIVES

Examine relational databases

Design related tables

Create one-to-many relationships

Create Lookup fields

Modify Text fields

Modify Number and Currency fields

Modify Date/Time fields

Modify validation properties

Create Attachment fields

Examining Relational Databases

The purpose of a relational database is to organize and store data in a way that minimizes redundancy and maximizes your flexibility when querying and analyzing data. To accomplish these goals, a relational database uses related tables rather than a single large table of data. At one time, the Sales department at Quest Specialty Travel tracked information about their tour sales and payments using a single Access table called Sales, shown in Figure E-1. This created data redundancy problems because of the duplicate tour, customer, and payment information entered into a single table. You decide to study the principles of relational database design to help Quest Specialty Travel reorganize these fields into a correctly designed relational database.

DETAILS

To redesign a list into a relational database, follow these principles:

- **Design each table to contain fields that describe only one subject**

  Currently, the table in Figure E-1 contains four subjects—tours, sales, customers, and payments—which creates redundant data. For example, the customer's name must be reentered every time that customer purchases a tour or makes a payment. The problems of redundant data include extra data-entry work, more data-entry inconsistencies and errors, larger physical storage requirements, and limitations on your ability to search for, analyze, and report on the data. You minimize these problems by implementing a properly designed relational database.

- **Identify a primary key field for each table**

  A **primary key field** is a field that contains unique information for each record. For example, in a customer table, the customer number field usually serves this purpose. Although using the customer's last name as the primary key field might work in a small database, names are generally a poor choice for a primary key field because the primary key could not accommodate two customers who have the same name.

- **Build one-to-many relationships**

  To tie the information from one table to another, a field must be common to each table. This linking field is the primary key field on the "one" side of the relationship and the **foreign key field** on the "many" side of the relationship. For example, a CustomerNo field acting as the primary key field in the Customers table would link to a CustomerNo foreign key field in a Sales table to join one customer to many sales. You are not required to give the linking field the same name in the "one" and "many" tables.

  The revised design for the database is shown in Figure E-2. One customer can purchase many tours, so the Customers and Sales tables have a one-to-many relationship based on the linking CustNo field. One tour can have many sales, so the Tours and Sales tables also have a one-to-many relationship based on the common TourID field (named TourNo in the Tours table). And one sale may have many payments, creating a one-to-many relationship based on the common SalesNo field.

FIGURE E-1: Single Sales table – redundant data

TourName	City	Cost	SalesNo	SaleDate	FName	LName	PaymentDate	PaymentAmt
Princess Bay Shelling	Captiva	$750	2	3/30/2012	Lisa	Wilson	3/2/2012	$50.00
Princess Bay Shelling	Captiva	$750	118	3/31/2012	Kristen	Collins	3/3/2012	$60.00
Story County Ski Club	Breckenridge	$850	1	4/5/2012	Kristen	Collins	4/2/2012	$70.00
Story County Ski Club	Breckenridge	$850	1	4/5/2012	Kristen	Collins	5/20/2012	$100.00
Princess Bay Shelling	Captiva	$750	120	4/29/2012	Naresh	Hubert	5/21/2012	$75.00
Princess Bay Shelling	Captiva	$750	86	4/30/2012	Lois	Goode	5/22/2012	$150.00
Story County Ski Club	Breckenridge	$850	1	4/5/2012	Kristen	Collins	6/2/2012	$200.00

Tour information is duplicated for each sale or payment

Sales information is duplicated for each payment

Customer information is duplicated for each sale or payment

Payment fields

FIGURE E-2: Related tables reduce redundant data

CustNo	FName	LName	Street	City	State	Zip
1	Gracita	Mayberry	52411 Oakmont Rd	Kansas City	MO	64144
2	Jacob	Alman	2505 McGee St	West Des Moines	IA	50288
3	Julia	Bouchart	5200 Main St	Kansas City	MO	64105
4	Kayla	Browning	8206 Marshall Dr	Lenexa	KS	66214
5	Samantha	Braven	600 Elm St	Olathe	KS	66031
6	Kristen	Collins	520 W 52nd St	Kansas City	KS	64105
7	Tom	Camel	66020 King St	Overland Park	KS	66210
8	Mark	Custard	66900 College Rd	Overland Park	KS	66210

One customer may purchase many tours

One tour may be purchased many times

TourNo	TourName	TourStartDate	Duration	City
1	Princess Bay Shelling	07/24/2012	7	Captiva
2	Red Reef Scuba	07/24/2012	6	Islamadora
3	Story County Ski Club	01/20/2013	7	Breckenridge
4	Boy Scout Troop 274	01/31/2013	14	Vail
5	Bridgewater Jaycees	03/05/2013	10	Aspen
6	Franklin Family Reunion	03/29/2013	7	Breckenridge

SalesNo	SaleDate	CustNo	TourID
1	4/5/2012	6	3
2	3/30/2012	32	1
3	5/31/2012	34	1
4	6/1/2012	6	47
5	6/1/2012	4	36
6	6/1/2012	8	36
7	6/1/2012	15	36
8	7/7/2012	6	51
9	7/8/2012	7	51

One sale may be paid with many payments

PaymentID	SalesNo	PaymentDate	PaymentAmt
1	2	3/2/2012	$50.00
2	118	3/3/2012	$60.00
3	1	4/2/2012	$70.00
4	1	5/20/2012	$100.00
5	120	5/21/2012	$75.00
6	86	5/22/2012	$150.00
7	1	6/2/2012	$200.00

Using many-to-many relationships

As you design your database, you might find that two tables have a **many-to-many relationship**. To join them, you must establish a third table called a **junction table**, which contains two foreign key fields to serve on the "many" side of separate one-to-many relationships with the two original tables. The Customers and Tours tables have a many-to-many relationship because one customer can purchase many tours and one tour can have many customers purchase it. The Sales table serves as the junction table to link the three tables together.

Modifying the Database Structure

Access 99

Designing Related Tables

After you develop a valid relational database design, you are ready to define the tables in Access. Using **Table Design View**, you can specify all characteristics of a table including field names, data types, field descriptions, field properties, Lookup properties, and primary key field designations. Using the new database design, you are ready to create the Payments table for Quest Specialty Travel.

STEPS

1. **Start Access, open the QuestTravel-E.accdb database, then enable content if prompted**
   The Customers, Sales, and Tours tables have already been created in the database. You need to create the Payments table.

2. **Click the Create tab on the Ribbon, then click the Table Design button in the Tables group**
   Table Design View opens, where you can enter field names and specify data types and field properties for the new table. Field names should be as short as possible, but long enough to be descriptive. The field name you enter in Table Design View is used as the default name for the field in all later queries, forms, and reports.

   QUICK TIP
   When specifying field data types, you can type the first letter of the data type to quickly select it.

3. **Type PaymentNo, press [Enter], click the Data Type list arrow, click AutoNumber, press [Tab], type Primary key field for the Payments table, then press [Enter]**
   The AutoNumber data type automatically assigns the next available integer in the sequence to each new record. This data type is often used as the primary key field for a table because it always contains a unique value for each record.

4. **Type the other field names, data types, and descriptions as shown in Figure E-3**
   Field descriptions entered in Table Design View are optional, but they are helpful in that they provide further information about the field.

   TROUBLE
   If you set the wrong field as the primary key field, click the Primary Key field button again to toggle it off.

5. **Click PaymentNo in the Field Name column, then click the Primary Key button in the Tools group**
   A **key symbol** appears to the left of PaymentNo to indicate that this field is defined as the primary key field for this table. Primary key fields have two roles: they uniquely define each record, and they may also serve as the "one" side of a one-to-many relationship between two tables. Table E-1 describes common examples of one-to-many relationships.

   QUICK TIP
   To delete or rename an existing table, right-click it in the Navigation Pane, then click Delete or Rename.

6. **Click the Save button 🖫 on the Quick Access toolbar, type Payments in the Table Name text box, click OK, then close the table**
   The Payments table is now displayed as a table object in the QuestTravel-E.accdb database Navigation Pane, as shown in Figure E-4.

Specifying the foreign key field data type

A foreign key field in the "many" table must have the same data type (Text or Number) as the primary key it is related to in the "one" table. An exception to this rule is when the primary key field in the "one" table has an AutoNumber data type. In this case, the linking foreign key field in the "many" table must have a Number data type. Also note that a Number field used as a foreign key field must have a Long Integer Field Size property to match the Field Size property of the AutoNumber primary key field.

FIGURE E-3: Table Design View for the new Payments table

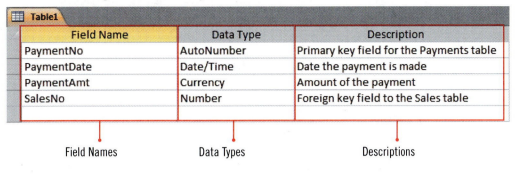

Field Name	Data Type	Description
PaymentNo	AutoNumber	Primary key field for the Payments table
PaymentDate	Date/Time	Date the payment is made
PaymentAmt	Currency	Amount of the payment
SalesNo	Number	Foreign key field to the Sales table

Field Names   Data Types   Descriptions

FIGURE E-4: Payments table in the QuestTravel-E database Navigation Pane

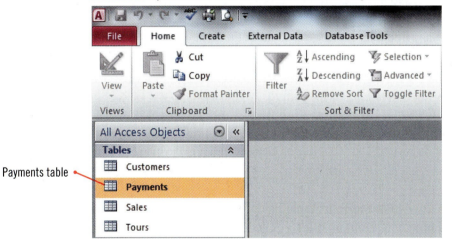

Payments table

TABLE E-1: Common one-to-many relationships

table on "one" side	table on "many" side	linking field	description
Products	Sales	ProductID	A ProductID field must have a unique entry in a Products table, but it is listed many times in a Sales table
Students	Enrollments	StudentID	A StudentID field must have a unique entry in a Students table, but it is listed many times in an Enrollments table as the student enrolls in multiple classes
Employees	Promotions	EmployeeID	An EmployeeID field must have a unique entry in an Employees table, but it is listed many times in a Promotions table as the employee is promoted over time

Creating One-to-Many Relationships

After creating the tables you need, you link them together in appropriate one-to-many relationships using the primary key field in the "one" table and the foreign key field in the "many" table. To avoid rework, be sure that your table relationships are finished before building queries, forms, or reports using fields from multiple tables. You are ready to define the one-to-many relationships between the tables of the QuestTravel-E.accdb database.

QUICK TIP
Drag the table's title bar to move the field list.

1. **Click the Database Tools tab on the Ribbon, click the Relationships button, click the Show Table button, double-click Customers, double-click Sales, double-click Tours, double-click Payments, then close the Show Table dialog box**

   The four table field lists appear in the Relationships window. The primary key fields are identified with a small key symbol to the left of the field name. With all of the field lists in the Relationships window, you're ready to link them in proper one-to-many relationships.

QUICK TIP
Drag the bottom border of the field list to display all of the fields.

2. **Click CustNo in the Customers table field list, then drag it to the CustNo field in the Sales table field list**

   Dragging a field from one table to another in the Relationships window links the two tables by the selected fields and opens the Edit Relationships dialog box, as shown in Figure E-5. Recall that referential integrity helps ensure data accuracy.

TROUBLE
Right-click a relationship line, then click Delete if you need to delete a relationship and start over.

3. **Click the Enforce Referential Integrity check box in the Edit Relationships dialog box, then click Create**

   The **one-to-many line** shows the link between the CustNo field of the Customers table and the CustNo field of the Sales table. The "one" side of the relationship is the unique CustNo value for each record in the Customers table. The "many" side of the relationship is identified by an infinity symbol pointing to the CustNo field in the Sales table. You also need to link the Tours table to the Sales table.

4. **Click TourNo in the Tours table field list, drag it to TourID in the Sales table field list, click the Enforce Referential Integrity check box, then click Create**

   Finally, you need to link the Payments table to the Sales table.

5. **Click SalesNo in the Sales table field list, drag it to SalesNo in the Payments table field list, click the Enforce Referential Integrity check box, click Create, then drag the Tours title bar down so all links are clear**

   The updated Relationships window should look like Figure E-6.

TROUBLE
Click the Landscape button on the Print Preview tab if the report is too wide for portrait orientation.

6. **Click the Relationship Report button in the Tools group, click the Print button on the Print Preview tab, then click OK**

   A printout of the Relationships window, called the **Relationships report**, shows how your relational database is designed and includes table names, field names, primary key fields, and one-to-many relationship lines. This printout is helpful as you later create queries, forms, and reports that use fields from multiple tables. Note that it is not necessary to directly link each table to every other table.

7. **Right-click the Relationships for QuestTravel-E report tab, click Close, click Yes to save the report, then click OK to accept the default report name**

   The Relationships for QuestTravel-E report is saved in your database, as shown in the Navigation Pane.

8. **Close the Relationships window, then click Yes if prompted to save changes**

FIGURE E-5: Edit Relationships dialog box

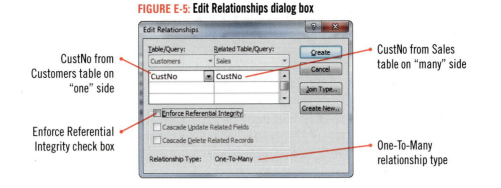

CustNo from
Customers table on
"one" side

CustNo from Sales
table on "many" side

Enforce Referential
Integrity check box

One-To-Many
relationship type

FIGURE E-6: Final Relationships window

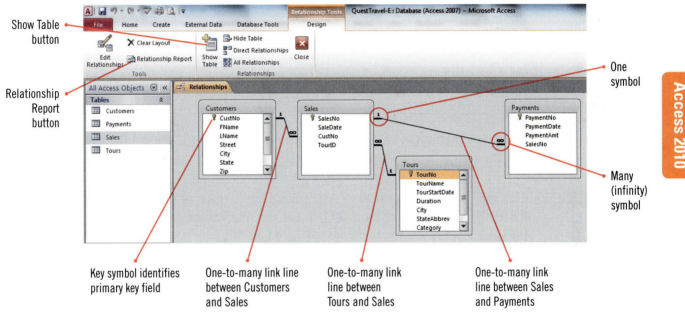

Show Table
button

Relationship
Report
button

One
symbol

Many
(infinity)
symbol

Key symbol identifies
primary key field

One-to-many link line
between Customers
and Sales

One-to-many link
line between
Tours and Sales

One-to-many link
line between Sales
and Payments

More on enforcing referential integrity

Recall that referential integrity is a set of rules to help ensure that no orphan records are entered or created in the database. An **orphan record** is a record in the "many" table (also called the **child table**) that doesn't have a matching entry in the linking field of the "one" table (also called the **parent table**). Referential integrity prevents orphan records in multiple ways. Referential integrity will not allow you to make an entry in the foreign key field of the child table that does not have a matching value in the linking field of the parent table. Referential integrity also prevents you from deleting a record in the parent table that has related records in the child table. You should enforce referential integrity on all one-to-many relationships if possible. Unfortunately, if you are working with a database that already contains orphan records, you cannot enforce this powerful set of rules unless you find and fix the data so that orphan records no longer exist. The process of removing and fixing orphan records is commonly called "scrubbing the database."

Creating Lookup Fields

A **Lookup field** is a field that contains Lookup properties. **Lookup properties** are field properties that supply a drop-down list of values for a field. The values can be stored in another table or directly stored in the **Row Source** Lookup property of the field. Fields that are good candidates for Lookup properties are those that contain a defined set of appropriate values such as State, Gender, or Department. You can set Lookup properties for a field in Table Design View using the **Lookup Wizard**. The FirstContact field in the Customers table identifies how the customer first made contact with Quest Specialty Travel such as being referred by a friend (Friend), finding the company through the Internet (Internet), or responding to a radio advertisement (Radio). Because the FirstContact field has only a handful of valid entries, it is a good Lookup field candidate.

STEPS

1. **Right-click the Customers table in the Navigation Pane, then click Design View**

   The Lookup Wizard is included in the Data Type list.

2. **Click the Text data type for the FirstContact field, click the Data Type list arrow, then click Lookup Wizard**

   The Lookup Wizard starts and prompts you for information about where the Lookup column will get its values.

3. **Click the I will type in the values that I want option button, click Next, click the first cell in the Col1 column, type Friend, press [Tab], then type the rest of the values as shown in Figure E-7**

   These are the values to populate the Lookup value drop-down list for the FirstContact field.

4. **Click Next, then click Finish to accept the default label and complete the Lookup Wizard**

   Note that the data type for the FirstContact field is still Text. The Lookup Wizard is a process for setting Lookup property values for a field, not a data type itself.

   <blockquote>
   QUICK TIP
   The Property Update Options button 📝 helps you propagate field property changes everywhere a field is used in the database.
   </blockquote>

5. **Click the Lookup tab in the Field Properties pane to observe the new Lookup properties for the FirstContact field, then double-click the Allow Value List Edits property to change the value from No to Yes as shown in Figure E-8**

   The Lookup Wizard helped you enter the correct Lookup properties for the FirstContact field, but you can always enter or edit them directly, too. The Row Source property stores the values that are provided in the drop-down list for a Lookup field. The **Limit To List** Lookup property determines whether you can enter a new value into a field with other Lookup properties, or whether the entries are limited to the drop-down list.

6. **Click the View button 🔲 to switch to Datasheet View, click Yes when prompted to save the table, press [Tab] eight times to move to the FirstContact field, then click the FirstContact list arrow as shown in Figure E-9**

   The FirstContact field now provides a list of four values for this field. To edit the list in Datasheet View, click the **Edit List Items button** 📝 below the list.

7. **Close the Customers table**

Creating multivalued fields

Multivalued fields allow you to make more than one choice from a drop-down list for a field. As a database designer, multivalued fields allow you to select and store more than one choice without having to create a more advanced database design. To create a multivalued field, enter Yes in the **Allow Multiple Values** Lookup property. This feature is only available for an Access database created or saved in the Access 2007 file format.

FIGURE E-7: Entering a list of values in the Lookup Wizard

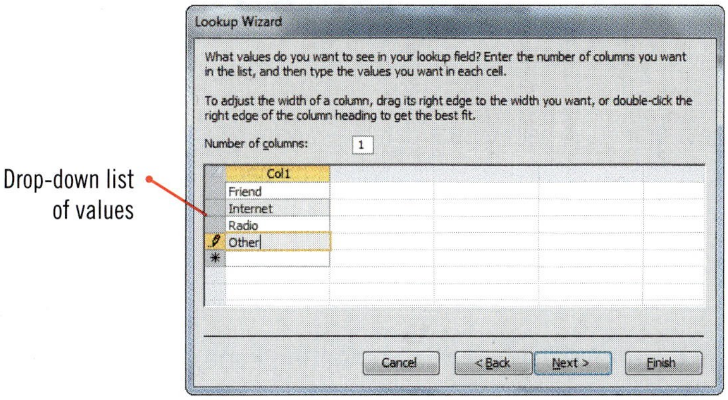

Drop-down list of values

Lookup Wizard

What values do you want to see in your lookup field? Enter the number of columns you want in the list, and then type the values you want in each cell.

To adjust the width of a column, drag its right edge to the width you want, or double-click the right edge of the column heading to get the best fit.

Number of columns: 1

Col1
Friend
Internet
Radio
Other

Cancel | < Back | Next > | Finish

FIGURE E-8: Viewing Lookup properties

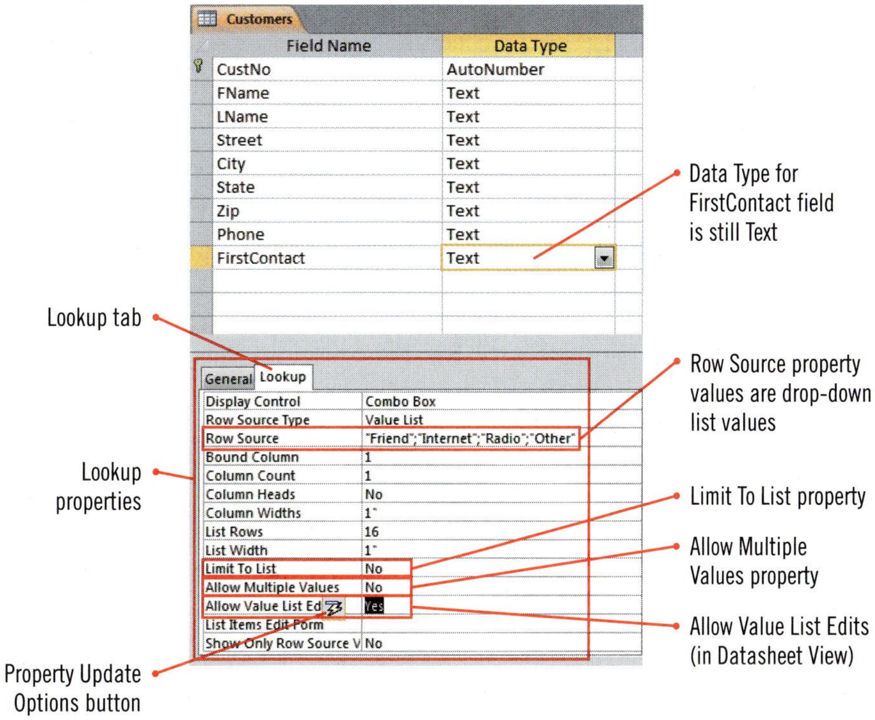

Customers

Field Name	Data Type
CustNo	AutoNumber
FName	Text
LName	Text
Street	Text
City	Text
State	Text
Zip	Text
Phone	Text
FirstContact	Text

Data Type for FirstContact field is still Text

Lookup tab

General | Lookup

Display Control	Combo Box
Row Source Type	Value List
Row Source	"Friend";"Internet";"Radio";"Other"
Bound Column	1
Column Count	1
Column Heads	No
Column Widths	1"
List Rows	16
List Width	1"
Limit To List	No
Allow Multiple Values	No
Allow Value List Ed	Yes
List Items Edit Form	
Show Only Row Source V	No

Lookup properties

Row Source property values are drop-down list values

Limit To List property

Allow Multiple Values property

Allow Value List Edits (in Datasheet View)

Property Update Options button

FIGURE E-9: Using a Lookup field in a datasheet

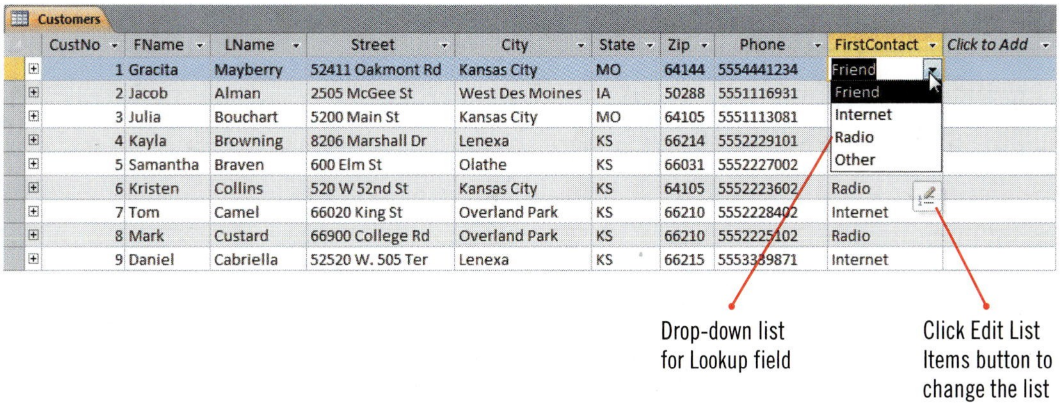

Customers

CustNo	FName	LName	Street	City	State	Zip	Phone	FirstContact	Click to Add
1	Gracita	Mayberry	52411 Oakmont Rd	Kansas City	MO	64144	5554441234	Friend	
2	Jacob	Alman	2505 McGee St	West Des Moines	IA	50288	5551116931	Friend	
3	Julia	Bouchart	5200 Main St	Kansas City	MO	64105	5551113081	Internet	
4	Kayla	Browning	8206 Marshall Dr	Lenexa	KS	66214	5552229101	Radio	
5	Samantha	Braven	600 Elm St	Olathe	KS	66031	5552227002	Other	
6	Kristen	Collins	520 W 52nd St	Kansas City	KS	64105	5552223602	Radio	
7	Tom	Camel	66020 King St	Overland Park	KS	66210	5552228402	Internet	
8	Mark	Custard	66900 College Rd	Overland Park	KS	66210	5552225102	Radio	
9	Daniel	Cabriella	52520 W. 505 Ter	Lenexa	KS	66215	5553339871	Internet	

Drop-down list for Lookup field

Click Edit List Items button to change the list

Modifying the Database Structure

Modifying Text Fields

Field properties are the characteristics that describe each field, such as Field Size, Default Value, Caption, or Row Source. These properties help ensure database accuracy and clarity because they restrict the way data is entered, stored, and displayed. You modify field properties in Table Design View. See Table E-2 for more information on Text field properties. After reviewing the Customers table with Samantha Hooper, you decide to change field properties for several Text fields in that table.

1. **Right-click the Customers table in the Navigation Pane, then click Design View on the shortcut menu**

   The Customers table opens in Design View. The field properties appear on the General tab on the lower half of the Table Design View window and apply to the selected field. Field properties change depending on the field's data type. For example, when you select a field with a Text data type, one visible property is the **Field Size property**, which determines the number of characters you can enter in the field. However, when you select a field with a Date/Time data type, Access controls the size of the data, so the Field Size property is not displayed. Many field properties are optional, but for those that require an entry, Access provides a default value.

2. **Press [↓] to move through each field while viewing the field properties in the lower half of the window**

   The **field selector button** to the left of the field indicates which field is currently selected.

3. **Click the FirstContact field name, double-click 255 in the Field Size property text box, type 8, click the Save button [icon] on the Quick Access toolbar, then click Yes**

   The maximum and the default value for the Field Size property for a Text field is 255. In general, however, you want to make the Field Size property for Text fields only as large as needed to accommodate the longest entry. You can increase the size later if necessary. In some cases, shortening the Field Size property helps prevent typographical errors. For example, you should set the Field Size property for a State field that stores two-letter state abbreviations to 2 to prevent errors such as TXX. For the FirstContact field, your longest entry is "Internet"—8 characters.

4. **Change the Field Size property to 30 for the FName and LName fields, click [icon], then click Yes**

   No existing entries are greater than 30 characters for either of these fields, so no data is lost. The **Input Mask** property provides a visual guide for users as they enter data. It also helps determine what types of values can be entered into a field.

TROUBLE

If the Input Mask Wizard is not installed on your computer, you can complete this step by typing !(999) 000-0000;;_ directly into the Input Mask property for the Phone field.

5. **Click the Phone field name, click the Input Mask property text box, click the Build button [...], click the Phone Number input mask, click Next, click Next, then click Finish**

   Table Design View of the Customers table should look like Figure E-10, which shows the Input Mask property entered for the Phone field.

6. **Right-click the Customers table tab, click Datasheet View, click Yes to save the table, press [Tab] enough times to move to the Phone field for the first record, type 5554441234, then press [Enter]**

   The Phone Input Mask property creates an easy-to-use visual guide to facilitate accurate data entry.

7. **Close the Customers table**

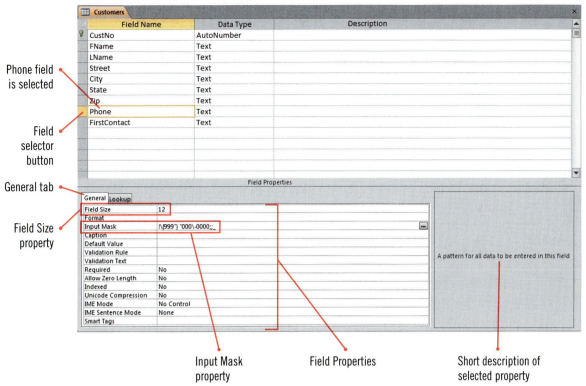

Phone field is selected

Field selector button

General tab

Field Size property

Input Mask property

Field Properties

Short description of selected property

TABLE E-2: Common Text field properties

property	description	sample field	sample property entry
Field Size	Controls how many characters can be entered into the field	State	2
Format	Controls how information will be displayed and printed	State	> (displays all characters in uppercase)
Input Mask	Provides a pattern for data to be entered	Phone	!(999) 000-0000;1;_
Caption	Describes the field in the first row of a datasheet, form, or report; if the Caption property is not entered, the field name is used to label the field	EmpNo	Employee Number
Default Value	Displays a value that is automatically entered in the given field for new records	City	Des Moines
Required	Determines if an entry is required for this field	LastName	Yes

Working with the Input Mask property

The Input Mask property provides a pattern for data to be entered, using three parts separated by semicolons. The first part provides a pattern for what type of data can be entered. For example, 9 represents an optional number, 0 a required number, ? an optional letter, and L a required letter. The second part determines whether all displayed characters (such as dashes in a phone number) are stored in

the field. For the second part of the input mask, a 0 entry stores all characters such as 555-7722, and a 1 entry stores only the entered data, 5557722. The third part of the input mask determines which character Access uses to guide the user through the mask. Common choices are the asterisk (*), underscore (_), or pound sign (#).

Access 2010

Modifying Number and Currency Fields

Although some properties for Number and Currency fields are the same as the properties of Text fields, each data type has its own list of valid properties. Number and Currency fields have similar properties because they both contain numeric values. Currency fields store values that represent money, and Number fields store values that represent values such as quantities, measurements, and scores. The Tours table contains both a Number field (Duration) and a Currency field (Cost). You want to modify the properties of these two fields.

STEPS

1. **Right-click the Tours table in the Navigation Pane, click Design View on the shortcut menu, then click the Duration field name**

   The default Field Size property for a Number field is **Long Integer**. See Table E-3 for more information on the Field Size property and other common properties for a Number field. Access sets the size of Currency fields to control the way numbers are rounded in calculations, so the Field Size property isn't available for Currency fields.

2. **Click Long Integer in the Field Size property text box, click the Field Size list arrow, then click Byte**

   Choosing a **Byte** value for the Field Size property allows entries from 0 to 255, so it greatly restricts the possible values and the storage requirements for the Duration field.

3. **Click the Cost field name, click Auto in the Decimal Places property text box, click the Decimal Places list arrow, click 0, then press [Enter]**

   Your Table Design View should look like Figure E-11. Because all of Quest's tours are priced at a round dollar value, you do not need to display cents in the Cost field.

4. **Save the table, then switch to Datasheet View**

   Because none of the current entries in the Duration field is greater than 255, which is the maximum value allowed by a Number field with a Byte Field Size property, you don't lose any data. You want to test the new property changes.

5. **Press [Tab] three times to move to the Duration field for the first record, type 800, then press [Tab]**

   Because 800 is larger than what the Byte Field Size property allows (0–255), an Access error message appears indicating that the value isn't valid for this field.

6. **Press [Esc] twice to remove the inappropriate entry in the Duration field, then press [Tab] four times to move to the Cost field**

   The Cost field is set to display zero digits after the decimal point.

7. **Type 750.25 in the Cost field of the first record, press [▼], then click $750 in the Cost field of the first record to see the full entry**

   Although the Decimal Places property for the Cost field specifies that entries in the field are *formatted* to display zero digits after the decimal point, 750.25 is the actual value stored in the field. Modifying the Decimal Places property does not change the actual data. Rather, the Decimal Places property only changes the way the data is *presented*.

8. **Close the Tours table**

Modifying the Database Structure

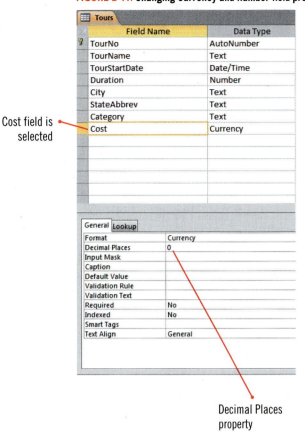

Cost field is selected

Decimal Places property

TABLE E-3: Common Number field properties

property	description
Field Size	Determines the largest number that can be entered in the field, as well as the type of data (e.g., integer or fraction)
Byte	Stores numbers from 0 to 255 (no fractions)
Integer	Stores numbers from –32,768 to 32,767 (no fractions)
Long Integer	Stores numbers from –2,147,483,648 to 2,147,483,647 (no fractions)
Single	Stores numbers (including fractions with six digits to the right of the decimal point) times 10 to the –38th to +38th power
Double	Stores numbers (including fractions with over 10 digits to the right of the decimal point) in the range of 10 to the –324th to +324th power
Decimal Places	The number of digits displayed to the right of the decimal point

Modifying fields in Datasheet View

When you work in Table *Datasheet* View, the Fields tab on the Ribbon provides many options to modify fields and field properties. For example, you can add and delete fields, change a field name or data type, and modify many field properties such as Caption, Default Value, and Format. Table *Design* View, however, gives you full access to *all* field properties such as all of the Lookup properties.

Access 2010

Modifying Date/Time Fields

Many properties of the Date/Time field, such as Input Mask, Caption, and Default Value, work the same way as they do in fields with a Text or Number data type. One difference, however, is the **Format** property, which helps you format dates in various ways such as January 25, 2013; 25-Jan-13; or 01/25/2013. You want to change the format of Date/Time fields in the Tours table to display two digits for the month and day values and four digits for the year, as in 05/05/2013.

STEPS

1. **Right-click the Tours table in the Navigation Pane, click Design View on the shortcut menu, then click the TourStartDate field name**

   You want the tour start dates to appear with two digits for the month and day, such as 07/05/2013, instead of the default presentation of dates, 7/5/2013.

2. **Click the Format property box, then click the Format list arrow**

   Although several predefined Date/Time formats are available, none matches the format you want. To define a custom format, enter symbols that represent how you want the date to appear.

3. **Type mm/dd/yyyy then press [Enter]**

   The updated Format property for the TourStartDate field shown in Figure E-12 sets the date to appear with two digits for the month, two digits for the day, and four digits for the year. The parts of the date are separated by forward slashes.

4. **Save the table, display the datasheet, then click the New (blank) record button on the navigation bar**

   To test the new Format property for the TourStartDate field, you can add a new record to the table.

5. **Press [Tab] to move to the TourName field, type Missouri Eagles, press [Tab], type 9/1/13, press [Tab], type 7, press [Tab], type Hollister, press [Tab], type MO, press [Tab], type Adventure, press [Tab], then type 700**

   The new record you entered into the Tours table should look like Figure E-13. The Format property for the TourStartDate field makes the entry appear as 09/01/2013, as desired.

TourStartDate field is selected

Field Name	Data Type
TourNo	AutoNumber
TourName	Text
TourStartDate	Date/Time
Duration	Number
City	Text
StateAbbrev	Text
Category	Text
Cost	Currency

General | Lookup

Format	mm/dd/yyyy
Input Mask	
Caption	
Default Value	
Validation Rule	
Validation Text	
Required	No
Indexed	No
IME Mode	No Control
IME Sentence Mode	None
Smart Tags	
Text Align	General
Show Date Picker	For dates

Custom Format property

Tours

TourNo	TourName	TourStartDate	Duration	City	StateAbbrev	Category	Cost
49	Golden State Tours	08/07/2012	10	Sacramento	CA	Cultural	$1,400
51	Bright Lights Expo	12/19/2012	3	Branson	MO	Site Seeing	$200
52	Missouri Bald Eagle Watc	08/31/2012	7	Hollister	MO	Adventure	$700
53	Bridges of Madison Count	10/25/2013	4	Winterset	IA	Site Seeing	$500
54	Branson Lights	12/01/2013	3	Branson	MO	Site Seeing	$300
55	Green Gathering	10/01/2013	3	Dallas	TX	Family	$300
56	Salmon Run Fishing	05/05/2013	4	Seattle	WA	Adventure	$800
57	Space Needle Fireworks	07/04/2013	3	Seattle	WA	Site Seeing	$500
58	Northwest Passage	08/01/2013	10	Vancouver	WA	Adventure	$2,000
59	Missouri Eagles	09/01/2013	7	Hollister	MO	Adventure	700
(New)							

Custom mm/dd/yyyy Format property applied to TourStartDate field

Using Smart Tags

Smart Tags are buttons that automatically appear in certain conditions. They provide a small menu of options to help you work with the task at hand. Access provides the Property Update Options Smart Tag to help you quickly apply property changes to other objects of the database that use the field. The Error Indicator

Smart Tag helps identify potential design errors. For example, if you are working in Report Design View and the report is too wide for the paper, the Error Indicator appears in the upper-left corner by the report selector button to alert you to the problem.

Access 2010

Modifying Validation Properties

The **Validation Rule** property determines what entries a field can accept. For example, a validation rule for a Date/Time field might require date entries on or after 6/1/2012. A validation rule for a Currency field might indicate that valid entries fall between $0 and $1,500. You use the **Validation Text** property to display an explanatory message when a user tries to enter data that breaks the validation rule. Therefore, the Validation Rule and Validation Text field properties help you prevent unreasonable data from being entered into the database. Samantha Hooper reminds you that all new Quest tours start on or after June 1, 2012. You can use the validation properties to establish this rule for the TourStartDate field in the Tours table.

STEPS

1. **Click the View button on the Home tab to return to Design View, click the TourStartDate field if it isn't already selected, click the Validation Rule property box, then type >=6/1/2012**

   This entry forces all dates in the TourStartDate field to be greater than or equal to 6/1/2012. See Table E-4 for more examples of Validation Rule expressions. The Validation Text property provides a helpful message to the user when the entry in the field breaks the rule entered in the Validation Rule property.

2. **Click the Validation Text box, then type Date must be on or after 6/1/2012**

   Design View of the Tours table should now look like Figure E-14. Access modifies a property to include additional syntax by changing the entry in the Validation Rule property to >=#6/1/2012#. Pound signs (#) are used to surround date criteria.

3. **Save the table, then click Yes when asked to test the existing data with new data integrity rules**

   Because no dates in the TourStartDate field are earlier than 6/1/2012, Access finds no date errors in the current data and saves the table. You now want to test that the Validation Rule and Validation Text properties work when entering data in the datasheet.

4. **Click the View button to display the datasheet, press [Tab] twice to move to the TourStartDate field, type 5/1/12, then press [Tab]**

   Because you tried to enter a date that was not true for the Validation Rule property for the TourStartDate field, a dialog box opens and displays the Validation Text entry, as shown in Figure E-15.

5. **Click OK to close the validation message**

   You now know that the Validation Rule and Validation Text properties work properly.

6. **Press [Esc] to reject the invalid date entry in the TourStartDate field**

7. **Close the Tours table**

FIGURE E-14: Entering Validation properties

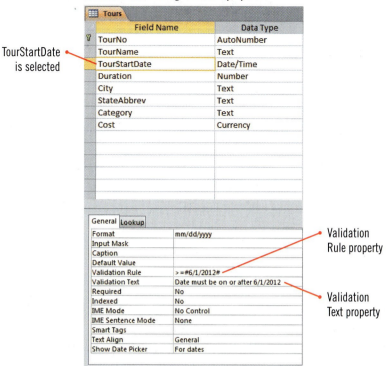

TourStartDate is selected

Validation Rule property

Validation Text property

FIGURE E-15: Validation Text message

Entering a TourStartDate before 6/1/2012

Validation Text property message

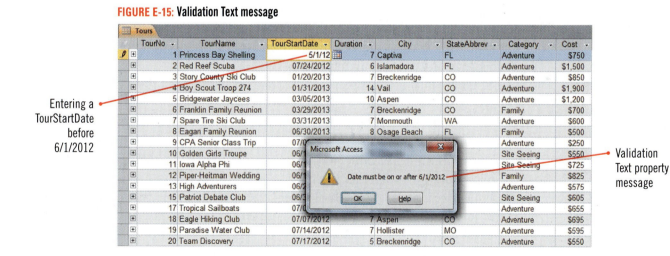

TABLE E-4: Validation Rule expressions

data type	validation rule expression	description
Number or Currency	>0	The number must be positive
Number or Currency	>10 And <100	The number must be greater than 10 and less than 100
Number or Currency	10 Or 20 Or 30	The number must be 10, 20, or 30
Text	"IA" Or "NE" Or "MO"	The entry must be IA, NE, or MO
Date/Time	>=#7/1/93#	The date must be on or after 7/1/1993
Date/Time	>#1/1/10# And <#1/1/12#	The date must be greater than 1/1/2010 and less than 1/1/2012

Creating Attachment Fields

An **Attachment field** allows you to attach an external file such as a Word document, PowerPoint presentation, Excel workbook, or image file to a record. Earlier versions of Access allowed you to link or embed external data using the **OLE** (object linking and embedding) data type. The Attachment data type is superior to OLE because it stores data more efficiently, stores more file formats such as JPEG images, and requires no additional software to view the files from within Access. Samantha Hooper asks you to incorporate images on forms and reports to help describe and market each tour. You can use an Attachment field to store JPEG images for customer photo identification.

STEPS

1. **Right-click the Customers table in the Navigation Pane, then click Design View**
   You can insert a new field anywhere in the list.

2. **Click the Street field selector, click the Insert Rows button on the Design tab, click the Field Name cell, type Photo, press [Tab], click the Data Type list arrow, then click Attachment as shown in Figure E-16**
   Now that you created the new Attachment field named Photo, you're ready to add data to it in Datasheet View.

3. **Click the Save button 💾 on the Quick Access toolbar, click the View button ▦ on the Design tab to switch to Datasheet View, then press [Tab] three times to move to the new Photo field**
   An Attachment field cell displays a small paper clip icon with the number of files attached to the field in parentheses. You have not attached any files to this field yet, so each record shows zero (0) file attachments. You can attach files to this field directly from Datasheet View.

4. **Right-click the attachment icon 📎 for the first record, click Manage Attachments on the shortcut menu, click Add, navigate to the drive and folder where you store your Data Files, double-click GMayberry.jpg, then click OK**
   The GMayberry.jpg file is now included with the first record, and the datasheet reflects that one (1) file is attached to the Photo field of the first record. You can add more than one file attachment to the same field. For example, you might add other pictures of this customer to this Photo Attachment field. You can view file attachments directly from the datasheet, form, or report.

5. **Double-click the attachment icon 📎 for the first record to open the Attachments dialog box shown in Figure E-17, then click Open**
   The image opens in the program that is associated with the .jpg extension on your computer such as Windows Photo Viewer. The **.jpg** file extension is short for **JPEG**, an acronym for Joint Photographic Experts Group. This association defines the standards for the compression algorithms that make JPEG files very efficient to use in databases and on Web pages.

6. **Close the window that displays the GMayberry.jpg image, click Cancel in the Attachments dialog box, close the Customers table, close the QuestTravel-E.accdb database, then exit Access**

FIGURE E-16: Adding an Attachment field

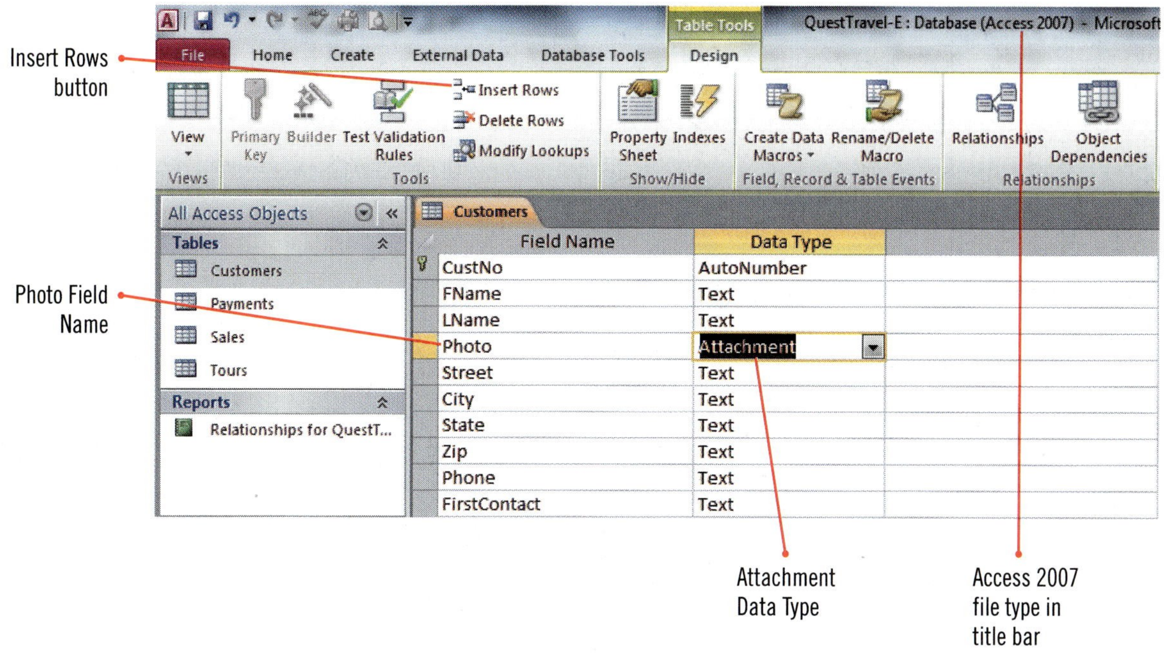

Insert Rows button

Photo Field Name

Attachment Data Type

Access 2007 file type in title bar

FIGURE E-17: Opening an attached file

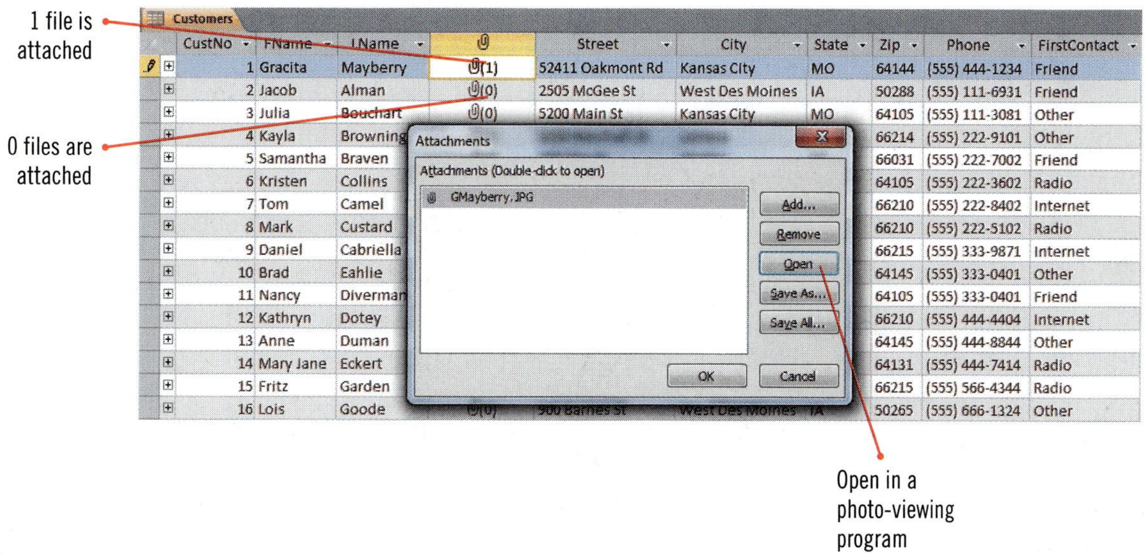

1 file is attached

0 files are attached

Open in a photo-viewing program

Working with database file types

When you create a new database in Microsoft Office Access 2010, Access gives the file an **.accdb** extension, and saves it as an Access 2007 database file type. This is why (Access 2007) is shown in the title bar of a database opened in Access 2010. Saving the database as an Access 2007 file type allows users of Access 2007 and 2010 to share the same database. Access 2007 databases are *not* readable by earlier versions of Access, however, such as Access 2000, Access 2002 (XP), or Access 2003. If you need to share your database with

people using Access 2000, 2002, or 2003, you can use the Save As command on the Office button menu to save the database with an Access 2000 file type, which applies an **.mdb** file extension to the database. Databases with an Access 2000 file type can be used by any version of Access from Access 2000 through 2010, but some features such as multivalued fields and Attachment fields are only available when working with an Access 2007 database.

Practice

For current SAM information, including versions and content details, visit SAM Central (http://www.cengage.com/samcentral). If you have a SAM user profile, you may have access to hands-on instruction, practice, and assessment of the skills covered in this unit. Since various versions of SAM are supported throughout the life of this text, check with your instructor for the correct instructions and URL/Web site for accessing assignments.

Concepts Review

Identify each element of the Relationships window shown in Figure E-18.

FIGURE E-18

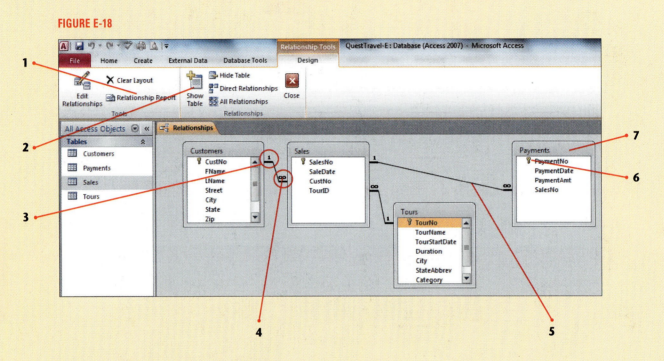

Match each term with the statement that best describes it.

8. Primary key field
9. Validation Rule
10. Table Design View
11. Row Source
12. Limit to List
13. Input Mask
14. Lookup properties
15. Multivalued field
16. Attachment field

a. Field that allows you to store external files such as a Word document, PowerPoint presentation, Excel workbook, or JPEG image

b. Field that holds unique information for each record in the table

c. Field that allows you to make more than one choice from a drop-down list

d. Determines whether you can enter a new value into a field

e. Field properties that allow you to supply a drop-down list of values for a field

f. Access window where all characteristics of a table, such as field names and field properties, are defined

g. Field property that provides a visual guide as you enter data

h. Field property that prevents unreasonable data entries for a field

i. Lookup property that determines where the Lookup field gets its list of values

Select the best answer from the list of choices.

17. Which of the following problems most clearly indicates that you need to redesign your database?
   a. The Input Mask Wizard has not been used.
   b. There is duplicated data in several records of a table.
   c. Not all fields have Validation Rule properties.
   d. Referential integrity is enforced on table relationships.

18. Which of the following is *not* done in Table Design View?
   a. Specifying the primary key field
   b. Setting Field Size properties
   c. Defining Field data types
   d. Creating file attachments

19. What is the purpose of enforcing referential integrity?
   a. To prevent incorrect entries in the primary key field
   b. To require an entry for each field of each record
   c. To prevent orphan records from being created
   d. To force the application of meaningful validation rules

20. To create a many-to-many relationship between two tables, you must create:
   a. A junction table.
   b. Two primary key fields in each table.
   c. Two one-to-one relationships between the two tables, with referential integrity enforced.
   d. Foreign key fields in each table.

21. The linking field in the "many" table is called the:
   a. Primary key field.
   b. Attachment field.
   c. Child field.
   d. Foreign key field.

22. The default filename extension for a database created in Access 2010 is:
   a. .acc10.
   b. .accdb.
   c. .mdb.
   d. .mdb10.

23. If the primary key field in the "one" table is an AutoNumber data type, the linking field in the "many" table will have which data type?
   a. AutoNumber
   b. Number
   c. Text
   d. Attachment

24. Which symbol is used to identify the "many" field in a one-to-many relationship in the Relationships window?
   a. Arrow
   b. Key
   c. Infinity
   d. Triangle

25. The process of removing and fixing orphan records is commonly called:
   a. Relating tables.
   b. Designing a relational database.
   c. Analyzing performance.
   d. Scrubbing the database.

Skills Review

1. **Examine relational databases.**

   a. List the fields needed to create an Access relational database to manage volunteer hours for the members of a philan-thropic club or community service organization.

   b. Identify fields that would contain duplicate values if all of the fields were stored in a single table.

   c. Group the fields into subject matter tables, then identify the primary key field for each table.

   d. Assume that your database contains two tables: Members and ServiceRecords. If you did not identify these two tables earlier, regroup the fields within these two table names, then identify the primary key field for each table, the foreign key field in the ServiceRecords table, and how the tables would be related using a one-to-many relationship.

2. **Design related tables.**

   a. Start Access 2010, then create a new database named **Service-E** in the drive and folder where you store your data files.

   b. Use Table Design View to create a new table with the name **Members** and the field names and data types shown in Figure E-19.

   FIGURE E-19

field name	data type
MemberNo	AutoNumber
FirstName	Text
LastName	Text
City	Text
Phone	Text
Email	Hyperlink
Birthdate	Date/Time
Gender	Text

   c. Specify MemberNo as the primary key field, save the Members table, then close it.

   d. Use Table Design View to create a new table named **ServiceHours** with the field names and data types shown in Figure E-20.

   FIGURE E-20

field name	data type
ServiceNo	AutoNumber
MemberNo	Number
ServiceDate	Date/Time
Location	Text
Description	Text
ServiceHours	Number
ServiceValue	Currency

   e. Identify ServiceNo as the primary key field, save the ServiceHours table, then close it.

3. Create one-to-many relationships.

  a. Open the Relationships window, double-click Members, then double-click ServiceHours to add the two tables to the Relationships window. Close the Show Table dialog box.

  b. Resize all field lists as necessary so that all fields are visible, then drag the MemberNo field from the Members table to the MemberNo field in the ServiceHours table.

  c. Enforce referential integrity, and create the one-to-many relationship between Members and ServiceHours. See Figure E-21.

FIGURE E-21

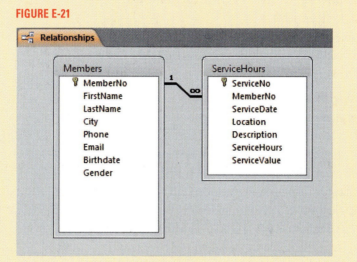

  d. Create a Relationships report for the Service-E database, add your name as a label to the Report Header section of the report in Report Design View, then print the report, if requested by your instructor.

  e. Save and close the Relationships report with the default name, Relationships for Service-E, then save and close the Relationships window.

4. Create Lookup fields.

  a. Open the Members table in Design View, then start the Lookup Wizard for the Gender field.

  b. Select the option that allows you to enter your own values, then enter **Female, Male,** and **Unknown** as the values for the Lookup column.

  c. Use the default **Gender** label, then finish the Lookup Wizard.

  d. Save and close the Members table.

5. Modify Text fields.

  a. Open the Members table in Design View.

  b. Use the Input Mask Wizard to create an Input Mask property for the Phone field. Choose the Phone Number Input Mask. Accept the other default options provided by the Input Mask Wizard. (*Hint*: If the Input Mask Wizard is not installed on your computer, type **!(999) 000-0000;;_** for the Input Mask property for the Phone field.)

  c. Change the Field Size property of the FirstName, LastName, and City fields to **30**. Change the Field Size property of the Phone field to **10**. Change the Field Size property of the Gender field to **6**. Save the Members table.

  d. Open the Members table in Datasheet View, and enter a new record with your name in the FirstName and LastName fields and your school's City and Phone field values. Enter your school e-mail address, **1/1/1995** for the Birthdate field, and an appropriate choice for the Gender field.

Skills Review (continued)

6. Modify Number and Currency fields.

    a. Open the ServiceHours table in Design View.

    b. Change the Decimal Places property of the ServiceHours field to **0**.

    c. Change the Decimal Places property of the ServiceValue field to **2**.

    d. Save and close the ServiceHours table.

7. Modify Date/Time fields.

    a. Open the ServiceHours table in Design View.

    b. Change the Format property of the ServiceDate field to **mm/dd/yyyy**.

    c. Save and close the ServiceHours table.

    d. Open the Members table in Design View.

    e. Change the Format property of the Birthdate field to **mm/dd/yyyy**.

    f. Save and close the Members table.

8. Modify validation properties.

    a. Open the Members table in Design View.

    b. Click the Birthdate field name, click the Validation Rule text box, then type **<1/1/2000**. (Note that Access automatically adds pound signs around date criteria in the Validation Rule property.)

    c. Click the Validation Text box, then type **Birthdate must be before 1/1/2000**.

    d. Save and accept the changes, then open the Members table in Datasheet View.

    e. Test the Validation Text and Validation Rule properties by tabbing to the Birthdate field and entering a date after 1/1/2000 such as 1/1/2001. Click OK when prompted with the Validation Text message, press [Esc] to remove the invalid Birthdate field entry, then close the Members table.

9. Create Attachment fields.

    a. Open the Members table in Design View, then add a new field after the Gender field with the field name **Photo** and an Attachment data type. Save the table.

    b. Display the Members table in Datasheet View, then attach a .jpg file of yourself to the record. If you do not have a .jpg file of yourself, use the **Member1.jpg** file provided in the drive and folder where you store your Data Files.

    c. Close the Members table.

    d. Use the Form Wizard to create a form based on all of the fields in the Members table. Use a Columnar layout, and title the form **Member Entry Form**.

    e. If requested by your instructor, print the first record in the Members Entry Form that shows the picture you just entered in the Photo field, then close the form.

    f. Close the Service-E.accdb database, then exit Access.

Modifying the Database Structure

Independent Challenge 1

As the manager of a music store's instrument rental program, you decide to create a database to track rentals to schoolchildren. The fields you need to track are organized with four tables: Instruments, Rentals, Customers, and Schools.

a. Start Access, then create a new blank database called **Music-E** in the folder where you store your Data Files.

b. Use Table Design View or the Fields tab on the Ribbon of Table Datasheet View to create the four tables in the MusicStore-E database using the information shown in Figure E-22. The primary key field for each table is identified with bold text.

c. Enter **>1/1/2011** as the Validation Rule property for the RentalStartDate field of the Rentals table. This change allows only dates later than 1/1/2011, the start date for this business, to be entered into this field.

d. Enter **Rental start dates must be after January 1, 2011** as the Validation Text property to the RentalStartDate field of the Rentals table. Note that Access adds pound signs (#) to the date criteria entered in the Validation Rule as soon as you enter the Validation Text property.

e. Save and close the Rentals table.

f. Open the Relationships window, add the Instruments, Rentals, Customers, and Schools tables to the window, and create one-to-many relationships as shown in Figure E-23. Be sure to enforce referential integrity on each relationship.

g. Preview the Relationships report, add your name as a label to the Report Header section, then print the report, if requested by your instructor, making sure that all fields of each table are visible.

h. Save the Relationships report with the default name, and close it. Save and close the Relationships window.

i. Close the Music-E.accdb database, then exit Access.

FIGURE E-22

table	field name	data type
Rentals	**RentalNo**	AutoNumber
	CustNo	Number
	SerialNo	Text
	RentalStartDate	Date/Time
Customers	FirstName	Text
	LastName	Text
	Street	Text
	City	Text
	State	Text
	Zip	Text
	CustNo	AutoNumber
	SchoolCode	Text
Instruments	Description	Text
	SerialNo	**Text**
	MonthlyFee	Currency
Schools	SchoolName	Text
	SchoolCode	**Text**

FIGURE E-23

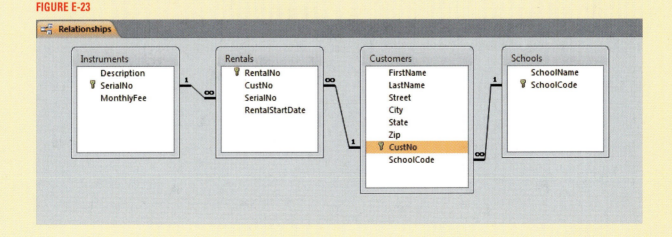

Independent Challenge 2

You want to create a database that documents blood bank donations by the employees of your company. You want to track information such as employee name, department, blood type, date of donation, and the hospital where the employee chooses to receive the donation. You also want to track basic hospital information, such as the hospital name and address.

a. Start Access, then create a new database called **BloodDrive-E** in the drive and folder where you store your Data Files.

b. Create an **Employees** table with fields and appropriate data types to record the automatic employee ID, employee first name, employee last name, and blood type. Make the employee ID field the primary key field.

c. Add Lookup properties to the blood type field in the Employees table to provide only valid blood type entries of **A+**, **A–**, **B+**, **B–**, **O+**, **O–**, **AB+**, and **AB–** for this field.

d. Create a **Donations** table with fields and appropriate data types to record an automatic donation ID, date of the donation, and an employee ID field to serve as a foreign key field. Make the donation ID the primary key field.

e. Create a **Hospitals** table with fields and appropriate data types to record a hospital code, donation ID (foreign key field), hospital name, street, city, state, and zip. Make the hospital code field the primary key field.

f. In the Relationships window, create a one-to-many relationship with referential integrity between the Employees and Donations table, using the common EmployeeID field.

g. In the Relationships window, create a one-to-many relationship with referential integrity between the Donations and Hospitals table, using the common DonationID field. The final Relationships window is shown in Figure E-24. (Your field names might differ.)

h. Preview the Relationships report, add your name as a label to the Report Header section, then print the report if requested by your instructor, making sure that all fields of each table are visible.

i. Save the Relationships report with the default name, and close it. Save and close the Relationships window.

j. Close BloodDrive-E.accdb, then exit Access.

FIGURE E-24

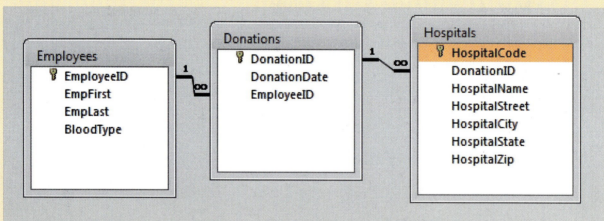

Modifying the Database Structure

Independent Challenge 3

This Independent Challenge requires an Internet connection.

You're a member and manager of a recreational baseball team and decide to create an Access database to manage player information, games, and batting statistics.

a. Start Access, then create a new database called **Baseball-E** in the drive and folder where you store your Data Files.

b. Create a **Players** table with fields and appropriate data types to record the player first name, last name, and uniform number. Make the uniform number field the primary key field.

c. Create a **Games** table with fields and appropriate data types to record an automatic game number, date of the game, opponent's name, home score, and visitor score. Make the game number field the primary key field.

d. Create an **AtBats** table with fields and appropriate data types to record hits, at bats, the game number, and the uniform number of each player. The game number and uniform number fields will both be foreign key fields. This table does not need a primary key field.

e. In the Relationships window, create a one-to-many relationship with referential integrity between the Games and AtBats table, using the common game number field.

f. In the Relationships window, create a one-to-many relationship with referential integrity between the Players and AtBats table, using the common uniform number field. The final Relationships window is shown in Figure E-25. (Your field names might differ.)

FIGURE E-25

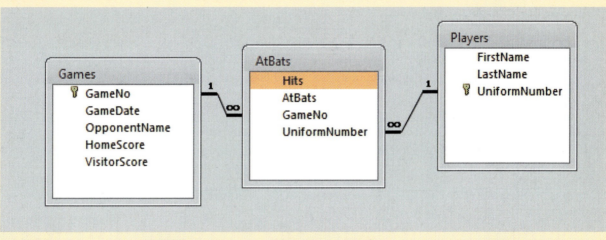

g. Preview the Relationships report, add your name as a label to the Report Header section, then print the report, if requested by your instructor, making sure that all fields of each table are visible.

h. Save the Relationships report with the default name, and close it. Save and close the Relationships window.

Advanced Challenge Exercise

- Enter your own name into the Players table, using **1** as the value for the UniformNumber field. Using an Internet search tool, find the roster for a baseball team in your area, and enter eight more baseball players into the Players table. Close the Players table.

- Research the games that this team has previously played, and enter one game record into the Games table. Close the Games table.

- Open the Players table and use subdatasheets to enter Hits and AtBats for GameNo 1 for each of the nine players. Your entries need not represent a real game, but they should be realistic. (*Hint*: Most players bat three or four times per game. A player cannot have more hits in a game than at bats.) In other words, each player will have one record in its subdatasheet that represents that player's batting statistics for GameNo 1.

i. Close the Baseball-E.accdb database, then exit Access.

Real Life Independent Challenge

An Access database can help record and track your job search efforts. In this exercise, you will modify two fields in the Positions table in your JobSearch database with Lookup properties to make data entry easier, more efficient, and more accurate.

a. Start Access, open the JobSearch-E.accdb database from the drive and folder where you store your Data Files, then enable content if prompted.

b. Open the Positions table in Design View. Click the EmployerID field, then start the Lookup Wizard.

c. In this situation, you want the EmployerID field in the Positions table to look up both the EmployerID and the CompanyName fields from the Employers table, so leave the "I want the lookup field to get the values from another table or query" option button selected.

d. The Employers table contains the fields you need. Select both the EmployerID field and the CompanyName field. Sort the records in ascending order by the CompanyName field.

e. Deselect the "Hide key column" check box so that you can see the data in both the EmployerID and CompanyName fields.

f. Choose EmployerID as the field to store values in and EmployerID as the label for the Lookup field. Click Yes when prompted to save relationships.

g. Save the table, and test the EmployerID field in Datasheet View. You should see both the EmployerID field as well as the CompanyName field in the drop-down list as shown in Figure E-26.

FIGURE E-26

Title	CareerArea	AnnualSalar	Desirability	EmployerID	PositionID	C
Marketing Representative	Computers	$35,000.00	5	1	1	
Systems Engineer	Computers	$37,000.00	5	1	2	
Office Specialist	Computers	$32,000.00	4	2	3	
Customer Service Rep	Computers	$31,000.00	4	2	4	
Technician	Computers	$30,500.00	3	2	5	
Professor	CSIT	$50,000.00	5	6	6	
Professor	CIS	$55,000.00	5	7	7	
Customer Service	CS	$30,000.00	3	8	8	
Analyst	HR	$35,000.00	4	9	9	
Advisor	Finance	$60,000.00	4	10	10	

4	DEC
9	Garmin
3	Hewlett Packar
5	Honeywell
1	IBM
6	JCCC
7	KCCC
8	Sprint
10	TMFS
2	Wang

Modifying the Database Structure

Real Life Independent Challenge (continued)

h. Return to Design View, click the Desirability field, and start the Lookup Wizard. This field stores the values 1 through 5 as a desirability rating. You will manually enter those values so choose the "I will type in the values that I want" option button.

i. Enter **1**, **2**, **3**, **4**, and **5** in the Col1 column, and accept the Desirability label for the Lookup field.

j. Save the table, and test the Desirability field in Datasheet View. You should see a drop-down list with the values 1, 2, 3, 4, and 5 in the list as shown in Figure E-27.

FIGURE E-27

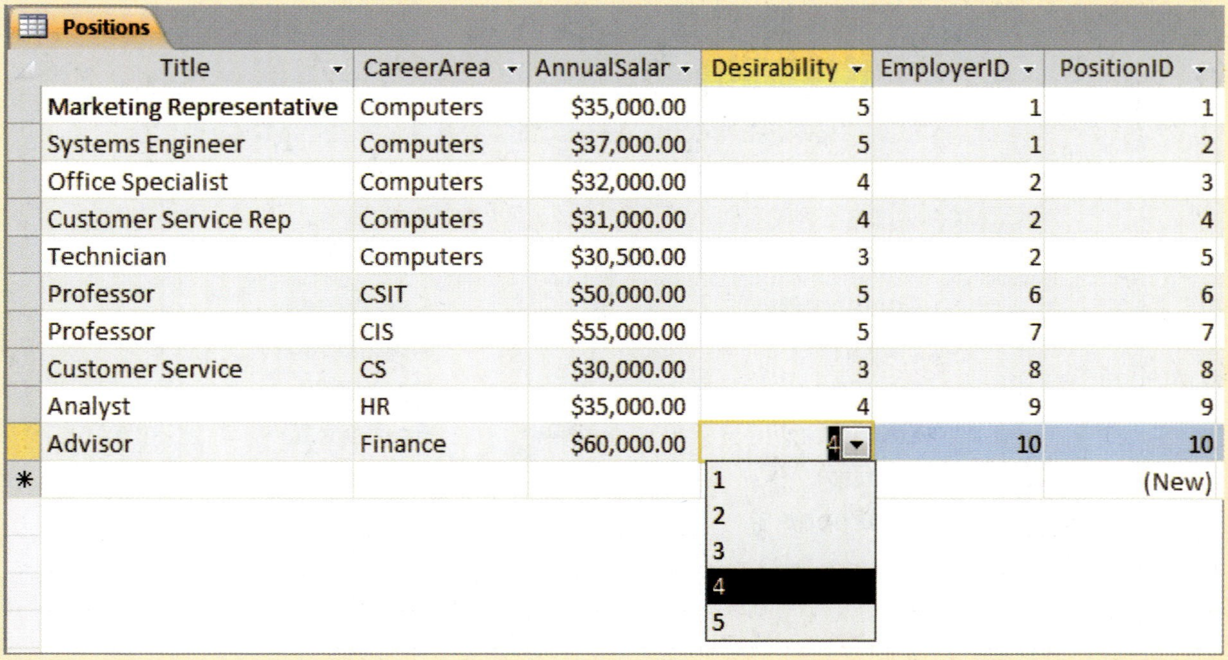

Title	CareerArea	AnnualSalar	Desirability	EmployerID	PositionID
Marketing Representative	Computers	$35,000.00	5	1	1
Systems Engineer	Computers	$37,000.00	5	1	2
Office Specialist	Computers	$32,000.00	4	2	3
Customer Service Rep	Computers	$31,000.00	4	2	4
Technician	Computers	$30,500.00	3	2	5
Professor	CSIT	$50,000.00	5	6	6
Professor	CIS	$55,000.00	5	7	7
Customer Service	CS	$30,000.00	3	8	8
Analyst	HR	$35,000.00	4	9	9
Advisor	Finance	$60,000.00	4	10	10
*			1 2 3 **4** 5		(New)

Real Life Independent Challenge (continued)

k. Return to Design View and modify the Limit To List Lookup property on the Lookup tab in the Field Properties pane for both the Desirability as well as the EmployerID fields to Yes.

l. Save the table, and test the Desirability and EmployerID fields. You should not be able to make any entries in those fields that are not presented in the list.

m. Close the Positions table, and open the Relationships window.

n. Double-click the link line created by the Lookup Wizard between the Employers and Positions tables, click Enforce Referential Integrity, then click OK. Your Relationships window should look like Figure E-28.

FIGURE E-28

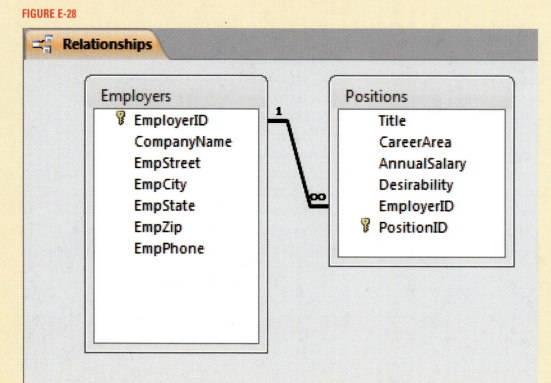

Real Life Independent Challenge (continued)

Advanced Challenge Exercise

- Use the Form Wizard to create a form/subform with all of the fields from both the Employers and Positions tables.
- View the data by Employers, and use a Datasheet layout for the subform.
- Title the form **Employers Entry Form** and the subform **Positions Subform**. View the form in Form View.
- In Form Design View, use your skills to move, resize, align, and edit the controls as shown in Figure E-29.
- Add a new record to the subform for the first company, IBM. Use realistic but fictitious data. Note that the EmployerID and PositionID values are automatically entered.

FIGURE E-29

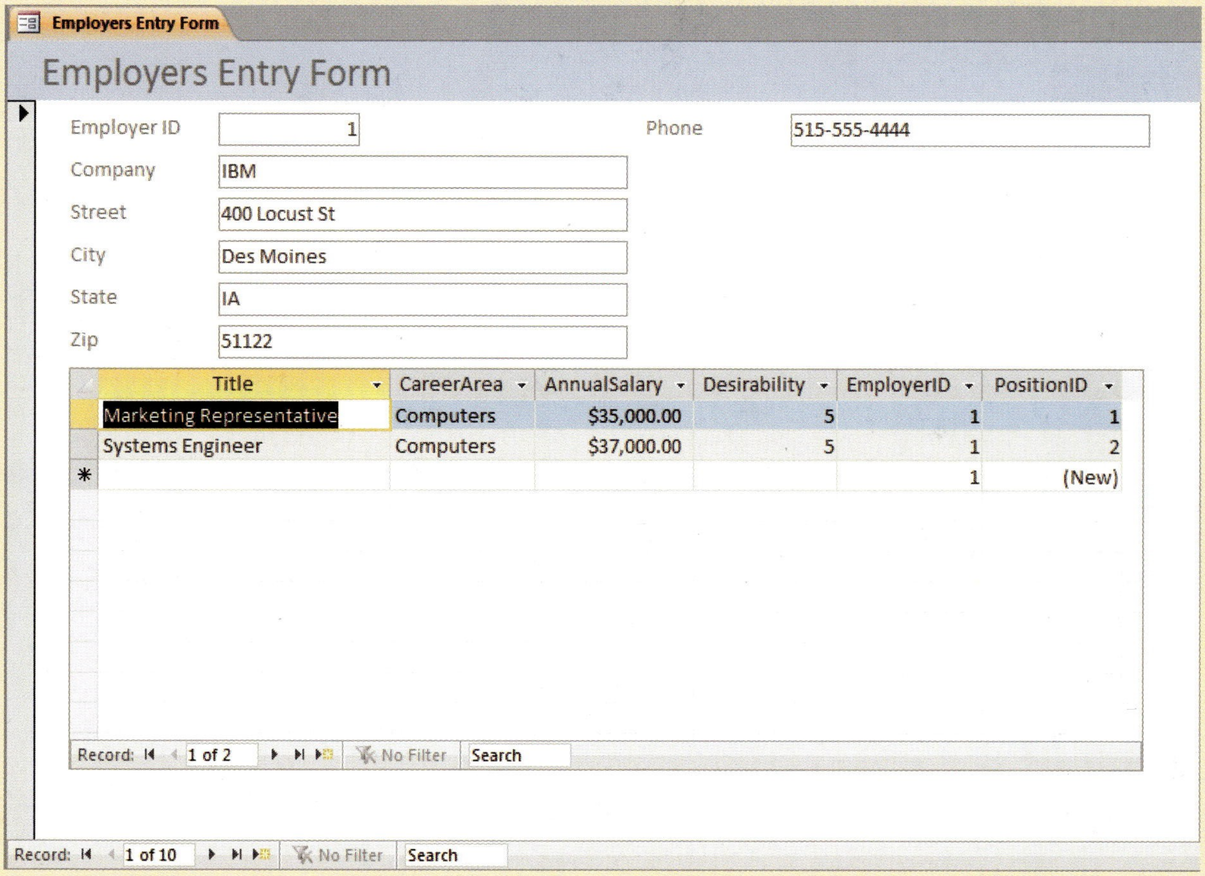

o. Save and close the Relationships window. Save and close the JobSearch-E.accdb database, and exit Access.

Visual Workshop

Open the Training-E.accdb database from the drive and folder where you store your Data Files, then enable content if prompted. Create a new table called **Vendors** using the Table Design View shown in Figure E-30 to determine field names and data types. Make the following property changes: Change the Field Size property of the VState field to **2**, the VZip field to **9**, and VPhone field to **10**. Change the Field Size property of the VendorName, VStreet, and VCity fields to **30**. Apply a Phone Number Input Mask to the VPhone field. Be sure to specify that the VendorID field is the primary key field. Relate the tables in the Training-E database as shown in Figure E-31, then view the Relationships report in landscape view. Move the tables in the Relationships window as needed so that the relationships printout fits on a single piece of paper. Add your name as a label to the Report Header section to document the Relationships report.

FIGURE E-30

Vendors	
Field Name	**Data Type**
VendorID	AutoNumber
VendorName	Text
VStreet	Text
VCity	Text
VState	Text
VZip	Text
VPhone	Text

FIGURE E-31

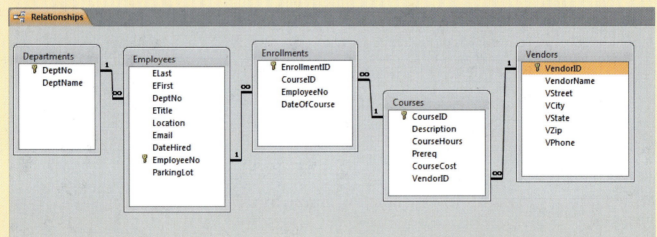

Working with Windows Live and Office Web Apps

Files You Will Need:

WEB-1.pptx
WEB-2.xlsx

If the computer you are using has an active Internet connection, you can go to the Microsoft Windows Live Web site and access a wide variety of services and Web applications. For example, you can check your e-mail through Windows Live, network with your friends and coworkers, and use SkyDrive to store and share files. From SkyDrive, you can also use Office Web Apps to create and edit Word, PowerPoint, Excel, and OneNote files, even when you are using a computer that does not have Office 2010 installed. You work in the Vancouver branch of Quest Specialty Travel. Your supervisor, Mary Lou Jacobs, asks you to explore Windows Live and learn how she can use SkyDrive and Office Web Apps to work with her files online.

(*Note*: SkyDrive and Office Web Apps are dynamic Web pages, and might change over time, including the way they are organized and how commands are performed. The steps and figures in this appendix were accurate at the time this book was published.)

OBJECTIVES

Explore how to work online from Windows Live

Obtain a Windows Live ID and sign in to Windows Live

Upload files to Windows Live

Work with the PowerPoint Web App

Create folders and organize files on SkyDrive

Add people to your network and share files

Work with the Excel Web App

Exploring How to Work Online from Windows Live

You can use your Web browser to upload your files to Windows Live from any computer connected to the Internet. You can work on the files right in your Web browser using Office Web Apps and share your files with people in your Windows Live network. You review the concepts and services related to working online from Windows Live.

DETAILS

- ### What is Windows Live?
  Windows Live is a collection of services and Web applications that you can use to help you be more productive both personally and professionally. For example, you can use Windows Live to send and receive e-mail, to chat with friends via instant messaging, to share photos, to create a blog, and to store and edit files using SkyDrive. Table WEB-1 describes the services available on Windows Live. Windows Live is a free service that you sign up for. When you sign up, you receive a Windows Live ID, which you use to sign in to Windows Live. When you work with files on Windows Live, you are cloud computing.

- ### What is Cloud Computing?
  The term **cloud computing** refers to the process of working with files online in a Web browser. When you save files to SkyDrive on Windows Live, you are saving your files to an online location. SkyDrive is like having a personal hard drive in the cloud.

- ### What is SkyDrive?
  SkyDrive is an online storage and file sharing service. With a Windows Live account, you receive access to your own SkyDrive, which is your personal storage area on the Internet. On your SkyDrive, you are given space to store up to 25 GB of data online. Each file can be a maximum size of 50 MB. You can also use SkyDrive to access Office Web Apps, which you use to create and edit files created in Word, OneNote, PowerPoint, and Excel online in your Web browser.

- ### Why use Windows Live and SkyDrive?
  On Windows Live, you use SkyDrive to access additional storage for your files. You don't have to worry about backing up your files to a memory stick or other storage device that could be lost or damaged. Another advantage of storing your files on SkyDrive is that you can access your files from any computer that has an active Internet connection. Figure WEB-1 shows the SkyDrive Web page that appears when accessed from a Windows Live account. From SkyDrive, you can also access Office Web Apps.

- ### What are Office Web Apps?
  Office Web Apps are versions of Microsoft Word, Excel, PowerPoint, and OneNote that you can access online from your SkyDrive. An Office Web App does not include all of the features and functions included with the full Office version of its associated application. However, you can use the Office Web App from any computer that is connected to the Internet, even if Microsoft Office 2010 is not installed on that computer.

- ### How do SkyDrive and Office Web Apps work together?
  You can create a file in Office 2010 using Word, Excel, PowerPoint, or OneNote and then upload the file to your SkyDrive. You can then open the Office file saved to SkyDrive and edit it using your Web browser and the corresponding Office Web App. Figure WEB-2 shows a PowerPoint presentation open in the PowerPoint Web App. You can also use an Office Web App to create a new file, which is saved automatically to SkyDrive while you work. In addition, you can download a file created with an Office Web App and continue to work with the file in the full version of the corresponding Office application: Word, Excel, PowerPoint, or OneNote. Finally, you can create a SkyDrive network that consists of the people you want to be able to view your folders and files on your SkyDrive. You can give people permission to view and edit your files using any computer with an active Internet connection and a Web browser.

FIGURE WEB-1: SkyDrive on Windows Live

Browser window

SkyDrive - Windows Live tab

By default, one folder is available on SkyDrive; you can create additional folders

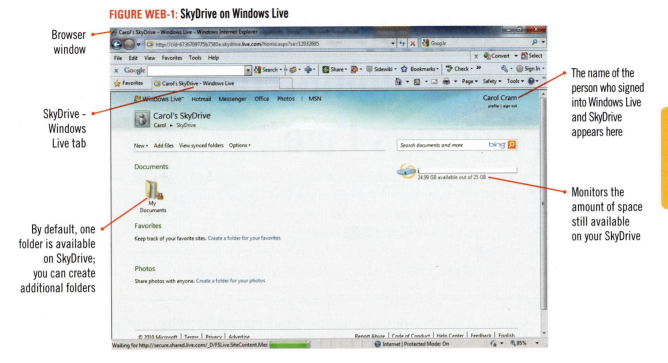

The name of the person who signed into Windows Live and SkyDrive appears here

Monitors the amount of space still available on your SkyDrive

FIGURE WEB-2: PowerPoint presentation open in the PowerPoint Web App

Browser window

Ribbon available in PowerPoint Web App

The presentation in PowerPoint Web App maintains the same look and feel as the same presentation in the desktop version of PowerPoint

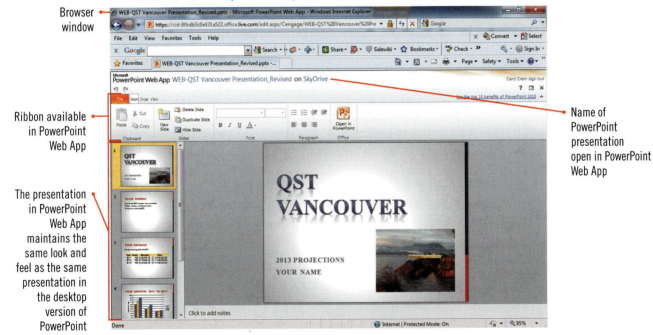

Name of PowerPoint presentation open in PowerPoint Web App

TABLE WEB-1: Services available via Windows Live

service	description
E-mail	Send and receive e-mail using a Hotmail account
Instant Messaging	Use Messenger to chat with friends, share photos, and play games
SkyDrive	Store files, work on files using Office Web Apps, and share files with people in your network
Photos	Upload and share photos with friends
People	Develop a network of friends and coworkers, then use the network to distribute information and stay in touch
Downloads	Access a variety of free programs available for download to a PC
Mobile Device	Access applications for a mobile device: text messaging, using Hotmail, networking, and sharing photos

Obtaining a Windows Live ID and Signing In to Windows Live

To work with your files online using SkyDrive and Office Web Apps, you need a Windows Live ID. You obtain a Windows Live ID by going to the Windows Live Web site and creating a new account. Once you have a Windows Live ID, you can access SkyDrive and then use it to store your files, create new files, and share your files with friends and coworkers. Mary Lou Jacobs, your supervisor at QST Vancouver, asks you to obtain a Windows Live ID so that you can work on documents with your coworkers. You go to the Windows Live Web site, create a Windows Live ID, and then sign in to your SkyDrive.

STEPS

QUICK TIP
If you already have a Windows Live ID, go to the next lesson and sign in as directed using your account.

1. **Open your Web browser, type home.live.com in the Address bar, then press [Enter]**

   The Windows Live home page opens. From this page, you can create a Windows Live account and receive your Windows Live ID.

2. **Click the Sign up button** *(Note: You may see a Sign up link instead of a button)*

   The Create your Windows Live ID page opens.

3. **Click the Or use your own e-mail address link under the Check availability button or if you are already using Hotmail, Messenger, or Xbox LIVE, click the Sign in now link in the Information statement near the top of the page**

4. **Enter the information required, as shown in Figure WEB-3**

   If you wish, you can sign up for a Windows Live e-mail address such as yourname@live.com so that you can also access the Windows Live e-mail services.

TROUBLE
The code can be difficult to read. If you receive an error message, enter the new code that appears.

5. **Enter the code shown at the bottom of your screen, then click the I accept button**

   The Windows Live home page opens. The name you entered when you signed up for your Windows Live ID appears in the top right corner of the window to indicate that you are signed in to Windows Live. From the Windows Live home page, you can access all the services and applications offered by Windows Live. See the Verifying your Windows Live ID box for information on finalizing your account set up.

6. **Point to Windows Live, as shown in Figure WEB-4**

   A list of options appears. SkyDrive is one of the options you can access directly from Windows Live.

TROUBLE
Click I accept if you are asked to review and accept the Windows Live Service Agreement and Privacy Statement.

7. **Click SkyDrive**

   The SkyDrive page opens. Your name appears in the top right corner, and the amount of space available is shown on the right side of the SkyDrive page. The amount of space available is monitored, as indicated by the gauge that fills with color as space is used. Using SkyDrive, you can add files to the existing folder and you can create new folders.

8. **Click sign out in the top right corner under your name, then exit the Web browser**

   You are signed out of your Windows Live account. You can sign in again directly from the Windows Live page in your browser or from within a file created with PowerPoint, Excel, Word, or OneNote.

FIGURE WEB-3: Creating a Windows Live ID

Click to sign in using a Hotmail, Messenger, or Xbox Live account

Once your registration is complete, you will be asked to verify your ID

A different code will appear on your screen

Type your e-mail address

You can choose to get a Windows Live e-mail address

Enter the information required

FIGURE WEB-4: Selecting SkyDrive

SkyDrive in the list of Windows Live options

Information about your Windows Live network

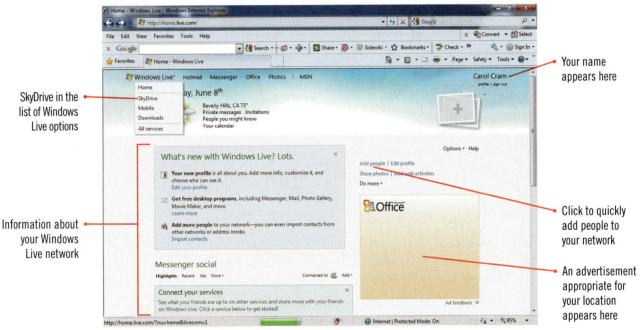

Your name appears here

Click to quickly add people to your network

An advertisement appropriate for your location appears here

Verifying your Windows Live ID

As soon as you accept the Windows Live terms, an e-mail is sent to the e-mail address you supplied when you created your Windows Live ID. Open your e-mail program, and then open the e-mail from Microsoft with the Subject line: Confirm your e-mail address for Windows Live. Follow the simple, step-by-step instructions in the e-mail to confirm your Windows Live ID. When the confirmation is complete, you will be asked to sign in to Windows Live, using your e-mail address and password. Once signed in, you will see your Windows Live Account page.

Working with Windows Live and Office Web Apps

Web Apps

Web Apps 5

Uploading Files to Windows Live

Once you have created your Windows Live ID, you can sign in to Windows Live directly from Word, PowerPoint, Excel, or OneNote and start saving and uploading files. You upload files to your SkyDrive so you can share the files with other people, access the files from another computer, or use SkyDrive's additional storage. You open a PowerPoint presentation, access your Windows Live account from Backstage view, and save a file to SkyDrive on Windows Live. You also create a new folder called Cengage directly from Backstage view and add a file to it.

STEPS

1. **Start PowerPoint, open the file WEB-1.pptx from the drive and folder where you store your Data Files, then save the file as WEB-QST Vancouver Presentation**

2. **Click the File tab, then click Save & Send**

   The Save & Send options available in PowerPoint are listed in Backstage view, as shown in Figure WEB-5.

3. **Click Save to Web**

   > **QUICK TIP**
   > Skip this step if the computer you are using signs you in automatically.

4. **Click Sign In, type your e-mail address, press [Tab], type your password, then click OK**

   The My Documents folder on your SkyDrive appears in the Save to Windows Live SkyDrive information area.

5. **Click Save As, wait a few seconds for the Save As dialog box to appear, then click Save**

   The file is saved to the My Documents folder on the SkyDrive that is associated with your Windows Live account. You can also create a new folder and upload files directly to SkyDrive from your hard drive.

6. **Click the File tab, click Save & Send, click Save to Web, then sign in if the My Documents folder does not automatically appear in Backstage view**

7. **Click the New Folder button in the Save to Windows Live SkyDrive pane, then sign in to Windows Live if directed**

8. **Type Cengage as the folder name, click Next, then click Add files**

9. **Click select documents from your computer, then navigate to the location on your computer where you saved the file WEB-QST Vancouver Presentation in Step 1**

10. **Click WEB-QST Vancouver Presentation.pptx to select it, then click Open**

    You can continue to add more files; however, you have no more files to upload at this time.

11. **Click Continue**

    In a few moments, the PowerPoint presentation is uploaded to your SkyDrive, as shown in Figure WEB-6. You can simply store the file on SkyDrive or you can choose to work on the presentation using the PowerPoint Web App.

12. **Click the PowerPoint icon on your taskbar to return to PowerPoint, then close the presentation and exit PowerPoint**

FIGURE WEB-5: Save & Send options in Backstage view

PowerPoint file

Save & Send area
in Backstage view

Save to Web
option

FIGURE WEB-6: File uploaded to the Cengage folder on Windows Live

Browser
window

Path to file

Current folder
menu bar

Uploaded file

Appendix
Web Apps
Office 2010

Working with the PowerPoint Web App

Once you have uploaded a file to SkyDrive on Windows Live, you can work on it using its corresponding Office Web App. **Office Web Apps** provide you with the tools you need to view documents online and to edit them right in your browser. You do not need to have Office programs installed on the computer you use to access SkyDrive and Office Web Apps. From SkyDrive, you can also open the document directly in the full Office application (for example, PowerPoint) if the application is installed on the computer you are using. You use the PowerPoint Web App to make some edits to the PowerPoint presentation. You then open the presentation in PowerPoint and use the full version to make additional edits.

STEPS

> **TROUBLE**
> Click the browser button on the task-bar, then click the Windows Live SkyDrive window to make it the active window.

1. **Click the WEB-QST Vancouver Presentation file in the Cengage folder on SkyDrive**

   The presentation opens in your browser window. A menu is available, which includes the options you have for working with the file.

2. **Click Edit in Browser, then if a message appears related to installing the Sign-in Assistant, click the Close button [X] to the far right of the message**

   In a few moments, the PowerPoint presentation opens in the PowerPoint Web App, as shown in Figure WEB-7. Table WEB-2 lists the commands you can perform using the PowerPoint Web App.

> **QUICK TIP**
> The changes you make to the presen-tation are saved automatically on SkyDrive.

3. **Enter your name where indicated on Slide 1, click Slide 3 (New Tours) in the Slides pane, then click Delete Slide in the Slides group**

   The slide is removed from the presentation. You decide to open the file in the full version of PowerPoint on your computer so you can apply WordArt to the slide title. You work with the file in the full version of PowerPoint when you want to use functions, such as WordArt, that are not available on the PowerPoint Web App.

4. **Click Open in PowerPoint in the Office group, click OK in response to the message, then click Allow if requested**

   In a few moments, the revised version of the PowerPoint slide opens in PowerPoint on your computer.

5. **Click Enable Editing on the Protected View bar near the top of your presentation window if prompted, select QST Vancouver on the title slide, then click the Drawing Tools Format tab**

> **QUICK TIP**
> Use the ScreenTips to help you find the required WordArt style.

6. **Click the More button [▼] in the WordArt Styles group to show the selection of WordArt styles, select the WordArt style Gradient Fill - Blue-Gray, Accent 4, Reflection, then click a blank area outside the slide**

   The presentation appears in PowerPoint as shown in Figure WEB-8. Next, you save the revised version of the file to SkyDrive.

7. **Click the File tab, click Save As, notice that the path in the Address bar is to the Cengage folder on your Windows Live SkyDrive, type WEB-QST Vancouver Presentation_Revised. pptx in the File name text box, then click Save**

   The file is saved to your SkyDrive.

> **TROUBLE**
> The browser opens to the Cengage folder but the file is not visible. Follow Step 8 to open the Cengage folder and refresh thelist of files in the folder.

8. **Click the browser icon on the taskbar to open your SkyDrive page, then click Office next to your name in the SkyDrive path, view a list of recent documents, then click Cengage in the list to the left of the recent documents list to open the Cengage folder**

   Two PowerPoint files now appear in the Cengage folder.

9. **Exit the Web browser and close all tabs if prompted, then exit PowerPoint**

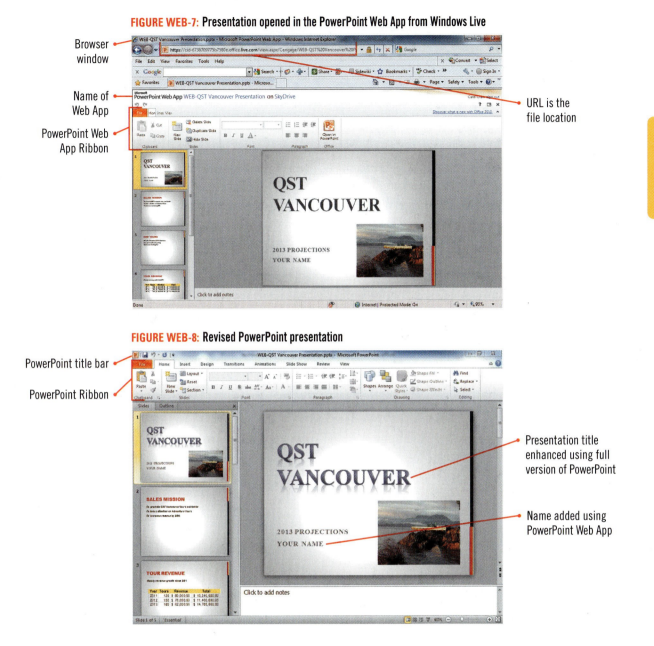

FIGURE WEB-7: Presentation opened in the PowerPoint Web App from Windows Live

Browser window

Name of Web App

PowerPoint Web App Ribbon

URL is the file location

FIGURE WEB-8: Revised PowerPoint presentation

PowerPoint title bar

PowerPoint Ribbon

Presentation title enhanced using full version of PowerPoint

Name added using PowerPoint Web App

TABLE WEB-2: Commands on the PowerPoint Web App

tab	commands available
File	• Open in PowerPoint: select to open the file in PowerPoint on your computer • Where's the Save Button?: when you click this option, a message appears telling you that you do not need to save your presentation when you are working on it with PowerPoint Web App. The presentation is saved automatically as you work. • Print • Share • Properties • Give Feedback • Privacy • Terms of Use • Close
Home	• Clipboard group: Cut, Copy, Paste • Slides group: Add a New Slide, Delete a Slide, Duplicate a Slide, and Hide a Slide • Font group: Work with text: change the font, style, color, and size of selected text • Paragraph group: Work with paragraphs: add bullets and numbers, indent text, align text • Office group: Open the file in PowerPoint on your computer
Insert	• Insert a Picture • Insert a SmartArt diagram • Insert a link such as a link to another file on SkyDrive or to a Web page
View	• Editing view (the default) • Reading view • Slide Show view • Notes view

Creating Folders and Organizing Files on SkyDrive

As you have learned, you can sign in to SkyDrive directly from the Office applications PowerPoint, Excel, Word, and OneNote, or you can access SkyDrive directly through your Web browser. This option is useful when you are away from the computer on which you normally work or when you are using a computer that does not have Office applications installed. You can go to SkyDrive, create and organize folders, and then create or open files to work on with Office Web Apps. 🎨 You access SkyDrive from your Web browser, create a new folder called Illustrated, and delete one of the PowerPoint files from the My Documents folder.

STEPS

TROUBLE
Go to Step 3 if you are already signed in.

1. **Open your Web browser, type home.live.com in the Address bar, then press [Enter]**
   The Windows Live home page opens. From here, you can sign in to your Windows Live account and then access SkyDrive.

TROUBLE
Type your Windows Live ID (your e-mail) and password, then click Sign in if prompted to do so.

2. **Sign into Windows Live as directed**
   You are signed in to your Windows Live page. From this page, you can take advantage of the many applications available on Windows Live, including SkyDrive.

3. **Point to Windows Live, then click SkyDrive**
   SkyDrive opens.

4. **Click Cengage, then point to WEB-QST Vancouver Presentation.pptx**
   A menu of options for working with the file, including a Delete button to the far right, appears to the right of the filename.

5. **Click the Delete button ⌧, then click OK**
   The file is removed from the Cengage folder on your SkyDrive. You still have a copy of the file on your computer.

6. **Point to Windows Live, then click SkyDrive**
   Your SkyDrive screen with the current selection of folders available on your SkyDrive opens, as shown in Figure WEB-9.

7. **Click New, click Folder, type Illustrated, click Next, click Office in the path under Add documents to Illustrated at the top of the window, then click View all in the list under Personal**
   You are returned to your list of folders, where you see the new Illustrated folder.

8. **Click Cengage, point to WEB-QST Vancouver Presentation_Revised.pptx, click More, click Move, then click the Illustrated folder**

9. **Click Move this file into Illustrated, as shown in Figure WEB-10**
   The file is moved to the Illustrated folder.

FIGURE WEB-9: Folders on your SkyDrive

Current location

Folders currently available

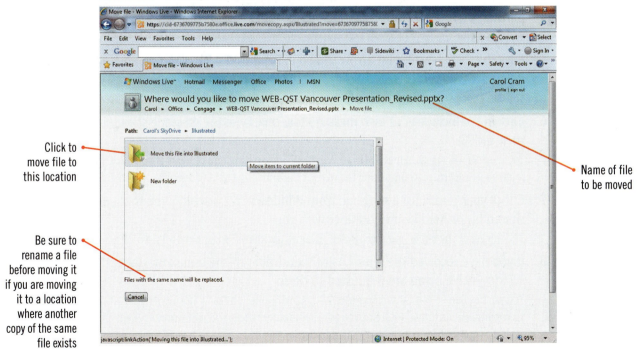

FIGURE WEB-10: Moving a file to the Illustrated folder

Click to move file to this location

Be sure to rename a file before moving it if you are moving it to a location where another copy of the same file exists

Name of file to be moved

Adding People to Your Network and Sharing Files

One of the great advantages of working with SkyDrive on Windows Live is that you can share your files with others. Suppose, for example, that you want a colleague to review a presentation you created in PowerPoint and then add a new slide. You can, of course, e-mail the presentation directly to your colleague, who can then make changes and e-mail the presentation back. Alternatively, you can save time by uploading the PowerPoint file directly to SkyDrive and then giving your colleague access to the file. Your colleague can edit the file using the PowerPoint Web App, and then you can check the updated file on SkyDrive, also using the PowerPoint Web App. In this way, you and your colleague are working with just one version of the presentation that you both can update. You have decided to share files in the Illustrated folder that you created in the previous lesson with another individual. You start by working with a partner so that you can share files with your partner and your partner can share files with you.

STEPS

TROUBLE
If you cannot find a partner, read the steps so you understand how the process works.

1. Identify a partner with whom you can work, and obtain his or her e-mail address; you can choose someone in your class or someone on your e-mail list, but it should be someone who will be completing these steps when you are

2. From the Illustrated folder, click Share

3. Click Edit permissions

   The Edit permissions page opens. On this page, you can select the individual with whom you would like to share the contents of the Illustrated folder.

4. Click in the Enter a name or an e-mail address text box, type the e-mail address of your partner, then press [Tab]

   You can define the level of access that you want to give your partner.

5. Click the Can view files list arrow shown in Figure WEB-11, click Can add, edit details, and delete files, then click Save

   You can choose to send a notification to each individual when you grant permission to access your files.

6. Click in the Include your own message text box, type the message shown in Figure WEB-12, then click Send

   Your partner will receive a message from Windows Live advising him or her that you have shared your Illustrated folder. If your partner is completing the steps at the same time, you will receive an e-mail from your partner.

TROUBLE
If you do not receive a message from Windows Live, your partner has not yet completed the steps to share the Illustrated folder.

7. Check your e-mail for a message from Windows Live advising you that your partner has shared his or her Illustrated folder with you

   The subject of the e-mail message will be "[Name] has shared documents with you."

QUICK TIP
You will know you are on your partner's SkyDrive because you will see your partner's first name at the beginning of the SkyDrive path.

8. If you have received the e-mail, click View folder in the e-mail message, then sign in to Windows Live if you are requested to do so

   You are now able to access your partner's Illustrated folder on his or her SkyDrive. You can download files in your partner's Illustrated folder to your own computer where you can work on them and then upload them again to your partner's Illustrated shared folder.

9. Exit the browser

FIGURE WEB-11: Editing folder permissions

Folder permissions will be changed for the Illustrated folder

Click to select network permission options

Type email address to continue to add people

Person whose permission status will change

Click to select person from list of contacts

Click to select permission option

FIGURE WEB-12: Entering a message to notify a person that file sharing permission has been granted

Sharing files on SkyDrive

When you share a folder with other people, the people with whom you share a folder can download the file to their computers and then make changes using the full version of the corresponding Office application.

Once these changes are made, each individual can then upload the file to SkyDrive and into a folder shared with you and others. In this way, you can create a network of people with whom you share your files.

Working with the Excel Web App

You can use the Excel Web App to work with an Excel spreadsheet on SkyDrive. Workbooks opened using the Excel Web App have the same look and feel as workbooks opened using the full version of Excel. However, just like the PowerPoint Web App, the Excel Web App has fewer features available than the full version of Excel. When you want to use a command that is not available on the Excel Web App, you need to open the file in the full version of Excel. ▟▟▟ You upload an Excel file containing a list of the tours offered by QST Vancouver to the Illustrated folder on SkyDrive. You use the Excel Web App to make some changes, and then you open the revised version in Excel 2010 on your computer.

STEPS

1. **Start Excel, open the file WEB-2.xlsx from the drive and folder where you store your Data Files, then save the file as WEB-QST Vancouver Tours**

    The data in the Excel file is formatted using the Excel table function.

> **TROUBLE**
> If prompted, sign in to your Windows Live account as directed.

2. **Click the File tab, click Save & Send, then click Save to Web**

    In a few moments, you should see three folders to which you can save spreadsheets. My Documents and Cengage are personal folder that contains files that only you can access. Illustrated is a shared folder that contains files you can share with others in your network. The Illustrated folder is shared with your partner.

3. **Click the Illustrated folder, click the Save As button, wait a few seconds for the Save As dialog box to appear, then click Save**

> **QUICK TIP**
> Alternately, you can open your Web browser and go to Windows Live to sign in to SkyDrive.

4. **Click the File tab, click Save & Send, click Save to Web, click the Windows Live SkyDrive link above your folders, then sign in if prompted**

    Windows Live opens to your SkyDrive.

5. **Click the Excel program button 🖼 on the taskbar, then exit Excel**

6. **Click your browser button on the taskbar to return to SkyDrive if SkyDrive is not the active window, click the Illustrated folder, click the Excel file, click Edit in Browser, then review the Ribbon and its tabs to familiarize yourself with the commands you can access from the Excel Web App**

    Table WEB-3 summarizes the commands that are available.

7. **Click cell A12, type Gulf Islands Sailing, press [TAB], type 3000, press [TAB], type 10, press [TAB], click cell D3, enter the formula =B3*C3, press [Enter], then click cell A1**

    The formula is copied automatically to the remaining rows as shown in Figure WEB-13 because the data in the original Excel file was created and formatted as an Excel table.

8. **Click SkyDrive in the Excel Web App path at the top of the window to return to the Illustrated folder**

    The changes you made to the Excel spreadsheet are saved automatically on SkyDrive. You can download the file directly to your computer from SkyDrive.

9. **Point to the Excel file, click More, click Download, click Save, navigate to the location where you save the files for this book, name the file WEB-QST Vancouver Tours_Updated, click Save, then click Close in the Download complete dialog box**

    The updated version of the spreadsheet is saved on your computer and on SkyDrive.

10. **Exit the Web browser**

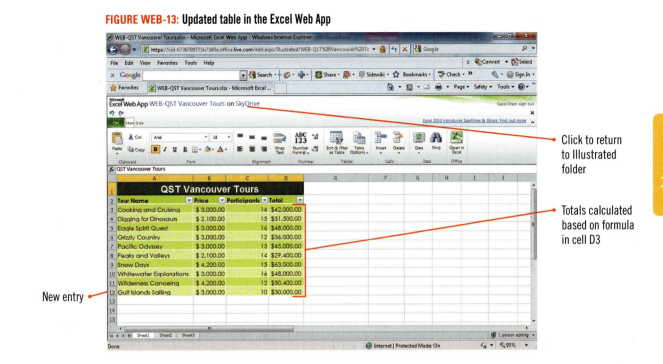

Click to return to Illustrated folder

Totals calculated based on formula in cell D3

New entry

TABLE WEB-3: Commands on the Excel Web App

tab	commands available
File	• Open in Excel: select to open the file in Excel on your computer • Where's the Save Button?: when you click this option, a message appears telling you that you do not need to save your spreadsheet when you are working in it with Excel Web App; the spreadsheet is saved automatically as you work • Save As • Share • Download a Snapshot: a snapshot contains only the values and the formatting; you cannot modify a snapshot • Download a Copy: the file can be opened and edited in the full version of Excel • Give Feedback • Privacy Statement • Terms of Use • Close
Home	• Clipboard group: Cut, Copy, Paste • Font group: change the font, style, color, and size of selected labels and values, as well as border styles and fill colors • Alignment group: change vertical and horizontal alignment and turn on the Wrap Text feature • Number group: change the number format and increase or decrease decimal places • Tables: sort and filter data in a table and modify Table Options • Cells: insert and delete cells • Data: refresh data and find labels or values • Office: open the file in Excel on your computer
Insert	• Insert a Table • Insert a Hyperlink to a Web page

Exploring other Office Web Apps

Two other Office Web Apps are Word and OneNote. You can share files on SkyDrive directly from Word or from OneNote using the same method you used to share files from PowerPoint and Excel. After you upload a Word or OneNote file to SkyDrive, you can work with it in its corresponding Office Web App. To familiarize yourself with the commands available in an Office Web App, open the file and then review the commands on each tab on the Ribbon. If you want to perform a task that is not available in the Office Web App, open the file in the full version of the application.

In addition to working with uploaded files, you can create files from new on SkyDrive. Simply sign in to SkyDrive and open a folder. With a folder open, click New and then select the Web App you want to use to create the new file.

Windows Live and Microsoft Office Web Apps Quick Reference

To Do This	Go Here
Access Windows Live	From the Web browser, type **home.live.com**, then click Sign In
Access SkyDrive on Windows Live	From the Windows Live home page, point to Windows Live, then click SkyDrive
Save to Windows Live from Word, PowerPoint, or Excel	File tab | Save & Send | Save to Web | Select a folder | Save As
Create a New Folder from Backstage view	File tab | Save & Send | Save to Web | New Folder button
Edit a File with a Web App	From SkyDrive, click the file, then click Edit in Browser
Open a File in a desktop version of the application from a Web App: Word, Excel, PowerPoint	Click Open in [Application] in the Office group in each Office Web App
Share files on Windows Live	From SkyDrive, click the folder containing the files to share, click Share on the menu bar, click Edit permissions, enter the e-mail address of the person to share files with, click the Can view files list arrow, click Can add, edit details, and delete files, then click Save

Glossary

.accdb The file extension that usually means the database is an Access 2007 format database.

Active The currently available document, program, or object; on the taskbar, when more than one program is open, the button for the active program appears slightly lighter.

Alignment command A command used in Layout or Design View for a form or report to either left-, center-, or right-align a value within its control, or to align the top, bottom, right, or left edge of the control with respect to other controls.

Allow Multiple Values A lookup property in a database in the Access 2007 file format that lets you create a multivalued field.

Alternate Back Color property A property that determines the alternating background color of the selected section in a form or report.

AND criteria Criteria placed in the same row of the query design grid. All criteria on the same row must be true for a record to appear on the resulting datasheet.

Argument Information that a function uses to create the final answer. Multiple arguments are separated by commas. All of the arguments for a function are surrounded by a single set of parentheses.

Attachment field A field that allows you to attach an external file such as a Word document, PowerPoint presentation, Excel workbook, or image file to a record.

AutoNumber A field data type in which Access enters a sequential integer for each record added into the datasheet. Numbers cannot be reused even if the record is deleted.

Avg function A built-in Access function used to calculate the average of the values in a given field.

Back Color property A property that determines the background color of the selected control or section in a form or report.

Backward-compatible Software feature that enables documents saved in an older version of a program to be opened in a newer version of the program.

Bound control A control used in either a form or report to display data from the underlying field; used to edit and enter new data in a form.

Byte A field size that allows entries only from 0 to 255.

Calculation A new value that is created by entering an expression in a text box on a form or report.

Calendar Picker A pop-up calendar from which you can choose dates for a date field.

Child table The "many" table in a one-to-many relationship.

Cloud computing When data, applications, and resources are stored on servers accessed over the Internet or a company's internal network rather than on user's computers.

Column separator The thin line that separates the field names to the left or right.

Combo box A bound control used to display a list of possible entries for a field in which you can also type an entry from the keyboard. It is a "combination" of the list box and text box controls.

Compatibility The ability of different programs to work together and exchange data.

Control Any element on a form or report such as a label, text box, line, or combo box. Controls can be bound, unbound, or calculated.

Control Source property A property of a bound control in a form or report that determines the field to which the control is connected.

Criteria Entries (rules and limiting conditions) that determine which records are displayed when finding or filtering records in a datasheet or form, or when building a query.

Criteria syntax Rules by which criteria need to be entered. For example, text criteria syntax requires that the criteria are surrounded by quotation marks (" "). Date criteria are surrounded by pound signs (#).

Current record The record that has the focus or is being edited.

Data type A required property for each field that defines the type of data that can be entered in each field. Valid data types include AutoNumber, Text, Number, Currency, Date/Time, and Memo.

Database designer The person responsible for building and maintaining tables, queries, forms, and reports.

Datasheet A spreadsheet-like grid that displays fields as columns and records as rows.

Datasheet View A view that lists the records of the object in a datasheet. Tables, queries, and most form objects have a Datasheet View.

Date function A built-in Access function used to display the current date on a form or report; enter the Date function as Date().

Design View A view in which the structure of the object can be manipulated. Every Access object (table, query, form, report, macro, and module) has a Design View.

Edit List Items button A button you click to add items to the combo box list in Form View.

Edit mode The mode in which Access assumes you are trying to edit a particular field, so keystrokes such as [Ctrl][End], [Ctrl][Home], [↑], and [↓] move the insertion point within the field.

Edit record symbol A pencil-like symbol that appears in the record selector box to the left of the record that is currently being edited in either a datasheet or a form.

Error indicator An icon that automatically appears in Design View to indicate some type of error. For example, a green error indicator appears in the upper-left corner of a text box in Form Design View if the text box Control Source property is set to a field name that doesn't exist.

Expression A combination of values, functions, and operators that calculates to a single value. Access expressions start with an equal sign and are placed in a text box in either Form Design View or Report Design View.

Field In a table, a field corresponds to a column of data, a specific piece or category of data such as a first name, last name, city, state, or phone number.

Field list A list of the available fields in the table or query that the field list represents.

Field name The name given to each field in a table.

Field properties Characteristics that further define the field.

Field selector The button to the left of a field in Table Design View that indicates the currently selected field. Also the thin gray bar above each field in the query grid.

Field Size property A field property that determines the number of characters that can be entered in a field.

Filter A way to temporarily display only those records that match given criteria.

Filter By Form A way to filter data that allows two or more criteria to be specified at the same time.

Filter By Selection A way to filter records for an exact match.

Focus The property that indicates which field would be edited if you were to start typing.

Foreign key field In a one-to-many relationship between two tables, the foreign key field is the field in the "many" table that links the table to the primary key field in the "one" table.

Form An Access object that provides an easy-to-use data entry screen that generally shows only one record at a time.

Form View View of a form object that displays data from the underlying recordset and allows you to enter and update data.

Form Wizard An Access wizard that helps you create a form.

Format property A field property that controls how information is displayed and printed.

Formatting Enhancing the appearance of the information through font, size, and color changes.

Function A special, predefined formula that provides a shortcut for a commonly used calculation, for example, SUM or COUNT.

Gallery A visual collection of choices you can browse through to make a selection. Often available with Live Preview.

Graphic image *See* Image.

Grouping A way to sort records in a particular order, as well as provide a section before and after each group of records.

Image A nontextual piece of information such as a picture, piece of clip art, drawn object, or graph. Because images are graphical (and not numbers or letters), they are sometimes referred to as graphical images.

Infinity symbol The symbol that indicates the "many" side of a one-to-many relationship.

Input Mask property A field property that provides a visual guide for users as they enter data.

Integrate To incorporate a document and parts of a document created in one program into another program; for example, to incorporate an Excel chart into a PowerPoint slide, or an Access table into a Word document.

Interface The look and feel of a program; for example, the appearance of commands and the way they are organized in the program window.

Is Not Null A criterion that finds all records in which any entry has been made in the field.

Is Null A criterion that finds all records in which no entry has been made in the field.

.Jpg The filename extension for JPEG files.

JPEG Acronym for Joint Photographic Experts Group, which defines the standards for the compression algorithms that allow image files to be stored in an efficient compressed format. JPEG files use the .jpg filename extension.

Join line The line identifying which fields establish the relationship between two related tables. Also called a link line.

Junction table A table created to establish separate one-to-many relationships to two tables that have a many-to-many relationship.

Key symbol The symbol appearing to the left of a primary key field.

Label An unbound control that displays text to describe and clarify other information on a form or report.

Label Wizard A report wizard that precisely positions and sizes information to print on a vast number of standard business label specifications.

Landscape orientation A way to print or view a page that is 11 inches wide by 8.5 inches tall.

Launch To open or start a program on your computer.

Layout View An Access view that lets you make some design changes to a form or report while you are browsing the data.

Left function An Access function that returns a specified number of characters, starting with the left side of a value in a Text field.

Like operator An operator used in a query to find values in a field that match the pattern you specify.

Limit to List A combo box control property that allows you to limit the entries made by that control to those provided by the combo box list.

Link line The line identifying which fields establish the relationship between two related tables.

Live Preview A feature that lets you point to a choice in a gallery or palette and see the results in the document without actually clicking the choice.

Logical view The datasheet of a query is sometimes called a logical view of the data because it is not a copy of the data, but rather, a selected view of data from the underlying tables.

Lookup field A field that has lookup properties. Lookup properties are used to create a drop-down list of values to populate the field.

Lookup properties Field properties that allow you to supply a dropdown list of values for a field.

Lookup Wizard A wizard used in Table Design View that allows one field to "look up" values from another table or entered list. For example, you might use the Lookup Wizard to specify that the Customer Number field in the Sales table display the Customer Name field entry from the Customers table.

.mdb The file extension for Access 2000 and 2002–2003 databases.

Macro An Access object that stores a collection of keystrokes or commands such as those for printing several reports in a row or providing a toolbar when a form opens.

Many-to-many relationship The relationship between two tables in an Access database in which one record of one table relates to many records in the other table and vice versa. You cannot directly create a many-to-many relationship between two tables in Access. To relate two tables with such a relationship, you must establish a third table called junction table that creates separate one-to-many relationships with the two original tables.

Module An Access object that stores Visual Basic programming code that extends the functions of automated Access processes.

Multiuser A characteristic that means more than one person can enter and edit data in the same Access database at the same time.

Multivalued field A field that allows you to make more than one choice from a drop-down list.

Name property A property that uniquely identifies each object and control on a form or report.

Navigation buttons Buttons in the lower-left corner of a datasheet or form that allow you to quickly navigate between the records in the underlying object as well as add a new record.

Navigation mode A mode in which Access assumes that you are trying to move between the fields and records of the datasheet (rather than edit a specific field's contents), so keystrokes such as [Ctrl][Home] and [Ctrl][End] move you to the first and last field of the datasheet.

Navigation Pane A pane in the Access program window that provides a way to move between objects (tables, queries, forms, reports, macros, and modules) in the database.

Object A table, query, form, report, macro, or module in a database.

Office Web App Versions of the Microsoft Office applications with limited functionality that are available online from Windows Live SkyDrive. Users can view documents online and then edit them in the browser using a selection of functions. Office Web Apps are available for Word, PowerPoint, Excel, and One Note.

OLE A field data type that stores pointers that tie files, such as pictures, sound clips, or spreadsheets, created in other programs to a record.

One-to-many line The line that appears in the Relationships window and shows which field is duplicated between two tables to serve as the linking field. The one-to-many line displays a "1" next to the field that serves as the "one" side of the relationship and displays an infinity symbol next to the field that serves as the "many" side of the relationship when referential integrity is specified for the relationship. Also called the one-to-many join line.

One-to-many relationship The relationship between two tables in an Access database in which a common field links the tables together. The linking field is called the primary key field in the "one" table of the relationship and the foreign key field in the "many" table of the relationship.

Online collaboration The ability to incorporate feedback or share information across the Internet or a company network or intranet.

OR criteria Criteria placed on different rows of the query design grid. A record will appear in the resulting datasheet if it is true for any single row.

Orphan record A record in the "many" table of a one-to-many relationship that doesn't have a matching entry in the linking field of the "one" table.

Parent table The "one" table in a one-to-many relationship.

Pixel (picture element) One pixel is the measurement of one picture element on the screen.

Portrait orientation A way to print or view a page that is 8.5 inches wide by 11 inches tall.

Previewing Prior to printing, seeing onscreen exactly how the printed document will look.

Primary key field A field that contains unique information for each record. A primary key field cannot contain a null entry.

Print Preview An Access view that shows you how a report or other object will print on a sheet of paper.

Property A characteristic that further defines a field (if field properties), control (if control properties), section (if section properties), or object (if object properties).

Property Sheet A window that displays an exhaustive list of properties for the chosen control, section, or object within the Form Design View or Report Design View.

Property Update Options A Smart Tag that applies property changes in one field to other objects of the database that use the field.

Query An Access object that provides a spreadsheet-like view of the data, similar to that in tables. It may provide the user with a subset of fields and/or records from one or more tables. Queries are created when the user has a "question" about the data in the database.

Query design grid The bottom pane of the Query Design View window in which you specify the fields, sort order, and limiting criteria for the query.

Query Design View The window in which you develop queries by specifying the fields, sort order, and limiting criteria that determine which fields and records are displayed in the resulting datasheet.

Read-only An object property that indicates whether the object can read and display data, but cannot be used to change (write to) data.

Record A row of data in a table.

Record source The table or query that defines the field and records displayed in a form or report.

Record Source property In a form or report, the property that determines which table or query object contains the fields and records that the form or report will display. It is the most important property of the form or report object. A bound control on a form or report has Control Source property. In this case, the Control Source property identifies the field to which the control is bound.

Referential integrity A set of Access rules that govern data entry and help ensure data accuracy.

Relational database software Software such as Access that is used to manage data organized in a relational database.

Relationships report A printout of the Relationships window that shows how a relational database is designed and includes table names, field names, primary key fields, and one-to-many relationship lines.

Report An Access object that creates a professional printout of data that may contain such enhancements as headers, footers, and calculations on groups of records.

Report View An Access view that maximizes the amount of data you can see on the screen.

Report Wizard An Access wizard that helps you create a report.

Row Source The Lookup property that defines the list of values for the Lookup field.

Ruler A vertical or horizontal guide that both appear in Form and Report Design View to help you position controls.

Save command A command on the File tab or Quick Access toolbar that saves the current object.

Save Object As command A command on the File tab that saves the current object with a new name.

Section A location of a form or report that contains controls. The section in which a control is placed determines where and how often the control prints.

Simple Query Wizard An Access wizard that prompts you for information it needs to create a new query.

Sizing handles Small squares at each corner of a selected control in Access. Dragging a handle resizes the control. Also known as handles.

Smart Tag A button that provides a small menu of options and automatically appears under certain conditions to help you work with a task, such as correcting errors. For example, the AutoCorrect Options button, which helps you correct typos and update properties, and the Error Indicator button, which helps identify potential design errors in Form and Report Design View, are smart tags.

Split form A form split into two panes; the upper pane allows you to display the fields of one record in any arrangement, and the lower pane maintains a datasheet view of the first few records.

SQL (Structured Query Language) A language that provides a standardized way to request information from a relational database system.

Subdatasheet A datasheet that is nested within another datasheet to show related records. The subdatasheet shows the records on the "many" side of a one-to-many relationship.

Sum function A mathematical function that totals values in a field.

Syntax Rules that govern how to enter property values and other information.

Tab Index property A form property that indicates the numeric tab order for all controls on the form that have the Tab Stop property set to Yes.

Tab order The sequence in which the controls on the form receive the focus when the user presses [Tab] or [Enter] in Form view.

Tab stop In Access, this refers to whether you can tab into a control when entering or editing data; in other words, whether the control can receive the focus.

Tab Stop property A form property that determines whether a field accepts focus.

Table A collection of records for a single subject, such as all of the customer records; the fundamental building block of a relational database because it stores all of the data.

Table Design View A view of a table that provides the most options for defining fields.

Template A sample file, such as a database provided within the Microsoft Access program.

Text Align property A control property that determines the alignment of text within the control.

Text box The most common type of control used to display field values.

Unbound A group of controls that do not display data.

Unbound control A control that does not change from record to record and exists only to clarify or enhance the appearance of the form, using elements such as labels, lines, and clip art.

User The person primarily interested in entering, editing, and analyzing the data in the database.

Validation Rule A field property that helps eliminate unreasonable entries by establishing criteria for an entry before it is accepted into the database.

Validation Text A field property that determines what message appears if a user attempts to make a field entry that does not pass the validation rule for that field.

Wildcard A special character used in criteria to find, filter, and query data. The asterisk (*) stands for any group of characters. For example, the criteria I* in a State field criterion cell would find all records where the state entry was IA, ID, IL, IN, or Iowa. The question mark (?) wildcard stands for only one character.

Index

F

G